Crime, Harm and Consumerism

This book offers a collection of cutting-edge essays on the relationship between crime, harm, and consumer culture. Although consumer culture has been addressed across the social sciences, it has yet to be fully explored in criminology. The editors bring to this field an impressive list of authors with original ideas and fresh perspectives. The collection first introduces the reader to three sets of ideas which will be especially useful to students and researchers piecing together theoretical frameworks for their studies. New concepts such as pseudo-pacification, the materialist libertine, and the commodification of abstinence can be used as foundation stones for new explanatory criminological analyses in the twenty-first century. The collection then moves on to present case studies based on rigorous empirical work in the fields of consumption and debt, 'outlaw' gangs, illegal drug markets, gambling, the mentality that drives investment fraudsters, and the relationship between social media and state surveillance. These case studies showcase the strength of the research skills and knowledge these scholars offer to the field of criminology. Written in a clear and direct style, this book will appeal to students and scholars in criminology, sociology, cultural studies, and social theory, and those interested in learning about the effects of consumer culture in modern society.

Steve Hall is an emeritus professor of criminology who worked at the universities of Northumbria, Durham, and Teesside, UK. Essentially a criminologist, he has also published in the fields of sociology, history, and radical philosophy. He is author of *Theorizing Crime and Deviance* and co-author of *The Rise of the Right*, *Revitalizing Criminological Theory*, *Riots and Political Protest*, *Rethinking Social Exclusion*, *Criminal Identities and Consumer Culture*, and *Violent Night*. He is co-editor of *New Directions in Criminology*.

Tereza Kuldova is a social anthropologist and senior researcher at the Work Research Institute, Oslo Metropolitan University, Norway. She is the author of the monographs *How Outlaws Win Friends and Influence People*, *Luxury Indian Fashion: A Social Critique*, and editor of *Fashion India: Spectacular Capitalism*, as well as *Urban Utopias: Excess and Expulsion in Neoliberal South Asia* and *Outlaw Motorcycle Clubs and Street Gangs: Scheming Legality, Resisting Criminalization*. She is the founder and editor-in-chief of the open-access peer-reviewed *Journal of Extreme Anthropology*.

Mark Horsley is a senior lecturer in criminology at the University of Chester, UK. He is the author of *The Dark Side of Prosperity*, a book about the causes and consequences of mass indebtedness in the run up to and aftermath of the 2008 Global Financial Crisis. In addition to other works on credit and debt, he has also published on criminological theory and the history of crime.

Routledge Studies in Crime and Society

Execution by Family
A Theory of Honor Violence
Mark Cooney

Changing Narratives of Youth Crime
From Social Causes to Threats to the Social
Bernd Dollinger

Human Enhancement Drugs
Edited by Katinka van de Ven, Kyle J.D. Mulrooney and Jim McVeigh

Organized Crime and Terrorist Networks
Edited by Vincenzo Ruggiero

Private Security and Domestic Violence
The Risks and Benefits of Private Security Companies Working with Victims of Domestic Violence
Diarmaid Harkin

The Human Factor of Cybercrime
Edited by Rutger Leukfeldt and Thomas J. Holt

Medical Misinformation and Social Harm in Non-Science Based Health Practices
A Multidisciplinary Perspective
Edited by Anita Lavorgna and Anna Di Ronco

Crime, Harm and Consumerism
Edited by Steve Hall, Tereza Kuldova and Mark Horsley

For more information about this series, please visit: www.routledge.com/Routledge-Studies-in-Crime-and-Society/book-series/RSCS

Crime, Harm and Consumerism

Edited by Steve Hall, Tereza Kuldova and Mark Horsley

Routledge
Taylor & Francis Group
LONDON AND NEW YORK

First published 2020
by Routledge
2 Park Square, Milton Park, Abingdon, Oxon OX14 4RN

and by Routledge
52 Vanderbilt Avenue, New York, NY 10017

Routledge is an imprint of the Taylor & Francis Group, an informa business

First issued in paperback 2021

British Library Cataloguing-in-Publication Data
A catalogue record for this book is available from the British Library

Library of Congress Cataloging-in-Publication Data
Names: Hall, Steve, 1955– editor. | Kuldova, Tereza, editor. | Horsley, Mark, editor.
Title: Crime, harm and consumerism / edited by Steve Hall, Tereza Kuldova, Mark Horsley.
Identifiers: LCCN 2019047245 | ISBN 9781138388628 (hardback) | ISBN 9780429424472 (ebook)
Subjects: LCSH: Consumption (Economics)—Case studies. | Criminology—Case studies.
Classification: LCC HB801 .C725 2020 | DDC 364.2/5—dc23
LC record available at https://lccn.loc.gov/2019047245

ISBN: 978-1-138-38862-8 (hbk)
ISBN: 978-1-03-208175-5 (pbk)
ISBN: 978-0-429-42447-2 (ebk)

Typeset in Times New Roman
by Apex CoVantage, LLC

Contents

Contributors

Tammy Ayres is an interdisciplinary scholar working in the area of drugs and drug policy at the University of Leicester, UK. Tammy has been undertaking research within the field of drugs for almost two decades, with extensive experience of investigating vulnerable populations, particularly problematic drug users, prisoners, and people with mental ill-health and trauma, both in the community and in prisons both in the UK and Guyana. Her research interests focus on the functionality of drug use, trauma, coping, and consumption.

Mark Featherstone is a senior lecturer in sociology at Keele University, UK. He is author of *Tocqueville's Virus: Utopia and Dystopia in Western Social and Political Theory* (Routledge, 2007), *Planet Utopia: Utopia, Dystopia, and the Global Imaginary* (Routledge, 2017), and a range of articles in journals including *Review of Education, Pedagogy, and Cultural Studies*; *Cultural Politics*; *Journal of Cultural Research*; and *Ctheory*.

Steve Hall is an emeritus professor of criminology who worked at the universities of Northumbria, Durham, and Teesside, UK. Essentially a criminologist, he has also published in the fields of sociology, history, and radical philosophy. He is author of numerous articles and *Theorizing Crime and Deviance* (Sage, 2012), and co-author of *The Rise of the Right* (Policy 2017), *Revitalizing Criminological Theory* (Routledge 2015), *Riots and Political Protest* (Routledge, 2015), *Rethinking Social Exclusion* (Sage, 2013), *Criminal Identities and Consumer Culture* (Routledge, 2008), and *Violent Night* (Berg, 2006). He is co-editor of *New Directions in Criminology* (Routledge, 2012).

Mark Horsley is a senior lecturer in criminology at the University of Chester, UK. He is the author of *The Dark Side of Prosperity* (Ashgate, 2015), a book about the causes and consequences of mass indebtedness in the run up to and aftermath of the 2008 Global Financial Crisis. In addition to other works on credit and debt, he has also published on criminological theory and the history of crime. He is currently writing a book-length critique of the concept of moral panic.

Justin Kotzé is a senior lecturer in criminology and criminal justice at Teesside University, UK. He was awarded his PhD in 2016 and has previously published work on the historical sublimation of violence and the consumption of steroids as a means of boosting bodily capital. He is also the author of *The Myth of the 'Crime Decline': Exploring Change and Continuity in Crime and Harm* (Routledge, 2019) and co-editor of *Zemiology: Reconnecting Crime and Social Harm* (Palgrave, 2018).

Tereza Kuldova is a social anthropologist and senior researcher at the Work Research Institute, Oslo Metropolitan University, Norway. She is the author of the monographs *How Outlaws Win Friends and Influence People* (Palgrave Macmillan, 2019) and *Luxury Indian Fashion: A Social Critique* (Bloomsbury, 2016) and editor of *Fashion India: Spectacular Capitalism* (Akademika Publishing, 2013), *Urban Utopias: Excess and Expulsion in Neoliberal South Asia* (Palgrave Macmillan, 2017), and *Outlaw Motorcycle Clubs and Street Gangs: Scheming Legality, Resisting Criminalization* (Palgrave Macmillan, 2018). She is the founder and editor-in-chief of the open-access peer-reviewed *Journal of Extreme Anthropology*.

Anthony Lloyd is a reader in criminology and sociology at Teesside University, UK. His research looks at reconfigured labour markets under neoliberal global capital and thus far has focused on call centres and the service economy. The connection between the sociology of work and labour markets, identity and subjectivity, and the fields of critical criminology, zemiology, and social harm forms the basis of his current research. His research monograph *Labour Markets and Identity on the Post-Industrial Assembly Line* was published in 2013 by Ashgate, and his latest book *The Harms of Work: An Ultra-Realist Account of the Service Economy* was published by Bristol University Press in 2018.

Leanne McRae is a research officer in critical disability studies at Curtin University in Western Australia. Her first book, *Terror, Leisure and Consumption: Spaces for Harm in a Post-Crash Era*, was published by Emerald in 2018. She is currently working on her second book with Emerald, due for publication in 2020, entitled *Crowd-Sourced Syllabus: A Curriculum for Resistance.*

Thomas Raymen is a senior lecturer in criminology at Northumbria University, UK. His interests span the fields of criminology, moral and political philosophy, political economy, psychoanalysis, and leisure studies. He is the author of *Parkour, Deviance and Leisure in the Late Capitalist City: An Ethnography* (Emerald, 2018) and co-editor of *Deviant Leisure: Criminological Perspectives on Leisure and Harm* (Palgrave, 2019). He is currently focused on developing a theory of social harm rooted in post-liberal ethics.

Oliver Smith is a reader in criminology at the University of Plymouth, UK. He has published widely in the field of deviant leisure and is the author of *Contemporary Adulthood and the Night Time Economy* (Palgrave, 2014). His current research examines the capacity for environmental harm in the context of commodified leisure markets.

Kate Tudor is a senior lecturer in criminology at Northumbria University in Newcastle Upon Tyne, UK. She has recently conducted empirical research with serious fraudsters that examines the relationship between late capitalism and illicit entrepreneurial forms. Her research interests broadly relate to the intersections between crime, harm, and political economy.

Introduction

Steve Hall, Tereza Kuldova, and Mark Horsley

Our everyday lives are shaped and framed by consumer culture, by the relentless manufacturing of consumer desire, and by the human and environmental destruction, emptiness and meaninglessness to which consumerism inevitably leads. Early consumer market sectors that during the west's industrial heyday relied exclusively on technological innovation to meet basic needs reached a saturation point by the 1970s. Once everyone open to the idea of buying a vacuum cleaner already had one, the mode of innovation changed. Of course, technological advances continued to be made, but running alongside these was the lifestyle symbolism attached to functional objects by the advertising and media industries. Symbolism knows no limits, therefore, by utilising sign-value and elevating its significance in the minds of consumers, the market was able to overcome the limitations of materiality. The gradual diminishment of use-value and the massive growth in the importance of lifestyle symbolism enabled the endless expansion of the market. Post-war working-class lives were liberated from the back-breaking toil that had beset previous generations. Working hours fell and incomes rose. Working conditions improved. Leisure time expanded, as did the range of commercialised cultural activities available for workers and their families. Amidst this cultural sea-change of displacement and renewal, consumer items became progressively more important in processes of identity-building. Consumerism's symbolism worked its way into what had hitherto been organic aspects of culture – family, class, community, nation, religion. Slowly, the importance of these signs grew, and more traditional aspects of common culture receded into history.

However, as neoliberalism's global market project took off in the 1980s and large regions of the west were deindustrialised, occupations became more unstable and wages flatlined relative to prices. In this difficult new context consumer desire was sustained by the importation of cheap goods and a vast ocean of debt. The new 'super-ego injunction to enjoy' (Žižek, 2009; see also Hall et al., 2008) became a cultural norm and encouraged us to feel guilty – not by indulging ourselves too much, but by missing even a single opportunity to do so. In this heady cultural climate consumer and household debts have grown enormously, even as incomes have fallen in real terms and job insecurity has established itself as a norm throughout the post-industrial west (Horsley, 2015). In basic financial terms, capital has claimed larger profits by suppressing wages. It has then used this surplus capital as a reserve 'cushion' on which banks and credit-card companies can issue sovereign currency as loans to workers – basically selling them interest-bearing money at a profit so they can continue to purchase the consumer items that are judged to be of such crucial cultural importance. Thus, a new investment mechanism was created, yet another source of huge profits that accrue from developing markets in consumer debt. These debts can be packaged, insured, and traded in derivatives markets, creating yet another source of profits. In the neoliberal era the entirety of the global economy is structured in relation to private debt, which has altered sectoral balances, expanding this debt and the consumption of symbolic goods as public expenditure has diminished.

In this neoliberal era, *consumer culture* or *consumerism* – throughout this collection the authors will use these terms interchangeably to signify not just the actual consumption of material goods but the sociosymbolic culture that accompanies it – has indeed become a way of life (Miles, 1998). Little has not been commodified and virtually nothing remains inalienable or sacred (see Kuldova, this volume). In a true iatrogenic process, there are no insecurities and anxieties that the market has not attempted to intensify and draw upon while it promises dubious transformative solutions in the shape of consumer goods. As Zygmunt Bauman (2003: 68) put it: 'modern markets do not suffer gladly the "non-market economy": the kind of life that reproduces itself without money changing hands'. Consumption defines and reifies identities as it fuels the economy with all its injustices, harms, and exploitations. But it also fuels everyday and serious organised forms of acquisitive crime, which figure highly in the statistics and are often associated with violence and other crimes and harms against the person (Hall et al., 2008). For more than two decades sociologists have spoken about 'consumer culture' and 'consumer society' (Bauman, 2007; Baudrillard, 2016; Featherstone, 1991; Smart, 2010), pointing out the myriad ways in which consumerism permeates the global north, especially in those nations that have fully embraced the principles of neoliberalism. Yet criminologists have either ignored consumerism or misunderstood its role in the constitution and reproduction of our current way of life. There has been a startling lack of recognition within criminology that consumerism is now integral to our global political economy, and very few criminologists have offered critical accounts of the vital functional and ideological roles consumerism has played throughout the history of capitalism. This is even more paradoxical given the fact that there is so much valuable literature that covers most aspects of consumerism. However, the illuminating concepts and analyses associated with this literature have only begun to be integrated into our discipline.

This collection of essays aims to place consumerism in the criminological spotlight and to begin to construct a framework in which we can attempt to understand a range of crimes and harms. If our discipline is to avail itself of new and enlightened models of socially contextualised motivation that are in keeping with the times, criminologists must try to understand consumerism's impact on our individual drives, desires, and social motivations – why and how we act and interact as social beings. Before we briefly outline the chapters in the volume, let us first sketch what we mean by consumerism, the harms associated with consumerism, and the gap within current criminological theory that this volume seeks to fill. After all, consumer culture is constantly active in those complex webs of meaning and interpretation and the broader macro-processes of mass mediation – infiltrating, persuading, humiliating, affirming, eroding, and reconstructing. We need to *rethink* consumerism from a criminological perspective, identify precisely its relationship to politics, economics, society, and culture, and locate it firmly in a conjuncture in which the certainties of modernity are rapidly receding into the past.

Consumerism, lack, and dissatisfaction

Consumerism has transformed many modern institutions (Beck and Beck-Gernsheim, 1995, 2001), our cultures, communities, and expectations of collective and political life (Baudrillard, 2016; Bauman, 2003, 2008). But consumerism does not only shape our material, economic, and political reality. More importantly, it has infiltrated our dreams (Hall et al., 2012), shaping our desires, fantasies, and aspirations. Our perceptions of ourselves and others, and our view of our place in the world, are mediated by commercials, films saturated with product placement, social media that bombard us with targeted marketing, and a vast landscape of astroturf marketing and its 'influencers' (Kuldova, 2016). Consumerism has displaced all alternative sources of meaning and furnished us with the symbols we use to understand our own value and social significance (Winlow and Hall, 2006, 2009). We should not underestimate the advertising industry's highly developed techniques of creating within us a desire for consumerism's symbol-laden objects (Lears, 1995; Ewen, 1998) and the various socio-cultural pressures imposed upon us – and indeed which we impose upon each other – to emotionally attach ourselves to these objects. Our desires are never fully our own. It is wrong to assume that they are simply a product of our will, choice, and imagination. Our desires are socially mediated. We desire what the other desires. The advertising industry's general understanding of these processes has enabled it to reformulate desire and thus expand consumer markets in increasingly sophisticated ways by identifying, creating or exacerbating social anxieties, and stimulating the deep sense of lack that lies at the core of the human subject (Hall et al., 2012).

In the context of rising inequality, poverty, disillusionment, and lack of hope for a better future, the fact that our ability to earn respect and recognition is increasingly dependent on our ability to display consumer goods has become a source of anxiety (Hall et al., 2012; Hall, 2012b). The same forces of capitalism that push some people into poverty and misery also push them towards sociosymbolic competition and relentless consumption of status symbols – a thoroughly criminogenic spiral (Hall et al., 2012). As Bauman put it, 'it is one thing to be poor in a society of producers and universal employment; it is quite a different thing to be poor in a society of consumers' (Bauman, 2005: 1). The desire for commodities and the social recognition and status they represent fuels much of today's acquisitive crime, both petty and grand, because consumerism mediates human relationships and informs the ways we perceive and interact with others (Miles et al., 1998; Boden, 2003; Illouz, 2007). It orders contemporary social hierarchies and mechanisms of exclusion (Hayward and Yar, 2006; Miles, 2014; Nadeem, 2014), reproducing the socially disruptive yet economically dynamic competitive individualism that is such a prominent feature of postmodern liberal societies (Hall and Winlow, 2013). In this context, 'conspicuous consumption' (Veblen, 1970) fulfils two main functions; fuelling the anxious, endlessly circular expression of desire that staves off the denigrated status of the 'flawed consumer' (Hall et al., 2012), whilst paradoxically signalling the pursuit of belonging, integration, and acceptance (Miles et al., 1998). We are pushed towards distinction, differentiation, individualism, and narcissistic subjectivity at the same time as we are pushed to belong to the 'herd' – a classic consumerist dynamic already identified by Georg Simmel (Simmel, [1904] 1957). Contradictory pressure is exerted simultaneously on all of us to both fit in with and stand out from social groups (Miles et al., 1998; Winlow and Hall, 2009). As we dress to reflect our unique choice of style, we also hope to triumph over others struggling to carry out precisely the same task. As we donate our energy and our money to consumer capitalism, we simultaneously and constantly disrupt the social collective in favour of an unstable milieu of competing individuals. We could aver that no previous cultural form has combined individual differentiation with social homogeneity in such a pervasive, inescapable, and economically dynamic relation (Hall, 2012a).

Consumerism, as (Baudrillard, 2016, see also Stiegler, 2009) noted, has replaced traditional systems of individuation to become a mode of rootless, free-floating, competitive differentiation. Its purpose is not the satisfaction of needs or desires. In a western culture dominated by advertising and mass media, we are relentlessly influenced to discard collective identities and exclusively pursue individuality through the symbols presented to us by consumerism's panoramic sign-value system. This inevitably leaves our 'individuality' anxious, incomplete, and, ultimately, a myth that reflects our growing distance from reality and our submersion in a commodified hyper-reality that has disrupted and displaced all collective forms and mutual interests. We have stepped outside history. These comprehensive changes to everyday social experience play a significant role in the gradual transformation of human subjectivity into one that prefers the surrogate and hyperreal world of consumer goods over a confrontation with the Real (Hall, 2012a, 2012b).

What is at stake here is not merely identifying the deleterious consequences of consumer culture, such as the proliferation of mental ill-health, depression, and anxiety (Sloan, 1996), and their various knock-on effects, which include obesity, body dysmorphia, anorexia, bulimia, self-harm, suicide, and so on (Schrecker and Bambra, 2015). Whilst of course avoiding crude mechanistic determinism, criminology must look beneath these symptoms to the underlying processual context, particularly the dominance of instrumentalism, cynicism, and narcissistic competition in our cultural lives. Consumerism's 'culture of now' (Hayward, 2007) encourages us to forget what we have lost and imagine instead a ceaseless procession of technological innovation and novel indulgences that will lead us into a bright future, improve our lives, and deliver to us enduring happiness. But, as it places individuals in competition with one another over symbols of social status, consumerism has eroded modern forms of civil society (Baudrillard, 2016; Stiegler, 2009) and played a significant role in the dissipation of modernity's collectivist and universalist political projects (Badiou, 2007). As the future looks bright up above, it also looks more unstable and fragile down below.

As some scholars have noted (see, for example, Bauman, 2007), the pleasures of consumerism tend to be quite fleeting. Consumerism is not simply about occasionally buying a few material goods that we want but do not need. It also involves the ritualised act of discarding consumer items that have lost their allure and attempting to humiliate those who still own them, only to begin the process all over again as new products enter the market (Appadurai, 2011). Consumerism holds out the prospect of satisfaction through ownership, but, quickly, we find ourselves yet again dissatisfied and assailed by new desires. New trinkets are placed before us, and the social dialogue that accompanies them inspires us to return yet again to the market in the hope that our latest shopping trip will assuage the anxieties that gnaw away at us from within, finally ensuring our socio-symbolic status. It never quite manages to deliver, however, as each momentary investment instead coalesces into a more or less permanent state of dissatisfaction, the market's principal psychological driver. In a sense, a 'consumer' is someone accustomed to dissatisfaction, to the emotional fix that precedes further acts of consumption as we endlessly oscillate between the poles of desire/enjoyment and satiation (McGowan, 2016).

Such salesmanship is not difficult. Lacanian psychoanalysts have long known that desire signifies a lack (Lacan, 2002), an absence, and as such is contingent, fragile, and ephemeral. As soon as we take ownership of the longed-for thing, we are destined to lose our desire for it. Desire, therefore, is dependent upon the absence of the desired object. Consumer markets are reliant upon this basic principle. Taking ownership of a car, a house, or a gadget we have longed for does not satisfy us, because desire is immediately reconstituted. We focus on another thing, or another experience, and desire begins again. Satisfaction, properly understood, threatens consumerism. If we ever reach a point at which we are no longer desirous of consumerism's products and services, capitalism would plunge into a major economic crisis. Even today's social movements, conceptually provisioned by social science's conservative and liberal theoretical frameworks, promote themselves by feeding on the desire for what the neoliberal market has made absent – community, authority, security, autonomy, politics, resistance, and so on. Consumerism cannot be understood without a clear understanding of the functions of lack, desire and dissatisfaction in the neoliberal economy.

Criminology and harm

Neoliberalism won its ideological battle with socialism in the 1980s by using mass media and the education system to persuade electorates that the painful aspects of economic 'dis-embedding' (Polanyi, [1944] 2001) were transitory and would soon give way to a continuation of post-war social improvements through renewed emphasis on opportunity, prosperity and the freedom to earn a lot of good things – to have fun and to enjoy ourselves. It's this promise that forms the political and economic bedrock of consumer culture even as it fosters the array of inequalities and injustices that have been a focal point for the social sciences ever since. In contrast, consumerism's harmful consequences and the way we understand harm have received scant attention. However, since the 1990s a zemiological movement has established a rather shaky foothold in sociology and, to a lesser extent, criminology. Zemiology, in very basic terms, is the study of harm. Its Ancient Greek root term *zemia* is broad and has multiple meanings, drawing together ways in which human beings experience and understand phenomena ranging from decay, wastage, attrition, lack, loss, and suffering to bodily damage, disaster, spoilage, ruin, and debt. Moreover, over the millennia *zemia* has been the unwritten and rarely spoken core concept that underpins our understanding of crime and our institutional practices of jurisprudence and punishment (Boukli and Kotzé, 2018). That such a venerable and ancient concept has been allowed to fade into the background indicates criminology's reluctance to remain connected to the conceptual ground on which it walks. To focus on crime and punishment without an adequate conception and a continuous empirical and philosophical investigation of the concept of harm is to accept social definitions established by past and present elites, quite often in their own interests (Hall, 2012; Raymen, 2016).

If criminology is to contribute to the renewal of interest in the concept of harm, simply constructing typologies of known harmful practices that may or may not warrant criminalisation is important but of limited use, and, until we establish an ongoing ontological, ethical, and epistemological framework around the concept, perhaps in the more ambiguous cases rather premature. However, we cannot simply reach up and pluck the abstract essence of *zemia* out of Plato's realm of Ideal Forms. Significant empirical and philosophical work needs to be carried out in a process of free and open enquiry to expand knowledge of real experiences and establish ontological, ethical, and epistemological principles – what is harm in the human experience and how can we produce at least a working knowledge of its varied yet commonly experienced forms and impacts? At a deeper level, can we approach consensus on the principles we use to give our concepts of harm some degree of ontological grounding?

The currently truncated political spectrum does not help us in this endeavour. Neoliberals sideline talk of harms such as global warming or underemployment because they believe the required interventions in the underlying systemic contexts will jeopardise their global economic project. Left liberals, on the other hand, worry that too much public talk of harm will fuel calls for further criminalisation and punishment. After all, if harms beyond the natural are being done, then some individuals or groups must be doing them. A generalised initial presumption of harmlessness in all ambivalent cases is better suited to the liberal way of doing things. Where harms are acknowledged, the standard liberal response is to posit them as nothing more than individual perceptions to be understood as interior traumas and addressed by psychotherapy and so on, which permanently distracts attention from external realities, underlying contexts, and collective or political solutions – for instance, those suffering from stress at work due to understaffing and impossible targets are encouraged to meditate rather than strike.

The only leftist alternative with any currency today is identity politics, a post-structural free-for-all where well-established activists claiming to represent numerous cultural interest-groups attempt to monopolise the ethical high-ground by placing their harms above others on the zemiological scale. This type of cultural politics aids piecemeal reformism and the partial equalisation of some post-structural social relations but distracts attention from deeper systemic contexts, even though each identitarian group seems to be claiming that the unequal relation they address has been the 'true social struggle' throughout history. Neoliberalism gains reproductive capital from this post-structural melee by using media and academia to foster competition between the various loci of social struggle, protecting itself from the formation of an organised, oppositional group that might actually inflict damage on its project. Zemiologists intent on establishing revised general principles and taking a harder look at what underlies our current perceived reality should prepare themselves for intense flak coming from numerous positions on neoliberalism's right and left spectrum (see Hall and Winlow, 2015).

As ultra-realists have argued for some time now, a vital first step is the networked ethnographic investigation of real human life-worlds to gather as much data as possible about zemiological experiences and unrecorded harms that can act as conceptual concrete universals with analytical generalisability – in very simple terms, experiences that many people in different locations would agree to be harmful (Hall and Winlow, 2015). It should also be understood that the cumulative impact of low-level incidents can have grave consequences (Kotzé, 2019) and that a reluctance to recognise situational harms closes the door on the investigation of underlying structural and processual contexts – for instance, a flash-flood that can be connected to a context constituted by global warming, fossil-fuel burning, industrialism, and consumer capitalism. In other words, many harms are symptoms of such complex underlying structures and processes, which then could be understood as *systemically and inherently zemiogenic*. For Reiner (2016), the obstacle facing criminologists is the morally tenuous – or in some cases arbitrary – means of distinguishing between legally defined crime and the non-criminalised harms hidden in various social spaces. In current labour markets, for instance, individuals can be seen wilting under the demands of monotonous, stressful, micro-managed jobs that are clear symptoms of an underlying context of insecurity, exploitation, and socioeconomic injustice (Lloyd, 2018). Harm is often one of those things that we might often be unsure of beforehand, but, despite relativist obfuscation, we know it when we see it, and we certainly know it when we feel it.

Even if some sort of partial consensus could be reached around which experiences should be understood as harmful, we can't proceed without some sort of prior working conceptual framework. Social science will not hand out funding or time to researchers to go out on a hunch or the vague claim that out there in the real world individuals already have some naturally consensual idea of what harm is, especially now that various post-structural lobby groups have convinced the funders that their harms are what really matter and they should get most of the support. Early attempts to construct grounded conceptual principles looked at social reproduction and human flourishing but proved to be rather vague. For Pemberton (2015), a step on the road to ontological clarity can be made by adopting a needs-based perspective – if a need is a goal that prevents a harm, it must be provisioned. However, whereas that claim would certainly clarify the issue of intervention and should not be rejected outright, it does not provide a firm conceptual understanding of harm itself. If any general conception of harm can be disrupted by relativists, the needs-based perspective can also be subjugated, as indeed it has been by negative liberty arguments, in which freedom trumps all and any freedom given up to provision need must be seen as a loss and therefore avoided, even though the exercise of extreme freedom as 'special liberty' is itself a major cause of harms (Hall, 2012; Lloyd, 2018).

Yar (2012) grounds harm in a theory of lack of social recognition, but this idea is trapped in a past when social and economic relations were more interdependent and, in some ways, reciprocal. In other words, where once masters needed slaves and were forced to take their opinions into account, now the globalised capitalist system has little use for many workers and their communities and regards physical resources as plentiful and of use only to profits. Neoliberalism has systematically disempowered organised workers and their political institutions (Slobodian, 2018), therefore traditional relations of interdependency have been severed and reciprocity is no longer necessary. Special liberty abounds, the sense that those who create wealth by whatever means can proceed in unrestricted ways, stretching or breaking laws and ethical codes where they deem it necessary. They define harm from on top in ways that can be brushed aside by combinations of relativism, negative liberty, and special liberty. Voices from below are rarely heard, while those that expose the system's core as inherently zemiogenic are not heard at all.

Is there a way out of the relativist trap, the hyper-idealist doctrine that denies universal objective truth and declares that perceptions from myriad cultural, sub-cultural, or individual positions are all we will ever have as our means of understanding the world and living in it? For some social scientists the path away from relativist chaos towards more clarity requires zemiology's ontology to be reconnected to a revived positive ethics (Lloyd, 2018; Raymen, forthcoming). If our understanding is correct, they seem to be pointing towards the social reorganisation and elevation of ethical conversations in different fields around what constitutes the good, a conversation that the broad liberal project has sidelined in favour of negative rights, liberty, and subjectivism. Relativism's true nemesis is the establishment of crucial conversations that must end with sets of decisions to be taken about coordinated actions on a large scale – the crucial responses to global warming or underemployment being the classic examples, both currently being mooted as interrelated issues in talks of a 'green new deal' (see, for example, Powell, 2019). When action to avoid a harm is agreed as a necessary good to be implemented as soon as possible, relativism dies. The initial question thus becomes concerned with which objectives are good in various fields of social life, such as health, ecology, economics, and so on, while the social decisions made to inform action through politics and policy must be made in an arena of free speech and rebalanced social power relations that actively disempower neoliberalism's global elite and find common ground underneath identitarian struggles. Where the good and harm associated with global warming are clear-cut – life versus death – more subtle categories require the opening up of democratised conversations to inform political actions in numerous other fields and sub-fields (Sparrow, 2014). If to some extent we know harms when we see them, we know them even better when we experience them and feel them receding, which requires accountable politicians who represent people rather than the agents of neoliberalism's economic project, along with constant action-centred conversations in the public realm.

Zemiology's conceptual framework is never fully settled but always a work in progress, but a work that must systematically avoid sailing into the political doldrums of relativism and subjectivism. Instead, it must help subjective experience to see outside itself and locate itself in the external structures and processes that often impact our lives in harmful ways. Although the past provides lessons to be learnt, conceptual frameworks and ethical decisions cannot be fully pre-empted and must be products of empirically rich and properly rebalanced representations of reality on which social conversations can be based. This requires the wholesale democratisation of politics, media, intellectual life, and financial/economic life, a situation that neoliberals have worked hard to prevent since the early 1980s. Criminology is one such field, with a number of sub-fields, that must enter the fully democratised arena to reignite conversations about specific goods and harms under the principles of free speech and rebalanced power relations, even though the 'elites' in these sub-fields are rarely neoliberals but activists who dominate the social conversations to their own end to force through their personal definitions of good and harm. This is not to disparage activism but to persuade activists to reach down and find unity in the systemic context that underlies most zemiological symptoms (Hall and Winlow, 2015).

The first move in any field is to throw all dominant assumptions into question, even the assumptions advocated by those who have become dominant in various fields yet still claim to be 'outsiders' and the agents of progress in waiting. The fundamental question is what allows room for the broad constellation of harms. Ultra-realists have already suggested that harms are not products of injustice or extreme inequality, but in fact injustice and extreme inequality are the products of the willingness or some 'misfelt' compulsion (see Winlow, 2014) to inflict harm or at least risk harm to others (Hall, 2012; Horsley, 2014). Consumerism, like the industrialism that rose up to meet its demands, expands and reproduces itself on the assumption of harmlessness, which justifies the willingness to risk harm in order to foster desires and sell goods. Raymen's (forthcoming) crucial contribution to zemiology is his recognition that the willingness to use liberal values and concepts such as liberty, relativism, and subjectivism to establish and reproduce an accepted order of thought and action in most fields, especially economic life, allows individuals to regularly deny or at least underestimate the potentially harmful consequences of their actions – we give ourselves permission to act as if we don't know what will happen, even when we have an inkling that what might happen will cause harm. Again, the denial or the constant postponement of the public declaration of firm knowledge about the human causes of climate-change or the political causes of insecurity and underemployment are classic examples. Raymen (forthcoming) reveals the essence of the problem in his prescient analysis of how liberal capitalism has separated ontology from ethics in such a way that our understanding of what exists, what should exist, and what we should do to bring it into real existence is no longer informed by an ongoing cultural discussion about what is good, but by the imperatives of a globalised market economy set up as a system of fragile interdependencies by a neoliberal elite who have already decided on our behalf what is the greatest good – negative liberty and individual wealth accumulation serviced by the free flow of money, goods, and people across the globe (Slobodian, 2018). In Raymen's (2019: 135) estimation,

> [T]he problem is not just that a consensus around social harm is hard to come by, but that the cynical individualism of liberal-postmodernism *fundamentally precludes any such consensus being reached.*

A revitalised social harm project requires the visiting of many everyday realities as its empirical basis, and a firm commitment to the construction of theory as these harms are connected to neoliberalism's structures, processes, and its (post) politics of minimal intervention, the context in which cynical individualism and special liberty thrive. But, more importantly, it must be reconnected to a revitalised ethical vision of the future:

> Social harm is not merely a concept that identifies what is socially, environmentally and politically-economically corrosive in our society. On the contrary, defining social harm is fundamentally bound up with constructing an imagination for the type of lives we want to lead, the society we want to live in, and the subjectivities we want to cultivate.
>
> (Raymen, 2019: 150)

In other words, the ontology of harm is the flipside of a collective enterprise based on an imagined good that has escaped the tarnished and collapsing neoliberal vision and requires political cooperation across the globe. It is opposed by neoliberalism's attempt to establish the assumption of harmlessness as a global norm in culture and political economy in order to intensify and expand individual desires and ambitions with only a bare minimum of ethical and political restraint. Ignoring specific harms while highlighting others that can be dealt with – or at least seen to be dealt with, or promised to be dealt with at some later date – while retaining the current socioeconomic and political order of things can create impoverished understandings and obscure important aspects of underlying structures and processes. This evasion confines thought, policy, and politics to pragmatic reforms in approved and tractable dimensions, the 'low-hanging fruit'. Therefore, harms that indicate inherent systemic problems are constantly swept under the carpet to resurface in more virulent forms. This category includes the more complex and subtle harms of consumerism.

Criminology and consumerism

Neoliberalism's globalised market economy is fuelled by constantly expanding consumer demand that long ago transcended basic needs to rely on the proliferation of individual desires. So many criminologists have ignored the zemiological aspect of consumerism that 'crime and consumerism' is one of the most neglected sub-fields in dire need of opening up to empirically inspired theoretical work on the subject of specific goods and harms (Boukli and Kotzé, 2018). We have already encountered the basic propositions that consumer culture is driven by sense of absence, and that absences can cause harms. Here we find the insight that criminologists ignore – by dissolving and superseding traditional forms of livelihood, communal security, and meaning, consumerism creates substantive absences in our cultural and political lives, as well as our intimate lives. So-called progressive liberalism helped neoliberalism to justify this process of dissolution and fulfil its principal political objective – to throw out the baby of strong political opposition along with the dirty bathwater of cultural prejudice – by labelling traditional forms as regressive because they harboured and reproduced prejudicial attitudes towards minorities. The harms produced by this absence of the social are now regarded as the normal and inevitable price of progress understood as increased consumption of symbolic goods and personal freedom (see Winlow and Hall, 2013; Bauman, 2008). The social and individual harms of deindustrialisation, insecure service work, community decay, and private debt in the west and intensively competitive labour markets in the developing world are often portrayed as outweighed by consumer capitalism's benefits. This volume will focus on a number of systemically derived harms associated with consumer capitalism.

It is quite remarkable that criminology has thus far avoided a serious and sustained encounter with what so obviously appears to be advanced capitalist culture's principal criminogenic context. Those who address consumerism do so only in the most basic way. For example, some criminologists have used the term *consumerism* to communicate only the basic need for goods (see Newburn et al., 2015). Some who place themselves on the criminological left have mistaken theoretical critiques of consumerism for some sort of condescension felt towards those who consume (see Cooper, 2012). Others approach it uncritically as the great gift capitalism has bestowed upon its populations (see Matthews, 2014) or even identify it as the new wellspring of political resistance (Hall, 1981; Littler, 2008). For over four decades many on the political left in Britain have embraced consumerism and focused on its supposedly liberating qualities. Many leftist social scientists (see, for example, Featherstone, 1995; Hall and Jefferson, 2006) have argued that consumer culture facilitated a 'rebellion into style', to bring choice and stylistic diversity to a dour and rather homogenous post-war cultural vista. Consumer symbols could be reworked into new meanings on which forms of subcultural togetherness could be founded. These post-1968 'new leftists' were convinced that all the while the consumer symbols that represented capital accumulation and systemic reproduction were being reworked and subverted by creative youth, even though the majority spent most of their disposable income on mass-produced consumer items and showed only passing interest in substantive alternative politics. This 'cultural turn' was in essence an intellectual and political wrong-turn that is only just recently beginning to be seen for what it is – a colossal mistake (Smith and Raymen, 2016; Raymen and Smith, 2016; Horsley, 2015). Wildly over-reacting to the failures of post-WWII state socialism and social democracy, the cultural turn founded itself negatively on the outright denial of the unavoidable fact that capitalism cannot be resisted at the point of consumption but only reproduced in novel forms that further expand the market.

The cultural turn was imported into many aspects of critical criminology, but it found its true expression in cultural criminology. To pare it down to its fundamental claims, cultural criminology tends to assume that the stereotypically marginalised 'criminal' is engaged in some sort of traditional, inarticulate sub-conscious fight against some permutation of capitalism, cultural homogeneity, and the broad system of oppressive social control (see Ferrell, 2019). This position romanticises the working-class deviant and imbues him with characteristics difficult to find in the prisons, police stations, and problem estates of the neoliberal era. Does the marginalised criminal truly or even vaguely understand the abstract system of capitalism and its social order, and is he so disgusted by his experiences of this capitalist reality that he structures his identity and social activity in opposition to it, even at the risk of significant punishment? Even more far-fetched is the claim that he is engaged in an inarticulate, unconscious, or 'preconscious' struggle against the system he does not understand (see Akram, 2014; Ferrell, 2019). Alternative research and theorisation suggests not (Treadwell et al., 2013; Ayres and Treadwell, 2012: Horsley, 2014; Smith, 2014) and offers the alternative perspective that most acquisitive crimes and even some violent crimes (see Hall and Wilson, 2014) are bound up with the logic of capitalism and the anxieties, drives, and desires it incites. Should we really continue with accounts of crime as resistance when reality indicates quite clearly that the desire to seek gratification in consumer capitalism's sign-value system is a well-established characteristic in most criminal cultures across the west? We think not, and the chapters that follow in this collection will offer synopses of theoretical arguments and empirical research that will explain why an alternative perspective is needed, and hopefully provide some concepts around which a new framework can be constructed.

The book is divided into two parts – the first focuses on historical and theoretical perspectives, the second on contexts and case studies. Steve Hall opens the volume with his chapter on *Consumer Culture and English History's Lost Object*, returning to the European beginnings of modernity/capitalism to trace the fundamental lost object of community and solidarity. In a cultural process which has dismantled all forms of political opposition that have risen up from time to time, the reproduction of this fundamental sense of social loss acts as the basis for the sense of lack and the competitive individualism that drives forward consumer culture. For Hall, the true irony of modernist/capitalist history is a sort of zemiological conversion, from a pre-modern culture that once normalised interpersonal violence to modern and postmodern cultures that reduced violence not to create social peace but to clear more space for non-violent subjugation, exploitation, and sociosymbolic competition, thus transforming the overall shape of crime and harm. Mark Featherstone, in his chapter on *The Libertine: Criminal Luxury, the Sadean System, and Materialist Horror*, also trawls through history to trace another fundamental cultural current that fuels consumer capitalism – the desire for criminal luxury that has been portrayed as a transgression of restrictive norms has established itself as normal, hegemonic, and highly functional cultural drive. The so-called heroic outsider challenging the old order is at the same time the decadent insider fuelling the engine of economic growth. Finally, Justin Kotzé, focusing on *The Commodification of Abstinence*, shows how even the act of abstaining from consumerism's procession of commodities and thus supposedly resisting consumer capitalism's hegemony can be recuperated and commodified. Those who imagine themselves to be acting politically actually come to enjoy their commodified acts of abstinence, thus withdrawing even further from effective politics into an 'interpassive' space and creating a gaping post-political fissure in which crimes and harms can proliferate.

The second part of the book then turns to concrete empirical cases, opening with a chapter by Mark Horsley and Anthony Lloyd on *Mass Indebtedness and the Luxury of Payment Means*, which explores late capitalism's prevailing strategy for maintaining consumer participation against the decline of its material productivity. Were it not for the rapid expansion of the credit industry since the early 1990s, they note, it's almost inconceivable that the neoliberal variant of capitalism could have sustained even relatively modest growth alongside falling incomes. Using elements of the authors' combined sets of data, the chapter shows how consumer culture rides on the potentially unresolvable assumption that all of us will, eventually, repay our debts. The profusion of debt-financed payment means has implicated every one of us, regardless of whether we individually carry outstanding debts, into a society-wide system of speculation that provides payment means only as a kind of 'systemic luxury', a transcendence of material circumstances that ultimately accentuates underlying inequalities and intensifies the criminogenic and zemiogenic aspects of neoliberal capitalism.

In her chapter entitled *Luxury Brands in the Wrong Hands: Of Harleys, Harm, and Sovereignty*, Tereza Kuldova invites us into the world of outlaw motorcycle clubs, such as the notorious Hells Angels MC, to think through the relation between class, capitalism, exploitation, harm, and luxury consumer objects. Kuldova not only looks at the perspectival illusion at the core of luxury, but also at luxury as a manifestation of the 'filthy sacred' which by its own nature depends on harm that is sublimated. She shows that luxury goods are sold today as a form of *commodified sovereignty* – a profoundly unsatisfying substitute for real experiences and moments of sovereignty that, in line with the logic of consumerism, always leave one wanting more. The case of the evolution of the outlaw motorcycle subculture in the post-war period illustrates the transition from real sovereignty to commodified sovereignty, and the ways in which branding has fundamentally transformed the subculture by enabling the rise of a transnational criminal enterprise and its manifold harms at the same time as preserving a semblance of the sacred, inalienable, and uncommodifiable in a world obsessed with consumer goods.

Tammy Ayres, in her chapter on *Substances: The Luxurious, the Sublime, and the Harmful*, continues this discussion on luxury and the sublime. She brings harm into the discussion by focusing more closely on the consumption and supply of different luxurious (il)licit substances. Ayres argues that these substances are a normal and integral part of surviving, succeeding, and creating a social identity in a consumer society. While drugs have been traditionally regarded by advocates on the right and left as relatively harmless, and seen again by some on the new left as 'subverting capitalism', Ayres shows that they have, on the contrary, been instrumental to its development and expansion. Substances act as 'sublime objects of ideology' that keep the neoliberal fantasy alive, their consumption and social use symptomatic of global neoliberal consumer culture, its harms, and its harmful subjectivities.

Thomas Raymen and Oliver Smith continue the debate by moving away from substances to practices, drawing our attention to *Gambling and Harm in 24/7 Capitalism: Reflections from the Post-Disciplinary Present*. Here they explore the shifting nature of the gambling industry as it moves out of the fixed geography of casinos and betting-shops into everyday life, becoming far more pervasive as it capitalises on the prevalence of online mobile computing technologies. The chapter begins with the suggestion that existing social-scientific work on gambling often fails to capture the realities of its digital form by relying on aging theoretical approaches that often see it as an exciting alternative cultural space fundamentally separate from – and in some cases resistant to – consumer capitalism's structural and emotional rhythms. However, few, if any, of Raymen and Smith's participants spoke of any kind of emotional high or monetary reward and instead seemed to gamble more as a way of switching their brains into neutral, of simply staving off boredom whilst remaining fully embedded in 24/7 capitalism's 'communication sensation-stimulus matrix'. What's more, they suggest, this shift into online spaces has allowed gambling to diffuse outwards from its traditional concentration points such as casinos to the extent that its harms – physical and mental illness, depression, alcohol abuse, damaged relationships, and escalating debts – increasingly fly under the radar of existing regulatory mechanisms.

Kate Tudor returns to the discussion of the profoundly unsatisfying, harmful, and destructive quest for sovereignty within the context of the pressures of neoliberalism, consumer capitalism, and widespread culture of anxiety in her chapter *Toxic Sovereignty: Understanding Fraud as the Expression of Special Liberty within Late Capitalism*. Drawing upon her work with those convicted for their involvement in investment fraud, she shows how the notion of sovereignty became central to their subjective experience, as a justification for fraud and their exercise of 'special liberty', the extreme personal freedom that enabled them to continue in their predatory acts despite the extreme economic and psychological harms they inflicted on their victims. Tudor also shows that their perspectives on consumer sovereignty, where the individual who self-governs consumptive choices is replaced by the individual characterised by the absolute right to pursue pleasure in an unrestrained way, has in turn eroded many personal and ethical barriers against harm and criminality.

Finally, Leanne McRae, in her chapter titled *Spy vs Spy: The Surveillance State of Social Media*, offers a criminological and zemiological analysis of social media that looks underneath the traditional themes of cyberbullying, trolling, fraud, identity theft, doxing, and protecting young people from online predators. McRae returns to the traditional critical criminological themes of social reaction, mass surveillance, and the harms of the state to ask whether the state's putative attempt to protect privacy has led to a worrying immersion in crime and harm discourses that paradoxically threaten to strip rights and promote persecution, while simultaneously distracting attention from the actual everyday harms that blight people's lives. Using Telegram as her main example, she examines how terrorists' use of social media in the planning and execution of attacks has prompted law enforcement systems to instigate types of legislation and regulatory practice that may jeopardise the principle of user privacy.

References

Akram, S. (2014) Recognizing the 2011 United Kingdom Riots as Political Protest: A Theoretical Framework Based on Agency, Habitus and the Preconscious. *British Journal of Criminology*, 54, 3: 375–92.

Appadurai, A. (2011) *The Social Life of Things: Commodities in Cultural Perspective*, Cambridge: Cambridge University Press.

Ayres, T. and Treadwell, J. (2012) Bars, Drugs and Football Thugs: Alcohol, Cocaine Use and Violence in the Night Time Economy Among English Football Firms. *Criminology and Criminal Justice*, 12, 1: 83–100.

Badiou, A. (2007) *The Century*, Cambridge: Polity Press.

Baudrillard, J. (2016) *The Consumer Society: Myths and Structures*, London: Sage.

Bauman, Z. (2003) *Liquid Love*, Oxford: Polity Press.

Bauman, Z. (2005) *Work, Consumerism and the New Poor*, Berkshire: Open University Press.

Bauman, Z. (2007) *Consuming Life*, Cambridge: Polity Press.

Beck, U. and Beck-Gernsheim, E. (1995) *The Normal Chaos of Love*, Oxford: Polity Press.

Beck, U. and Beck-Gernsheim, E. (2001) *Individualization*, London: Sage.

Boden, S. (2003) *Consumerism, Romance and the Wedding Experience*, New York: Palgrave Macmillan.

Boukli, A. and Kotzé, J. (2018) *Zemiology: Reconnecting Crime and Social Harm*, London: Palgrave Macmillan.

Cooper, C. (2012) Understanding the English Riots of 2011: Mindless Violence or 'Mekin Histri' in Austerity Britain? *Youth and Policy*, 109, 6: 6–26.

Ewen, S. (1998) *PR! A Social History of Spin*, London: Basic Books.

Featherstone, M. (1991) *Consumer Culture and Postmodernism*, London: Sage.

Featherstone, M (1995) *Undoing Culture: Globalisation, Postmodernism and Identity*, London: Sage.

Ferrell, J. (2019) In Defence of Resistance. *Critical Criminology*. doi:10.1007/s10612-019-09456-6

Hall, S. (1981) Notes on Deconstructing the Popular. In R. Samuel (ed.) *People's History and Socialist Theory*, London: Routldge and Kegan Paul.

Hall, S. (2012a) The Solicitation of the Trap: On Transcendence and Transcendental Materialism in Advanced Consumer-Capitalism. *Human Studies*, 35, 3: 365–81.

Hall, S. (2012b) *Theorizing Crime and Deviance: A New Perspective*, London: Sage.

Hall, S. and Jefferson, T. (2006) *Resistance Through Rituals: Youth Subcultures in Post*, 2nd edn., Abingdon: Routledge.

Hall, S. and Wilson, D. (2014) New Foundations: Pseudo-Pacification and Special Liberty as Potential Cornerstones for a Multi-Level Theory of Homicide and Serial Murder. *European Journal of Criminology*, 11, 5: 635–55.

Hall, S. and Winlow, S. (2013) *Rethinking Social Exclusion: The End of the Social?* London: Sage.

Hall, S. and Winlow, S. (2015) *Revitalizing Criminological Theory*, London: Routledge.

Hall, S. and Winlow, S. (2018) Big Trouble or Little Evils: The Ideological Struggle Over the Concept of Harm. In J. Kotzé and A. Boukli (eds.) *Zemiology: Critical Criminological Perspectives*, Cham: Palgrave Macmillan, 107–26.

Hall, S., Winlow, S. and Ancrum, C. (2008) *Criminal Identities and Consumer Culture: Crime, Exclusion and the New Culture of Narcissism*, London: Willan/Routledge.

Hayward, K.J. (2007) Situational Crime Prevention And Its Discontents: Rational Choice Theory Versus The 'Culture of Now'. *Social Policy & Administration*, 41, 1: 232–250.

Hayward, K.J. and Yar, M. (2006) The Chav Phenomenon: Consumption, Media and the Construction of a New Underclass. *Crime, Media, Culture*, 2, 1: 9–28.

Horsley, M. (2014) The 'Death of Deviance' and the Stagnation of 20th Century Criminology. In M. Dellwing, J. Kotarba and N. Pino (eds.) *The Death and Resurrection of Deviance*, London: Palgrave Macmillan.

Horsley, M. (2015) *The Dark Side of Prosperity*, Farnham: Ashgate.

Illouz, E. (2007) *Cold Intimacies: The Making of Emotional Capitalism*, New York: Polity Press.

Kotzé, J. (2019) *The Myth of the Crime Decline: Exploring Change and Continuity in Crime and Harm*, London: Routledge.

Kuldova, T. (2016) Directing Passions in New Delhi's World of Fashion: On the Power of Ritual and 'Illusions Without Owners'. *Thesis Eleven*, 133, 1: 96–113.

Lacan, J. (2002) *The Subversion of the Subject and the Dialectic of Desire in the Freudian Unconscious. Écrits*, trans. B. Fink, New York: W.W. Norton, 671–702.

Lears, J. (1995) *Fables of Abundance: A Cultural History of Advertising in America*, London: Basic Books.

Littler, J. (2008) *Radical Consumption: Shopping for Change in Contemporary Culture*, Maidenhead: Open University Press.

Lloyd, A. (2018) *The Harms of Work: An Ultra-Realist Account of the Service Economy*, Bristol: Bristol University Press.

Matthews, R. (2014) *Realist Criminology*, London: Palgrave Macmillan.

McGowan, T. (2016) *Capitalism and Desire: The Psychic Cost of Free Markets*, New York: Columbia University Press.

Miles, S. (1998) *Consumerism: A Way of Life*, London: Sage.

Miles, S. (2014) Young People, 'Flawed Protestors' and the Commodification of Resistance. *Critical Arts*, 28, 1: 76–87.

Miles, S., Cliff, D. and Burr, V. (1998) 'Fitting in and Sticking out': Consumption, Consumer Meanings and the Construction of Young People's Identities. *Journal of Youth Studies*, 1, 1: 81–96.

Nadeem, S. (2014) Fair and Anxious: On Mimicry and Skin-Lightening in India. *Social Identities*, 20, 2: 224–38.

Newburn, T., Cooper, K., Deacon, R. and Diski, B. (2015) Shopping for Free? Looting Consumerism and the 2011 English Riots. *British Journal of Criminology*, 55, 5: 987–1004

Pemberton, S. (2015) *Harmful Societies: Understanding Social Harm*, Bristol: Policy Press.

Polanyi, K. ([1944] 2001) *The Great Transformation: The Political and Economic Origins of Our Times*, Boston, MA: Beacon Press.

Powell, D. (2019) Rebooting the UK's Green New Deal. *The New Economics Foundation*. Available at: https://neweconomics.org/2019/01/a-green-new-deal-for-the-uk (Accessed: 1 August 2019)

Raymen, T. (2019) 'The Enigma of Social Harm and the Barrier of Liberalism: Why Zemiology needs a theory of the Good'. In *Justice, Power and Resistance: The Journal of the European Group for the Study of Deviance and Social Control*, 3, 1: 133–161.

Raymen, T. (2016) Designing-in Crime by Designing-out the Social? Situational Crime Prevention and the Intensification of Harmful Subjectivities. *British Journal of Criminology*, 56, 3: 497–514.

Raymen, T. and Smith, O. (2016) What's Deviance Got to Do with It? Black Friday Sales, Violence and Hyper-Conformity. *British Journal of Criminology*, 56, 2: 389–405.

Reiner, R. (2016) *Crime*, Cambridge: Polity Press.

Schrecker, T. and Bambra, C. (2015) *How Politics Makes Us Sick: Neoliberal Epidemics*, London: Palgrave Macmillan.

Simmel, G. ([1904] 1957) Fashion. *American Journal of Sociology*, 62, 6: 541–58.

Sloan, T. (1996) *Damaged Life: The Crisis of the Modern Psyche*, London: Routledge.

Slobodian, Q. (2018) *Globalists: The End of Empire and the Birth of Neoliberalism*, London: Harvard University Press.

Smart, B. (2010) *Consumer Society*, London: Sage.

Smith, O. (2014) *Contemporary Adulthood and the Night-Time Economy*, London: Palgrave.

Smith, O. and Raymen, T. (2016) Deviant Leisure: A Criminological Perspective. *Theoretical Criminology*, 22, 1: 63–82.

Sparrow, T. (2014) *The End of Phenomenology: Metaphysics and the New Realism*, Edinburgh: Edinburgh University Press.

Stiegler, B. (2009) *Acting Out*, Stanford: Stanford University Press.

Treadwell, J., Briggs, D., Winlow, S. and Hall, S. (2013) Shopocalypse Now: Consumer Culture and the English Riots of 2011. *British Journal of Criminology*, 53, 1: 1–17.

Veblen, T. (1970) *The Theory of the Leisure Class: An Economic Study of Institutions*, London: Unwin Books.

Winlow, S. (2014) Trauma, Guilt and the Unconscious: Some Theoretical Notes on Violent Subjectivity. In L. Ray and J. Kilby (eds.) *Sociological Review Monograph: Violence and Society: Towards a New Sociology*, Chichester: Wiley, 32–49.

Winlow, S. and Hall, S. (2006) *Violent Night: Urban Leisure and Contemporary Culture*, Oxford: Berg.

Winlow, S. and Hall, S. (2009) Living for the Weekend: Youth Identities in Northeast England. *Ethnography*, 10, 1: 91–113.

Winlow, S. and Hall, S. (2013) *Rethinking Social Exclusion: The End of the Social?* London: Sage.

Yar, M. (2012) Recognition as the Grounds for a General Theory of Crime as Social Harm'. In S. O'Neill and N. Smith (eds.) *Recognition Theory as Social Research*, London: Palgrave Macmillan.

Žižek, S. (2009) *The Ticklish Subject*, London: Verso.

Part 1

Historical and theoretical perspectives

1 Consumer culture and English history's lost object

Steve Hall

Introduction

Although the motivations behind many serious newsworthy crimes continue to be diverse and individualistic, much of today's mundane volume crime is driven by consumer desire (Hall et al., 2008). Contrary to the eternally optimistic liberal narrative, there has been no real decline in consumer-driven criminal markets (Kotzé, 2019). Localised criminal markets that expanded during the early years of neoliberalism's destructive course and operate largely under the statistical radar are now joined by new online markets that supply goods to consumers worldwide – illegal goods such as drugs and weapons, counterfeits such as clothes and image-enhancing pharmaceuticals, or legal goods distributed illegally (see Hall and Antonopoulos, 2016; Large, 2019). As anxious consumers unsure of their identities and concerned about their personal images crave corporate capitalism's consumer objects as the symbolic props for their very sense of being in the world, the old liberal-leftist idea of 'resistance at the point of consumption' now seems increasingly tenuous.

Criminology, still adhering to romantic notions of organic resistance, is short of a convincing theory of late capitalism's committed consumer subject, and, therefore, unable to either explain the persistence of everyday criminal activity that permeates the social structure, but, more specifically, has in many working-class locales displaced the industrial era's fragile solidarity projects (Hall et al., 2008; Treadwell et al., 2013; Ellis, 2016; Kotzé, 2019). This brief chapter suggests that, in order to regain its intellectual and political efficacy in difficult times for the left, criminology must reject romantic notions of organically 'resistant' consumer subjectivity and misfiring Foucauldian notions of clean cultural/epistemological breaks in history. Instead, it must begin to construct a theoretical framework able to explain the longue durée historical development of modernity's anxious, apolitical, and – in situations of deprivation or excessive opportunity – crime-prone consumer subject.

What follows defies the postmodernist command to construct historical metanarratives. This relatively modest metanarrative begins in Late Mediaeval England and includes insights into events and processes that might well have been real. I'm not suggesting that this juncture I will shortly outline is an 'origin' or a 'source' but a point in history that shifted English and eventually European culture, economy, and politics in a slightly different direction. It contributes an important factor in the overall explanation of the country's early proto-capitalist development – the pseudo-pacified subject, the root of today's forms of adaptive and flimsily pacified criminality. It does not attempt to displace the standard factors behind the early development of the market economy in the transition from Feudalism to Capitalism – technological developments in production and communication, revival of science, European trading options, production for trade, flaws in the feudal system and so on – but simply draws attention to rather neglected culturo-legal and subjective aspects that might be useful for criminological theory.

Given that over time slightly different directions often become substantially different and enduring directions, we will hopefully gain some insights into how the cultural norms and subjectivity set in motion at that juncture have evolved to the present. History is of course a mixture of continuities and discontinuities, but here I claim that we are looking at a major continuity. The trajectory was set by important shifts in the economic and culturo-legal methods by which key economic players were motivated, restrained, and pacified. The principal shifts can be described in very basic terms as 1) the transfer of the primary economic object of desire and repository of value from land to money, and 2) the transfer of the primary source of social status from the violent defence of land and community to the personal pseudo-pacified struggle for social distinction gauged by the degree of success achieved by the individual in the competitive market economy.

The socioeconomic tumour

Despite the violence and political tyranny that afflicted the English population for two centuries after the eleventh-century Norman invasion, alternative forms of ideology, practice, and subjectivity struggled for breath in the nooks and crannies of everyday socioeconomic life. Named 'Distributism' centuries later by G.K. Chesterton (2009), many of these practices drew upon peasant customs yet were also encouraged by some of the more progressive Catholic authorities. In keeping with other European regions, usury – the practice of charging excessive interest on loans, especially personal loans – met with disapproval from the Church. In villages where embryonic Distributist projects enjoyed a brief existence in this period, popular voices concurred with the Church authorities to insist on the tight regulation of usury and the establishment of a 'just and fixed price' for goods, initially established by markets but heavily regulated to prevent overcharging, profiteering and hoarding to raise prices. Price undercutting and the expansion of businesses beyond a reasonable number of employees were also forbidden.

These anti-monopolistic regulations allowed the slow but relatively stable redevelopment and expansion of the old Roman production centres and trading arteries, and a more even and inclusive social distribution of labour and business opportunities at the point of production. We can discern the beginnings of a manifested *agape*, the attempt to diffuse the social ideal of care in the family and community outwards into the broader economy, to operate in the interests of social justice and civility. The Distributist movement did not endure, but its motivating ideals were briefly manifested as a direct and substantive opposition to the harnessed individual greed that drives the current deregulated market, now recognised by some criminologists as today's primary criminogenic context (Reiner, 2007; Currie, 2015).

However, after the Norman invasion many English kings began to allow usury and the subsequent indebting of subjects in order to raise funds, expand business, and levy taxes on the credit issuers. The imperatives that structured individuals' lives began to shift from communal relations to financial transactions. This opened the door for the eventual intrusion of the market in most aspects of human life, the establishment of money as the universal unit of exchange, and the application of energy to the constant repayment of the debt that was necessary to expand business and obtain shelter (Horsley, 2015). Moves such as this prepared the way for the dynamic forces of the market to prevail over Distributism's attempt to combine customs and laws into an ethical socioeconomic project.

The early market economy – production for trade, accounting, the profit motive, mobile labour, and the private ownership of land – benefitted from the active commitment of the more mobile and entrepreneurial peasants. It was in the first stages of its establishment by the thirteenth century (Macfarlane, 1978). The lax Norman warlords were too concerned with war, prayer, courts, and tribute to bother with the everyday details of estate management. This lofty negligence left unattended spaces in which peasants and artisans were able to establish private ownership and administration of the means of production, learning the business skills and accumulating the capital necessary for their eventual entry to the nascent bourgeoisie. It's quite wrong to assume that most peasants resisted these early moves towards the market economy and remained committed to their traditional lives, or to assume that Late Mediaeval society was so rigid and restrictive that modest forms of social mobility were impossible (Dyer, 2000). As production entered the early stage of privatisation, some of the wealthier peasants bought urban residences in towns to seek opportunities for private wealth accumulation in burgeoning consumer markets. Their rejection of communal village life was firm and enduring.

If we briefly shift the analysis over to the culturo-legal dimension, we can begin to discern an important but often neglected factor that prepared England for the initial transition to capitalism. This factor is a process of what looks like cell division – rather than simple vertical mobility as a means of breaking through the class barrier – which was initiated by the economic ejection of sons and daughters from the family and community and the injunction to seek out a living elsewhere. Macfarlane (1978) posits the initial drive behind English bourgeois individualism as a product of the separation of *homo economicus* from the traditional productive-defensive unit constituted by families in the geographically bound community. In the twelfth century the introduction of the laws of primogeniture and entail throughout the social structure – in Europe they were confined to the upper class – effectively broke up the family. In this legal system the first-born inherited the family estate whilst the other siblings lost their guarantee of inheritance. The relations of sociability, security, and love conditional only on the defence of the family's honour and land were tainted by what could be described as a norm of institutionalised betrayal. Other European cultures were slower to separate economics from morality and politics or eject the individual from the fundamental geographically bound reproductive units of land, family, and community – indeed, some Mediterranean regions still hang on to vestiges of this traditional way of doing things (Tsantiropoulos, 2008).

The process that rests on the splitting of the family and community to produce the insecure, anxious, and ambitious individual could be described as a socioeconomic tumour, a growth produced by rapid cell-splitting spreading from dissolving institutions where hyperactive binary fission creates an eruption too rapid and intensive for the traditional social body to control. The individual experienced this tumour as a traumatising maelstrom of undirected activity, unpredictable in every way except the continuation of its growth and the establishment of its dominance. Familial relations were disrupted to the extent that the death of the father became a literally manifested mythology, a misandristic urge for latter-born siblings to commit parricide; alongside incest one of the two primary Oedipal crimes. Because the early death of the father was common in war-torn times and the mother was the first in line for inheritance and control of family property and business, the leap from misandry to misogyny was not difficult. Siblings lower down the pecking order were totally dependent on either parent's autonomous and unpredictable generosity or sense of justice. Unpredictability often reached terrifying proportions – a case of dementia afflicting the surviving parent, for instance, could result in the disinheritance of the whole family.

These culturo-legal processes and their impact on the subject's anxiety, fear, resentment, and desire contributed to the disruption and eventual trituration of traditional communities, further encouraging movement into market towns. As early as the thirteenth century twenty per cent of peasants permanently inhabited towns as entrepreneurs and consumers, developing their tastes for food, clothes, and novelties as status symbols. The nascent urban bourgeoisie began to emulate and compete with the aristocracy. We must accept the fact that, historically, 'resistance' has been practiced as a struggle for economic opportunities and social distinction, an escape not only from the clutches of the ruling class but also from the Church, the community, and their embryonic practices of social justice (Hall, 2012, 2014). In this period the rapidly developing market economy became reliant on both domestic and international trade, producing over twenty-five per cent of the GNP (Dyer, 2000). The relative decline of smaller village markets necessitated the transport of goods and coinage between larger towns, which in turn required more effective means of protecting property. From 1285, following the Statute of Winchester, Edward I reformed the criminal justice system and introduced early community policing measures such as watch and ward, hue and cry, and assizes of arms under the control of shire reeves and constables, which combined with measures such as the coppicing of roadsides to increase safety. We can see here the early establishment of the legal and physical infrastructure in which what we will encounter later in this analysis as an anthropologically unique *pseudo-pacified subject* – economically acquisitive and socially competitive yet physically more pacified – became normal.

In the aftermath of the Plague from the mid-fourteenth century, the rapid population decline caused numerous economic problems in both production and consumption. Aristocrats were forced to make concessions, which increased the flow of entrepreneurial peasants into the market as private producers and traders – accumulating capital, expanding consumption, and fuelling the demand for, and supply of, symbols of social distinction. The Enclosure Movement gathered pace to incentivise producers and revive production. However, the majority who were unable to raise funds to buy land or initiate production centres remained vulnerable to eviction and insecure lives as wage-labourers. This vulnerability fuelled anxiety, envy, and social conflict, and altered the more traditional communal sense of social justice to one associated with the individual's social mobility rights. Anxiety, opportunism, and the rejection of common fate combined to create the subjective fuel for embryonic capitalism's destructive socio-economic dynamism.

The fifteenth century saw an upward spiral of production and consumption (Sassatelli, 2007). English manorial estates were full-blown capitalist enterprises run exclusively for profit. Ownership was individualised and legalised, and where wives had rights to one-third of the estate, children still had none and could not prevent either parent selling it. This tense sociolegal situation fuelled a very active market in land. Entrepreneurialism, social climbing by conspicuous consumption, hatred of regulation and taxation, the toleration of non-violent economic crime, and the dismantling of the customary moral authority held by the commons and religious orders combined to establish a proto-libertarian mentality that was to become one of the psychocultural cornerstones in the development of capitalism. Although the post-plague years saw higher wages and job mobility, there was also evidence of de-skilling, the cultural reframing of work as drudgery, and the social diffusion of the appreciation of leisure, luxury, and unregulated enterprise. Class conflict certainly existed as the less successful peasants were evicted or indebted and bought out to be ejected as landless wage labourers, but much of this class oppression and exploitation was the work of the newly mobile peasantry that, together with the merchant class, was ascending the social hierarchy.

In the fifteenth-century gentrification process, successful merchants and entrepreneurial peasants began to identify with the Lords, eventually intermarrying and competing with them in every dimension. Younger, less ruthless and competitive children were often disinherited and cast out into an insecure market where social mobility was expected and vital for survival. By this time the socioeconomic tumour had spread throughout most of the social body. The social divisiveness that now underpins competitive individualism and the class relation was reproduced in the constantly splitting cell of the family itself. Favoured sons and daughters inherited or were able to buy more land whilst disfavoured siblings joined the ranks of the landless labourers, with land rights and subsistence removed, their whole livelihoods dependent on the vagaries of the emerging market economy and the whims of their masters. This familial splitting became a push-factor in emigration, and in the sphere of the market no external structural force oppressed the peasant class. The atomisation of the peasantry into competitive, pseudo-pacified monads that we understood as 'the bourgeoisie' was the product of an internally generated process.

For the poorer peasants, initial decisions to migrate to the urban areas were not always the products of free choice. By the seventeenth century the wretched wages and conditions of the putting-out system combined with enclosure to further increase the flow of landless labourers into towns in search of better work, fuelling the early stage of the urbanisation process that was to accelerate in the nineteenth century. However, the new urban labouring class, despite their precarity and the social injustices inflicted on them, was not driven by dreams of solidarity or a nascent organised political opposition but the need to maximise individual opportunities. The precarious mobile worker, denied charity outside the boundaries of his parish of birth, was forced or at least found it wise to develop some degree of personal initiative and financial sense. Immersed in a rapidly developing market system replete with proliferating opportunities as well as injustices, the more alert and enterprising workers quickly learned to operate with varying degrees of success in the world of urban commerce. This process of self-improvement and social mobility was invigorating and to some quite lucrative, but it was also brutally competitive, divisive, and corrosive to the traditional ethico-social customs that acted as impediments to personal success.

The organic intellectual, communicative, and organisational means by which the new urban workers could become a proletariat, a group with the potential to become a class for itself, were simply absent. The urban workers' failure to construct their own identity was not a product of 'false consciousness' so much as the dawning of a cynical consciousness that had become averse to the idea of collectivism, which of course had in their historical memory betrayed and failed them. It had cast them out as individuals in an emerging economy that was precarious yet simultaneously full of opportunities for those who decided to commit themselves to business and the new trades that were burgeoning alongside consumer culture. An eye for new consumer markets, styles, and fashions became an essential means of survival in the material sense as a producer/trader and in the cultural sense as an accumulator and exhibitor of consumerism's social symbols.

Resentment and cynicism had another root in family relations. Before the eighteenth century, when high infant and child mortality rates had accustomed parents to loss and created a psychocultural defence mechanism to alleviate its pain, parents' sentimental attachment to their children was significantly restrained (Ariès, 1996). This exacerbated the fragile conditionality of familial relations created by culturo-legal change and added more subjective fuel to the development of a cultural climate conducive to capitalism's competitive, unforgiving socioeconomic dynamic and the psychogenesis of the 'hardened' subject (see Crank and Jacoby, 2014). The child of the pre-industrial family did not matter to parents in the same way as a child seems to matter in today's child-centred western cultures.

Psychosocial loss and the hardened subject of modernity/capitalism carry many fundamental criminological implications, up to now poorly researched.

However, was Ariès correct to suggest that this attitude subsequently changed in any substantive way beyond the personal relationship? For sure, parents' love of their children has been enriched in the modern era, but hardened attitudes and conditional love are still prevalent in the attitudes of many ambitious parents towards their children's *external* educational and economic performances. The position of the child – one in which the parents' unconditional love expressed in legal and material rights, bonding, support, and gestures of affection became the primary *lost object* – has not been entirely displaced during the course of modernity. Personal affective relations have generally improved, but the lost object, the psychological proto-symbol that gives initial symbolic shape to the subject's fundamental sense of lack, has not been fully recovered. As I have argued elsewhere:

> Haunted by the spectral presence of the father's judgement that continues even after the father's death, rendering the symbolic figure of the father as 'undead', the sons and daughters are activated to reproduce the father's wishes yet to keep on trying to kill the spectral image with myriad *sinthomes*, minute joys or stupid pleasures, expressed in great detail in the poetry of Sylvia Plath. These harmless expressions are on their own little objects of *jouissance* symbolising the guilt felt by the repressed knowledge that the subject is a blind follower of the coalesced obscene underside of bourgeois culture; stimulated and systematised by advanced capitalism's consumer culture, however, they combine and expand exponentially into the immensely potent psychosocial force that continues to drive forward capitalism.
>
> (Hall, 2012: 229)

The culture of cynical, competitive individualism was institutionalised by Protestantism in the sixteenth and seventeenth centuries, but, as we have seen, it had been active from the twelfth century, from which point 'the social' lacked any firm foundation in England. Substantive love, rights, and security were replaced by the gestural culture of sentimentalism and an educational ethos based on the obligation to prepare the individual for a tough and insecure independent life in the competitive world of commerce. The cultural norm of 'tough love' evolved as a sublimated and economised form of child-rearing, disparaging and degrading any type of dependency that might linger into adulthood. Continued help, where it could be offered by wealthier parents, had to be clandestine and firmly disavowed to avoid embarrassment. This cultural norm, destructive of both aristocratic and peasant traditions, is the precursor to the modern detestation of *dependency culture*, the disparaging bourgeois term for the supportive relation between a collective body and the individual. Whereas dependency was once a dignified and ethically sanctioned relation between the individual and the community, in the modern era it became anathema. The debt to the community was erased, to be replaced by debts to financial organisations and extraneous individuals.

Honour, the third space, and the pseudo-pacification process

From the late fourteenth century, as land was enclosed, social crimes – the angry and potentially proto-political reaction to poverty, insecurity, and class oppression – and the number of landless labourers prone to 'sturdy vagabondage' proliferated (Thompson, 1975). The customs of food-gathering and hunting were criminalised, which of course produced more criminals as defined by changing laws and statistical records. The Waltham Black Acts, for instance, which initially entered the statute in 1723, added over fifty new offences to the book, most of which were criminalised means of obtaining food (Thompson, 1975). This 'criminalisation process' aimed by the powerful at the poor and dispossessed has been critical criminology's conceptual bedrock and touchstone since the 1970s, but of course it tells us very little about the subjective motivations to the more harmful types of crime back then and absolutely nothing about them as they operate today. As I have argued elsewhere, it provides no answers to the fundamental criminological question of why some individuals are orientated to socially divisive interpersonal competition rather than solidarity and the organisation of a collective struggle out of their predicament (Hall, 2012).

We can begin to construct a theoretical framework in which initial answers to that question can be found. If we take the period from the late fourteenth century to the mid-1950s, we can discern a downward trend in homicide and high-harm violence accompanied by an upward trend in non-violent volume crime (Ellis, 2019). Rather than explain this trend as the outcome of a straightforward 'civilising process', for criminological purposes it's more useful to locate it in the context of a historical shift in the means of establishing honour – from the violent defence of land to the social establishment of the self as a successful player in the market, signified by the display of consumer symbolism (Hall et al., 2008). Spierenburg (2008) simply explained away honour-based violence in his crude and ontologically bereft thesis that it had somehow been 'spiritualised' in the historical move away from the traditional defence of body and land. Elias (1994) was more circumspect with his thesis that the violent defence of honour was 'stored behind the scenes' to emerge only in decivilising spurts of collective violence.

However, Hirschman (1977) relocated honour in capitalism's shifting economic context, a formulation that is glaringly absent not only from the two popular theories just mentioned but also from liberal-postmodernist sociology's poorly embedded and politically fatal cultural theories established in cautious celebration of reflexive modernisation and global cosmopolitanism (see for instance Beck, 2000). This macro-theoretical framework simply cannot deal with the issues of economically grounded insecurity and threats to honour. Hirschman's trawl through Renaissance writings on the development of civility and cosmopolitanism revealed the pivotal cultural concept of *la doceur du commerce* – a concerted attempt to domesticate the 'rude' peoples of Europe in order to create a cultural context conducive to the expansion of pacified commercial activity.

Hirschman seems to be talking about a normalised subjectivity that became the functional outcome of what I call the *pseudo-pacification process* (Hall, 2014).

To explain this process, we need to return to the beginning of this metanarrative to explore a parallel path and draw out a few important criminological inferences. Contrary to revisionist notions of peaceable accommodation and freedom, the European Middle Ages after the demise of the Roman Empire became a vast ungoverned paraspace, replete with structural and random violence as warlords struggled for land and power (Ward-Perkins, 2005). In the later period of the Middle Ages, intimidation and violence had become principal structuring forces in politics and social relations (Maddern, 1992). In England, violent social ordering techniques were also emulated by those who sought localised power in the spaces that opened and closed amid the sparse legal and cultural codes that, as we have already seen, were in constant flux during the social disruption caused by the Norman invasion (Hall, 2014). The original proto-capitalist move away from violent honour towards pseudo-pacified civility – a civility that pacified subjects principally in order to allow the intensification and democratisation of sociosymbolic competition in emerging markets – was an essential requirement for the renewal of economic prosperity, which was to be grounded in the revival and expansion of the derelict nodes and arteries of the old Roman production and trading network.

The pseudo-pacified subject functioned on the supply and demand sides of the economy, lobbying for the reduction of violence to 1) protect newly privatised property and allow safer production and trading, and 2) to encourage the social diffusion of sociosymbolic competition without violent retribution or rebellion (Hall, 2014). Modernity's shift from violence to its prevailing type of pseudo-pacified volume crime was built into the new culture and subjectivity emerging in the earliest stage of the transition to capitalism. Early signs of what was to become the predominant form of criminality can be seen in the informal market that was developing alongside the official market from the twelfth century. Economic transactions took place outside towns and licensed markets – in fields, inns, and other secret meeting places while poaching began to proliferate on newly privatised land. A substantial amount of hidden trade outside official market venues and institutions avoided rents, tolls, and taxes. Major consumers didn't seem too averse to these early criminal suppliers; some Priories obtained less than five per cent of their goods from official markets (Dyer, 2000).

As Sombart (1967) reminded us, the development of luxury urban consumption was also a vital factor in capitalist development, creating cities as consumer nodes in trade arteries and generating increased demand for new sectors of production and trade. As elite urban courtiers became wealthier and earned disposable income over and above subsistence, they became essential to the expansion of the consumption that boosted trade and attracted investment in new productive industries. If *la doceur du commerce* ensured pacified commercial activity, the broader pseudo-pacification process and its dominant subjectivity also ensured the evacuation of violence from the sociosymbolic practices of conspicuous consumption in which significance and honour could be won. As it began to spread throughout Europe, the pseudo-pacification process's early subjectivities were celebrated in Renaissance literature as the intrepid bourgeois pioneers of civilised progress (Hall, 2012). However, in everyday socioeconomic reality the process generated immense undialectical tension, stimulating and sublimating desire in equally intense measures, which laid down the cultural context not for a new civilised subjectivity but a reformed type of hardened subjectivity, one that was in the throes of substituting the physically violent practices that had risen to prominence during the Middle Ages with the less violent but ruthless competitive practices of the market. Today's mobile entrepreneur/consumer is not a product of the outright rejection of violence but, as we have seen, its sublimation into an intensive and quite relentless pseudo-pacified sociosymbolic competition.

On a purely technical economic level, capitalism should have arisen first in the regions that were eventually to become Italy. The invention of double entry book-keeping and the growth of production centres and the market towns populated by socially mobile merchants who served the Crusaders and enjoyed easier access to western terminals of Silk Road commerce gave these Mediterranean regions a head start. However, the crucial factors of familial/communal cell-splitting and pseudo-pacification were far less advanced – these regions retained strong familial and communal ties but also violent social ordering methods, and they suffered from violent bandits hampering market activity well into the sixteenth century. The cultural contrast between the two countries elicited some cutting comments from a Genoese visitor in 1497, which I have discussed elsewhere:

> [The] visitor's impression of the English proto-bourgeois individual was a self-confident, arrogant and suspicious character, out for himself and with no sincere and solid friendships. He displayed a lack of trust, was uncommunicative and would not reveal private affairs. Our visitor was horrified by the lack of affection in families and the willingness to put young children out to apprenticeships, most of whom did not return to the family because of the widespread adoption of primogeniture, which meant they had little hope of parental inheritance. These individuals were suited to a harsh economic meritocracy of compulsory 'undertaking' that leads to greed, anxiety, competitiveness and the tendency of either sex to marry for money. Most saw nobility and status in transcending manual work and becoming a 'master' of others, so the chance to dominate and wield authority over others seemed to trump even the allure of Veblen's leisure class. England was more prosperous than its continental neighbours, but English commentators tended to see value only in prosperity and social mobility and judged Europe accordingly. The good points of autonomous and spontaneous individualism, prosperity and social mobility were outweighed by a notable lack of sympathy for others and public-spiritedness and sympathy for others; the early rise and self-affirmed triumph of *homo economicus*.
>
> (Hall, 2012: 222/3)

Our visitor's rather cutting assessment reveals a subject that is not fully civilised but pacified, yet harsh and competitive in specific ways for specific economic purposes. The culture laid down by the pseudo-pacification process developed its own hierarchy of competence and success. Private inner desires and life-projects replaced the old communal ethics and sentiments (Shorter, 1975) as resentful children ignored and opposed the wishes of the parents who were seen to have betrayed them. This is a pivotal aspect of cultural development because it marks the emergence and normalisation of the type of privatised desire that could be manipulated by the external forces of consumer culture, which offered a surrogate source of social status and significance (Hall et al., 2008). This insular privatism was not entirely new, as Goody (1983) reminds us, because early traces of it could be seen in Middle-Age England, probably an outcome of the Roman invaders' disruption of communalism and the eventual withdrawal from Christianity, which was rejoined later but only as a ritualised Ideal rather than a communal practice. However, in the later Middle Ages and Early Modernity, the institutionalisation of this privatised individualism in the cold rationality of law, bureaucracy, economy, and in the culture of social competition and mobility through conspicuous consumption, enabled the English individual to embrace the rise of capitalism with great enthusiasm.

As we have seen, by the seventeenth century the traditions of collective ownership and collective power had withered while the ethos and subjectivity that had grown on the old platform dissipated and died off. The long period from the end of the Civil War to the mid twentieth century was characterised by a persistent decline in homicide and high-harm violence (Ellis, 2019) but a concomitant rise in property crimes. This provides us with further evidence that the pseudo-pacification process was relatively successful in its redirection of anxiety, honour, and hostility from physically violent encounters to the socioeconomic competition that was furnished with its symbolic structure by consumer culture. Much has been made of the Protestant Ethic as capitalism's cultural driver from the seventeenth century onwards, but, in the work of Sombart and others (see Sassatelli, 2007), we can quite clearly see the early diffusion of consumer desire throughout the social body at the same time as Protestant asceticism was supposed to restrict it. Weber (2002) dismissed the narcissistic adventurer/speculator as 'not a real Protestant' – a classic 'no true Scotsman' fallacy – but the dispute about whether urban business owners were upstanding citizens creating wealth for all or disreputable spivs and narcissistic consumers is rather pointless. These two poles of the pseudo-pacification process – the pacified citizen seeking to respect and serve the other and the pacified yet ruthless competitor seeking to undermine the other in both business and the display of consumer symbolism – were active in all but the most rebellious bourgeois subjects.

We can see quite clearly that the anxious, socially disembedded individual thrust into the urban maelstrom of rapidly expanding markets and consumer symbolism in the absence of any real collective oppositional identity or political organisation had little choice but committed adoption of the new democratised consumer identity. It's difficult to detect a true opposition to the pseudo-pacification process in any social group during the run-up to full-blown industrial capitalism. In the eighteenth century, English middle-class culture had moved into an age of contrived sentiment alongside reason. The display of refined sensibilities such as pity and benevolence accrued high cultural capital amongst those who considered themselves to be the progressive movement in polite society (Eagleton, 2009). A rather apprehensive cultural elite, worried about the potential outcomes of the divisive and unstable energy of ambition and the hostile interpersonal competition energising the masses, concerned themselves with the construction of safe apolitical regulatory forces.

All this unpredictable libidinal energy unleashed into the social body was to be sublimated and made safe by Frances Hutcheson's 'calm desire for wealth' (Eagleton, 2009: 15), the libidinal partner policed by the super-ego form of *la doceur du commerce*. For urban life to be less turbulent and hostile the often debt-ridden subjects of the commercial maelstrom had to be seen to act in a civilised manner, otherwise the possible reactions of violence and unrest could jeopardise the project of accumulating property and money. Calm was not simply an agreeable consequence of prosperity but a functional necessity. Thus Pocock's (1989) ideology of *commercial humanism* developed, the attempt to establish the liberal progressive continuum of civilised, rule-bound, competitive individualism that remains with us today. The entrepreneurial consumer subject was to be ruthlessly competitive and acquisitive yet sociable and civilised. A powerful yet fragile tension is built into the core of the culture that grew amid urban commerce. The rather sanctimonious yet socially active benevolentists and sentimentalists, who from the eighteenth century established themselves as the politically tolerated agents of civilization, tried to construct a mediatory cultural realm in which a contrived and rather fragile bonhomie could be sustained in the *third space* between 1) the principal drivers of id-driven accumulation and anxiety-driven narcissism, and 2) the peripheral insulating sleeve of norms that had been constructed from the remains of the deracinated values of *agape*, which were once active at the heart of families and communities.

The ethical tension that pervades this third space and the desperate idealism required to maintain faith in it can be revealed with only a cursory glance at liberal thought. In the nineteenth century, despite social disruption, poverty, imperialism, and war, European liberalism took a distinctly Utopian turn. Kant averred that the liberal project of reason, freedom, and prosperity must be sufficiently strong and vigilant to deal with a 'race of devils', always prepared to call on the 'cunning of reason' to ensure 'perpetual peace' by pacifying and harnessing the egotistical energies of 'intelligent devils'. Evil exists in all of us, and it should be put to good use. It was imagined that God would bless this move, and, to add a pragmatic dimension, perhaps this is the only way that Good can survive amongst fallen creatures. From Mandeville to Friedman, the nervously liberalised conservative establishment preached the idea that it is Good, in both the intrinsic and consequential sense, to invoke private vices and turn them into public virtue through the magic of the market. Private vices should generally be assumed to be harmless except in the instances where they appear as direct harmful manifestations, as individual crimes, and even then their consequential harms tend to played down in liberal culture (see Raymen, forthcoming), often with the justification that the over-identification of harm as crime would fuel punitiveness and popular unrest.

From its inception, progressive liberalism was a dream of the Imaginary, neither an autonomous emotional drive nor a symbolic law, a dream that is sustained only by denying the intensity with which the pseudo-pacification process had stimulated and recruited the obscene Id to pump its predatory energy into the economy and turn a substantial proportion of subjective desire towards capitalism's endless procession of consumer objects. The losers left hanging on at the margins deserved sympathy, according to the progressive liberal benevolentists, but it could never be said that they deserved antecedent political intervention at the deep structural level – banking, investment, production, markets, consumer desire. That would risk inefficiency and potential loss of economic growth and accumulation. We could make gestures of solidarity, and we could even offer real help in the form of welfare and an education that prepared the individual to compete, but solidarity must never be real in the unholy realm of political economy. Neither must it ever be allowed to interfere with capital accumulation, nor the efficient cultural reproduction of the pseudo-pacified hedonistic-solipsistic subject whose libidinal priority must continue to be the consumption of a constant stream of novelties carrying some degree of social status.

Liberal capitalism's primary psychocultural move was to deracinate love as *agape* – a fundamental human drive and a social glue – by separating desire and morality (Raymen, forthcoming). There were more profitable uses to which desire could be put. The one optimistic possibility that the capitalist continuum has bequeathed us is that the object of *agape* has not been lost forever but relocated from the position of core values to peripheral 'insulating norms' that perform a restricted and *ex post facto* pseudo-pacifying function (Hall et al., 2008). However, one strict rule, established in capitalism's formative centuries, is still assiduously and unconditionally applied – *agape* and its manifested fellow-feeling should never be extended to our economic relations and transactions (Winlow and Hall, 2019). In their agreement with this golden rule the benevolentists and sentimentalists eschewed all intervention in the market and its social outcomes beyond charity and welfare. Therefore, they functioned politically as soft ideologues, tirelessly promising the impossibilities of fairness and justice within the liberal-capitalist system as it stood and finding excuses for the system's inevitable failure to deliver them in any substantive form. They created a cultural buffer zone between the devil as *avarus praedo* and the angel as *agape*. Capitalists had learnt their principal lesson very well; violence and altruism both presented extreme danger to the efficient functioning of the system, while the third space populated by the disempowered producer and the pseudo-pacified consumer subject was the location in which the system functioned at peak efficiency.

Conclusion: crime, harm, and the neoliberal consumer subject

The sociological upshot is that in the period between the Norman invasion and the industrial revolution, England ceased to be a 'peasant society'. Caught up in the socioeconomic tumour caused by fundamental culturo-legal, organisational and technological changes, the traditional socioeconomic position of *villeinage* was diverted to a trajectory that would lead to the normalisation of a hyper-individualistic subject (see Bloch, 1967). The subject found itself in the position of having to adapt or fall into poverty and social insignificance. Those committed to adaptation to this nascent new world established themselves as successful players. Dumont (1986) reminds us that the culture of the capitalist era is characterised by a shift from direct ethical relations between individuals in communal settings to relations mediated by private property, money, and the market, a 'nominalist' culture that encourages people to see themselves first and foremost as competitive individuals rather than members of a social group.

We can begin the process of intellectual renewal with the observation that many criminals not necessarily on the brink of starvation or even extreme financial difficulties – the latter a possibility that haunts us all in an insecure world (Horsley, 2015) – seemed to commit themselves to economic crime as a solution to the difficult double-bind that had appeared in capitalist modernity's mutating codes of honour. It is a universal anthropological principle that those who cannot exchange socially recognised symbols cease to exist in the eyes of others who value those symbols (Baudrillard, 1993). Throughout much of human history, especially for males who carried the breadwinner burden, the fear that social and legal repercussions which might befall any individual who took an illegal short-cut to wealth and status had often been outweighed by the fear of the social disgrace that inevitably followed failing altogether as a socioeconomic actor.

We must consider the possibility that this ancient fear has been simultaneously aggravated and domesticated in a reconfigured capitalist social order that became more permeable and therefore imposed more expectations of success on individuals. All those 'liberated' into the position of competitive economic actors in business or labour markets now feel the same honorific pressure, which can fuel harmful acts ranging from aggressive street crime to harmful management practices in neoliberal organisations (see Lloyd, 2019). Acts of choosing to be involved in criminal activities – a higher proportion of which inflict more harm on fellow citizens than many critical criminologists are willing to admit (Raymen, forthcoming) – are now increasingly driven by the powerful emotional injunction to save face in the context of consumer culture. Some people seem able to cope with 'lowly' social positions that have been symbolically devalued in the capitalist continuum – especially the neoliberal phase that places the successful entrepreneur on a pedestal above all others – while others seem most emphatically unable to cope (see Tudor, this volume).

In the decades between World Wars I and II, when conditions for indebted individuals or unemployed and landless labourers were still dire and constantly threatened destitution, the combination of desperation and lack of choice still made a convincing aetiological argument in criminological theory. However, in the post-war welfare state characterised by social support mechanisms, full employment, and projects of political solidarity up to the 1980s, credit and unprecedently cheap consumer goods, it applies to fewer individuals, and it is even less convincing given that even in today's age of post-crash austerity only a small proportion of the relatively poor resort to crime. Critical criminology seems to be reluctant to explore the possibility of more sophisticated aetiological explanations based on the development of pseudo-pacified subjectivities within the modernist-capitalist continuum, with its many traumatic events and shifting socioeconomic processes and structures (Ellis et al., 2017).

The modern subject has become accustomed to this continuing trauma as if it is the natural way of things. Amid such unpredictability, adoption of firm moral guidance becomes a potentially fatal threat to the individual's survival. Who knows what one might need to do should the currently unknown situation demand it? As Georg Simmel argued, the individual caught in this maelstrom of unpredictable events without guidance is constantly exposed to the temptations of impulse (Simmel, 1978). If impulse can be sublimated, dragged away from the dangerous territory of acting out autonomously in everyday reality and cathected to an order of symbols, it is a powerful psychological force in the expansion of demand in the capitalist marketplace. The post-war advertising industry is an efficient machine designed to perform precisely that operation of cathexis/sublimation whilst also performing the accompanying ideological move of convincing the individual that authentic acting out is still the norm (Hall et al., 2008).

Although mass consumerism was a twentieth-century post-war phenomenon, we have seen that the embryonic consumer subject was the product of a long bourgeois continuum, gradually diffused throughout the social body as capitalism's productive progress into an era of affordable luxury made the democratisation of the sociosymbolic competition possible. By the 1980s, the last vestiges of alternative sources of value in community and mass political projects were erased. Liberal-postmodernist theorists, desperate to avoid the social antagonism and brutal politics of the recent past, hastily reframed the pseudo-pacification process's third space as a realm of freedom, in which the sovereign individual could exercise her choice and forge her personal and social identity. This intellectual project failed, as did its associated politics. In late capitalism's current reality of precarity and anxiety, this third space reveals itself to be what it has always been – an unforgiving psychic energy trap. Here, for the majority, the promissory dream is rapidly turning sour. The pseudo-pacification process can sustain itself only if the mass media and education system can sustain the narrative of progress and an exhausted material reality can continue to be displaced by a virtual surrogate social world that distributes the symbols individuals crave.

The psychosocial aspect of this culture, based on the glorification of entrepreneurialism and the anxious, adrift subject, is most interesting for criminology. Throughout the long historical continuum outlined here the individual subject struggled to free itself from the existing social order because it had become anything but social (Winlow and Hall, 2013). We could be forgiven for concluding that this subject sounds remarkably like the ancestor of today's libertarian, the subject who after World War II was lauded and cultivated as the foundation of neoliberalism (Slobodian, 2018). For Crank and Jacoby (2014), the 'hardened subject' is the central player in today's global and local criminal markets. For ultra-realists such as Winlow (2001), Lloyd (2018), Ellis (2016), and Kuldova

(2019), the pseudo-pacified subject, the individual in the grip of a domesticated and recuperated form of hardness, is the central player in these markets, in locations ranging from neoliberal management regimes to post-proletarian 'outlaw' cultures. Already, in the 1980s, the old industrial world had seen an explosion of crime, dampened down from the mid-1990s only by a combination of oppressive securitisation and statistical chicanery (Kotzé, 2019). Now violent crime is once again on the increase in many economically abandoned locales across the UK and Europe (Ellis, 2016; Briggs and Gamero, 2017). Far-right politics once thought consigned to history's dustbin are on the ascent (Winlow et al., 2017). Neoliberalism is failing. Criminology's central theoretical task is to examine, in detail and with a hitherto repressed honesty, the breakdown of the pseudo-pacification process and the diverse reactions of the uniquely hardened consumer subject as it competes in consumerism's surrogate social world to acquire sociopolitically sterilised substitutes for its lost object.

References

Ariès, P. (1996) *Centuries of Childhood: A Social History of Family Life*, London: Pimlico.

Baudrillard, J. (1993) *Symbolic Exchange and Deatt*, London: Sage.

Beck, U. (2000) *What Is Globalization?* Oxford: Wiley-Blackwell.

Bloch, M. (1967) *Land and Work in Mediaeval Europe*, London: Routledge and Kegan Paul.

Briggs, D. and Gamero, R.M. (2017) *Dead-End Lives: Drugs and Violence in the City Shadows*, Bristol: Policy Press.

Chesterton, G.K. (2009[1910 *passim*]) *Three Works on Distributism*, Createspace Independent Publishing Platform. Available at: https://www.amazon.co.uk/Three-Works-Distributism-G-Chesterton/dp/1449511228

Crank, J.P. and Jacoby, L.S. (2014) *Crime, Violence and Global Warming*, London: Routledge.

Currie, E. (2015) *The Roots of Danger: Violent Crime in Global Perspective*, Oxford: Oxford University Press.

Dumont, L. (1986) *Essays on Individualism: Modern Ideology in Anthropological Perspective*, Chicago: University of Chicago Press.

Dyer, C. (2000) *Everyday Life in Mediaeval England*, London: Hambledon and London.

Eagleton, T. (2009) *Trouble with Strangers: A Study of Ethics*, Chichester: Wiley-Blackwell.

Elias, N. (1994) *The Civilizing Process*, Oxford: Blackwell.

Ellis, A. (2016) *Men, Masculinities and Violence: An Ethnographic Study*, London: Routledge.

Ellis, A. (2019) A Decivilizing Reversal or System Normal? Rising Lethal Violence in Post-Recession Austerity United Kingdom. *British Journal of Criminology*. doi:10.1093/bjc/azz001

Ellis, A., Winlow, S. and Hall, S. (2017) 'Throughout My Life I've Had People Walk All Over Me': Trauma in the Lives of Violent Men. *Sociological Review*, 65, 4: 699–713.

Goody, J. (1983) *The Development of the Family and Marriage in Europe*, Cambridge: Cambridge University Press.

Hall, S. (2012) *Theorizing Crime and Deviance: A New Perspective*, London: Sage.

Hall, S. (2014) The Socioeconomic Function of Evil. In L. Ray and J. Kilby (eds.) *Sociological Review Monograph: Violence and Society: Towards a New Sociology*, Chichester: Wiley, 13–31.

Hall, A. and Antonopoulos, G.A. (2016) *Fake Meds Online: The Internet and the Transnational Market in Illicit Pharmaceuticals*, London: Palgrave Macmillan.

Hall, S., Winlow, S. and Ancrum, C. (2008) *Criminal Identities and Consumer Culture: Crime, Exclusion and the New Culture of Narcissism*, London: Willan/Routledge.

Hirschman, A. (1977) *The Passions and the Interests: Political Arguments for Capitalism Before its Triumph*, Princeton: Princeton University Press.

Horsley, M. (2015) *The Dark Side of Prosperity: Late Capitalism's Culture of Indebtedness*, Farnham: Ashgate.

Kotzé, J. (2019) *The Myth of the Crime Decline: Exploring Change and Continuity in Crime and Harm*, London: Routledge.

Kuldova, T. (2019) *How Outlaws Win Friends and Influence People*, London: Palgrave Macmillan.

Large, J. (2019) *The Consumption of Counterfeit Fashion*, London: Palgrave Macmillan.

Lloyd, A. (2018) *The Harms of Work: An Ultra-Realist Account of the Service Economy*, Bristol: Bristol University Press.

Lloyd, A. (2019) Harm at Work: Bullying and Special Liberty in the Retail Sector. *Critical Criminology*. doi:10.1007/s10612-019-09445-9

Macfarlane, A. (1978) *The Origins of English Individualism. The Family, Property and Social Transition*, Oxford: Blackwell.

Maddern, P. (1992) *Violence and Social Order: East Anglia 1422–1442*, Oxford: Oxford University Press.

Pocock, J. (1989) Civic Humanism and Its Role in Anglo-American Political Thought. In J. Pocock (ed.) *Politics, Language and Time: Essays on Political Thought and History*, Chicago: University of Chicago Press.

Raymen, T. (forthcoming) The Enigma of Social Harm and the Barrier of Liberalism: Why Zemiology Needs a Theory of the Good. *Justice, Power, and Resistance: The Journal of the European Group for the Study of Deviance and Social Control*.

Reiner, R. (2007) *Law and Order: An Honest Citizen's Guide to Crime and Control*, Cambridge: Polity Press.

Sassatelli, R. (2007) *Consumer Culture; History, Theory and Politics*, London: Sage.

Shorter, E. (1975) *The Making of the Modern Family*, New York: Basic Books.

Simmel, G. (1978 [1900]) *The Philosophy of Money*, trans. T. Bottomore and D. Frisby, London: Routledge and Kegan Paul.

Slobodian, Q. (2018) *Globalists: The End of Empire and the Birth of Neoliberalism*, Cambridge, MA: Harvard University Press.

Sombart, W. (1967[1913]) *Luxury and Capitalism*, Ann Arbor: University of Michigan Press.

Spierenburg, P. (2008) *A History of Murder: Personal Violence in Europe from the Middle Ages to the Present*, Cambridge: Polity Press.

Thompson, E.P. (1975) *Whigs and Hunters: The Origin of the Black Act*, London: Allen Lane.

Treadwell, J., Briggs, D., Winlow, S. and Hall, S. (2013) Shopocalypse Now: Consumer Culture and the English Riots of 2011. *British Journal of Criminology*, 53, 1: 1–17.

Tsantiropoulos, A. (2008, April) Collective Memory and Blood Feud: The Case of Mountainous Crete. *Solon Online Journal*, 2: 1.

Ward-Perkins, B. (2005) *The Fall of Rome and the End of Civilization*, Oxford: Oxford University Press.

Weber, M. (2002[1905]) *The Protestant Ethic and the Spirit of Capitalism*, trans. S. Kalberg, Oxford: Blackwell.

Winlow, S. (2001) *Badfellas: Crime, Tradition and New Masculinities*, Oxford: Berg.

Winlow, S. and Hall, S. (2013) *Rethinking Social Exclusion: The End of the Social?* London: Sage.

Winlow, S. and Hall, S. (2019) Why the Left Must Change: Right-Wing Populism in Context. In W.S. DeKeseredy and E. Currie (eds.) *Progressive Justice in an Age of Repression: Strategies for Challenging the Rise of the Right*, London: Routledge.

Winlow, S., Hall, S. and Treadwell, J. (2017) *The Rise of the Right: English Nationalism and the Transformation of Working-Class Politics*, Bristol: Policy Press.

2 The libertine

Criminal luxury, the Sadean system, and materialist horror

Mark Featherstone

Criminal luxury

How can we define luxury? If there is something necessarily transgressive about the luxurious, and luxury means moving beyond utility, what are we to make of French luxury brand, Maison de Sade, and its use of the name *Sade* to sell fine wines, brandies, and beers? A descendent of the infamous Marquis and owner of Maison de Sade, Count Hugues de Sade, has also reportedly held talks with global brand Victoria's Secret about producing a line of luxury lingerie bearing the Sade name. Now anybody who has ever read *Sade* or even heard the name knows that the Marquis was into excess, and predominantly sexual excess, but we can be more or less certain that he would not have been particularly interested in imagining his famous libertine heroine Justine wearing Victoria's Secret. The reason for this may be less clear to the reader with only a passing interest in the Marquis. Surely Victoria's Secret is part of a global, capitalist, erotic-sexual, luxury industry defined by the industrial production of desire and fantasy to stir consumption and swell the bottom line, which we might think about in terms of the realisation of Sade's vision of a sexual utopia?

Although it may well be the case that the sale of luxury lingerie represents the high end of what we might call a contemporary erotic utopia, I think that the reason Sade would *not* have been interested in Justine wearing Victoria's Secret is because his vision of sexual luxury was absolutely concerned with the brutal transgression of norms, the blasphemous smashing of rules, and the destruction of the other. There is no artifice, no eroticism, no seduction about sex in Sade because the other is meaningless, an empty vehicle for *his* violent transgression of the normal. This is precisely how Sade understood pleasure. There is no pleasure without breaking rules because rules sketch out the sphere of utility and there is nothing here that could interest the libertine. In Sade's work the luxury of sexual pleasure able to suspend the world of utility does not, therefore, reside in sex itself, but rather in sex that breaks rules – sex that is somehow pointless, blasphemous, and monstrous. This is *criminal sex*, which produces the only real kind of luxury (criminal luxury beyond the norm where everything has a use) and the only real kind of pleasure (criminal pleasure beyond the norm where everything has a reason), and delivers what Sade really wants – confirmation of his essential freedom from *all* restriction and regulation. This is the criminal luxury of the libertine, and I would argue Sade represents the most developed theory of libertinism in western thought. Thus, if we want to understand the relationship between crime and luxury, or *criminal luxury*, we must, I think, begin with Sade.

Following this advice, my objective in this chapter is to explore Sade's project, the figure of the libertine, and the notion of criminal luxury in the context of first, the Marquis' own historical moment, eighteenth-century revolutionary France, where luxury was simultaneously a criminal and institutional form subject to fierce debate about the morality and economic value of extreme consumption. Moving beyond the eighteenth century, my next move is to project Sade forward into a second moment of revolutionary transgression, the events of 1968, where he became a kind of heroic, criminal figure, able to represent a new utopian future based upon his theory of the libertine, sexual luxury, and essential freedom. However, keeping in mind the tension between Sade's criminal luxury and the safe, comfortable model of erotic luxury represented today by brands such as Victoria's Secret, in this, the second part of the chapter, I seek to draw out the hyper-rational, systemic aspect of Sade outlined by Klossowski (1991), Blanchot (2004), and Adorno and Horkheimer (1997), which aligns his criminality with the institutional form of luxury capitalism that first emerged in early modern France. My objective here is to show how Sade's version of criminal luxury may be seen to contain the seeds of the contemporary neoliberal capitalist system, where luxury, and the transgression of norms, is paradoxically absolutely normal and (ironically) completely necessary to global economic growth. This is the case to the extent that it is possible to say that there is no real sense of luxury and no real sense of crime, and where the regulation of behaviour is a purely technical matter founded upon shifting interpretations of utility, the luxurious, and what is very clearly *constructed* as normal, acceptable, and lawful. In order to explain this theory, where Sade becomes the ultimate insider, the secret architect of a system based on luxurious transgression and the everyday breaking of rules, I move on to consider the works of the contemporary French writer Michel Houellebecq. By picking up Sadean themes in Houellebecq's novels, and centrally focusing upon the hopelessness of sex represented in *Whatever* (1999), *Atomised* (2001), *Platform* (2003), and *The Possibility of an Island* (2005), I look to show what happens when Sade's system of transgression and criminal luxury becomes hegemonic and part of the mainstream. Where is luxury under these conditions?

Although Sade was extreme in his own historical context, he was also a man of his time, and his behaviour was supported by the socioeconomic structures of eighteenth-century feudal France, where sovereignty and the sign of nobility were founded upon the ability to waste, squander, and wallow in luxury. However, in much same way that eighteenth-century France was in the process of shifting from a feudal, theocratic society where luxury was centrally opposed to utility, into a more rational, enlightenment system, where excess would be understood through reasoned thought, Sade was similarly a borderline character, who loved his absolute liberty and looked down upon everybody else, but also could not help becoming caught up in systems and structures of his own making that essentially represented the modern future to come. This is precisely how Marcel Henaff (1999) understands Sade in his work on the libertine body.

For Henaff, Sade's feudal libertine body, the body pushing towards absolute freedom and criminal luxury through its opposition to every system that might try to contain it, simultaneously ended up creating its own highly rationalised system based upon endless transgression into pleasure followed by the desperate need to return to self in order to confirm mastery, unity, and self-identity. Since this return to self only confirmed the enclosure of the libertine, and in a sense his flesh-bound lack of freedom, Henaff explains that Sade was compelled to repeat the same process of transgression and return to identity endlessly in the creation of a highly rational, circular system Klossowski (1998) would later identify with the Nietzschean vicious circle and before him Freud (2003) would write about in terms of the *Sadistic* death drive, Thanatos. It is because of this endless circularity that, in Klossowski's (1991) view, the other – the neighbour – became so important for Sade. Despite his libertinism that meant he thought of himself as absolutely free, beyond any form of dependence or social relation, Klossowski explains that Sade *needed* the neighbour in order to maintain both his own integral self-identity and to pursue the luxurious transgression of limits, which is where the 'other' comes into the picture.

Where Sade remains the master, and maintains a haughty sense of self, the neighbour becomes the eternal victim who experiences every form of violence, degradation, and destruction in the name of pleasures that reside beyond the controlled self of the master. The master experiences these luxurious pleasures vicariously through the neighbour, who becomes a vehicle for his thirst for annihilation and also confirms his absolute superiority and freedom from all constraint through her total and utter subordination and ruination. But since the neighbour is always a vehicle, a living symbol, through which the master experiences the pleasure of complete destruction and nothingness *and* absolute freedom and infinite control, Sade never escapes Klossowski's (1991, 1998) vicious circle, but only repeats it on the level of a violent, anti-social relation with the neighbour. Although there was nothing *necessarily* completely rational about this process, Klossowski (1991), Blanchot (2004), and Henaff (1999) similarly focus upon Sade's rationalisation of violence, torture, and extraction of luxury value, which we can attribute to the master's constant need to 1) reinforce his own freedom and control and 2) endlessly experience the criminal luxury of pushing through the limits of the normal through perverse violence and the destruction of the neighbour's self. This rationalisation was located in the historical context of Enlightenment Europe, where the cybernetic fusion of man and relentless machine had already been set up by La Mettre in the 1740s.

Caught between feudalism and modernity, the old regime and the revolution, Henaff's (1999) libertine body is, therefore, a borderline body in the process of becoming something else. On the one hand, the libertine's superiority and nobility, his belief in his ability to say and do anything, were founded in the feudal system. On the other hand, his rationality, his coldness, and his mechanical cruelty were products of an early modern social, political, and economic system where luxury had become not simply a symbol of extreme wealth and the ability to waste, squander, and live a life of luxurious abandon, but also a socio-politico-economic strategy set up to advance the economic position of France in Europe. Writing on the shift from feudalism to modernity in the seventeenth and eighteenth centuries, Steve Hall (2012) develops C. B. Macpherson's (2010) theory of possessive individualism, which shows how Hobbes and Locke imagined the projection of the natural violence of the state of nature into the early capitalist economy in order to create a vision of useful competition through his theory of pseudo-pacification.

Explaining this process, Hall (2012) argues that the enlightenment, modernity, and emergence of the capitalist economy seemed to reduce violence, but the truth is they only projected or sublimated these conditions into the nascent market economy with the result that they created a 'safe space' for pacified competition. In this space free of violent retribution, competition could be intensified and expanded, enriching the winners but inflicting inequality, poverty, misery, and the struggle to survive upon those who found themselves on the losing side of the new contract-based war of all against all. Pseudo-pacification allowed the Feudal subjective form of 'special liberty', the aristocratic warlord's entitled and unrestricted venting of the libido controlled only by a sense of righteousness, to be integrated into capitalism's socioeconomic competition and acted out in ways that inflicted myriad harms on others but usually stopped at the border of physical violence. Following Hall's line of reasoning, where Feudal crime, violence and 'special liberty' become pacified, legalised, and normalised in the new Early Modern capitalist society, I think it is also possible to make the same argument about the development of feudal luxury, which went from an extra-economic, excessive, and transgressive element of an ancient social and political system to a fully integrated aspect of the early modern consumer capitalism of eighteenth-century France under Louis XIV through Louis XV up to Louis XVI when the drive for luxury, excess, and the finance necessary to prop this system up brought about the revolution, Robespierre, and a new kind of terrible social and political dynamic: the terror.

The Sadean system

But the pseudo-pacification process also fostered discontents. The slow erosion of religious power in the face of Enlightenment philosophy threw the libertine into a situation where there was absolutely no ethical check on the power of special liberty, which is precisely why Annie Le Brun (1990) imagines Sade on the edge of a sudden abyss, caught between nothingness and infinity, represented by perhaps *the* monument to Sadean criminal luxury, the dark castle Silling from *The 120 Days of Sodom* (2016). Where the Feudal warlord inflicted violence on the other publicly and unashamedly, in this castle concealed from the eyes of an inefficient and almost apologetic secular legal system, the four libertines could carry out their unspeakable tortures and torments. By imagining the horrors of Silling, which was modelled on the Chateau de Lacoste now coincidentally owned by

French-Italian designer Pierre Cardin, Sade's objective was to write an encyclopaedia of real criminal luxury beyond pseudo-luxury things one might easily buy and sell and thus escape every possible form of utility. Only this would confirm Sade's mastery and demonstrate his position outside of any system that might constrain his freedoms.

According to historian and Sade biographer Maurice Lever (1993) the Marquis' libertine obsession with criminal luxury emerged in his childhood years. He explains that Sade hated his mother and soon came to believe he was absolutely superior to others, who he treated with disdain. In Lever's account little Sade was haughty, unable to communicate, and never really grew up. Rather than benefitting from an 'upbringing', Lever tells us that little Sade was subject to endless 'uprooting' by his libertine uncle who exposed him to the use of prostitutes and the violent pleasures of criminal luxury. Centrally, Uncle Sade never really gave his nephew a proper home. Schooled in libertinism, where the objective is to endlessly uproot and escape from constraint through outrageous rule-breaking and the assertion of freedom, it is thus possible that Sade spent the rest of his life negatively searching for some kind of home through the constant attack on projections of his mother, who had left him in his early years.

Given his libertine 'uprooting', it is no surprise that Sade sought to escape his deeply repressed pain through endless expressions of criminal luxury capable of simultaneously taking him outside of himself and confirming that he was in fact free of his mother, who he constantly destroyed through the monotonous attack on living symbolic representations. In this respect Lever (1993) paints a picture of a man who was completely 'locked in' and understood others as so many objects put in the world for his use and centrally to support his escape attempts from the horror of lack and loss. Lever's (1993) Sade is, therefore, driven by a negative Oedipus complex. On the basis of this psychological system, the libertine plunges into criminal luxury – blasphemous sex, torture, every kind of perversion imaginable, and endless repetitious orgasm – in the name of escape from himself and his ruined identity.

It is this economic system that cycles through lack, loss, excess, and exorbitance that leads Sade to plunge his reader into an abyss of degradation. This is Sade's criminal luxury economy, which from Klossowski's (1991) point of view, must be understood in terms of a kind of Satanic Spinozism. Whereas Spinoza had led the radical enlightenment through his claim that God was in fact nature, Sade explained that God was the stupid invention of a terrified creature (man) unable to face up to the horrors of the natural world, which is the ultimate luxury system. As Blanchot (2004) points out, Sade's rational taste for systems fundamentally revolved around a deeply pessimistic vision of nature that creates in order to destroy in order to create once more, ad infinitum. Since there is no end to this luxury system that produces for no reason other than to destroy in order to produce forevermore into the future, Sade wanted to 'say it all' in his writings and create an encyclopaedia of natural perversions that would have made Hegel blush in its ambition to totalitarianism. But ironies and paradoxes abound in Sade's work and the flipside of the implicit, systemic totalitarianism found in *The 120 Days of Sodom* (2016) and other works is his 'locked in' defence of libertine individualism, which leads Klossowski (1991) and Blanchot (2004) to write about a morality of absolute solitude based upon the Marquis' own theory of isolism. Here, the other is an object, and must be treated in this way, because there is absolutely no way to reach it.

According to Sade's philosophy the core feature of human life is loneliness, and the only way to cope with this situation is through the escape into pleasure and luxury that confirms individual significance, control, and domination. On the basis of this theory of solitude, Sade's ethos of luxurious consumption suggested that it is fundamentally ethically correct for every individual to pursue his or her own pleasure regardless of the impact on others, who are impossible to reach. As a result of radical solitude and the individual's 'locked-in' nature, an ethic of otherness is pointless and senseless. From the libertine's point view, the pain of the other is irrelevant. Why should he care about the destruction of the other, who he can never really know, when his own pleasure is under consideration? The result of this ethos is therefore a system of universal prostitution where self and other are able, and in fact compelled by their thirst for luxury, to use and abuse each other with complete abandon. Although there appears to be some kind of social contract implicit in Sade's suggestion, which would lead to a primitive sexual communist utopia, the truth is that his vision was actually completely conditioned by his feudal uprooting, where some are always more equal than others, and that this entirely undercut any possibility of sexual communism. The truth is that in the system of universal prostitution the naturally strong, or feudal elites, would do the fucking and the naturally weak, or stupid masses, would be fucked and used up in the name of the extraction of their surplus or luxury value. This is also why Sade, as Klossowski (2017) famously pointed out in his essay on the relationship between the Marquis and Charles Fourier, never imagined the generalisation of his sexual utopia. On the contrary, Sade's fantasy of luxurious sexual abandon was always a *counter-utopia*, a secret society, which he represented through the infamous *Society of the Friends of Crime*, where a group of like-minded libertines would secure women to use and abuse and would never be part of wider society.

It is this principle of *opposition* that leads the reader of Sade back to the ultimate contradiction of his thought, outlined by Klossowski (1991). Despite everything, the libertine needs his neighbour. He needs his opponent; he needs his victim who he can negate in order to keep his luxurious system moving, transgressing, and breaking boundaries. This is nowhere clearer than in Sade's atheism. Despite his professed enlightenment lack of belief, Sade was ultimately a borderline character who believed enough to hate God and to try to offend him at every turn in the name of asserting his own mastery. Against God – who torments humans, telling them *not* to do this, *not* to do that, and *not* to do the other – Sade thought that true nature is endlessly luxurious. Contrary to what God says, nature is never about prohibition, but endless excess, and in this respect, it is evil on a molecular, atomic level. Given this proto-Darwinian thesis, Sade's response to God's legal system was to say that there is paradoxically nothing evil about evil and in fact humans *should* be evil because this is precisely what nature commands. You must be evil!

But this elevation of nature led Sade towards one final paradox: how could the libertine tolerate subjection to nature? More importantly, how could he escape this subjection, since every evil, every crime he could commit, every luxurious move he could make, would only confirm his submission to a system that is in itself set up to pursue evil? This is precisely why sodomy has such an important place in Sade's system of criminal luxury and perversion – because in his view this was not simply blasphemous, but also offensive to nature because of its suspension of reproductive sexual difference. Through sodomy Sade sought to seize the initiative, sought to take evil away from nature and make it his own. He wanted to break the link between sexual ecstasy and abandon and the utilitarianism of reproduction able to keep nature moving and to conceive of a plan to deliver the ultimate in criminal luxury – extinction, the abyss of nothingness – even though he knew that nature would survive even this and continue to push forward relentlessly into a post-human future.

Regardless of the possibility of this post-human future, Sade sought to escape the final system of nature through the elevation of sodomy to the ultimate criminally luxurious offence. In Klossowski's (1991) view the purpose of this move was to keep the possible in play, save his counter-utopianism, and also establish his own libertine freedom. Of course, Sade was never able to escape his debt to the other – the neighbour, the sodomised, the offended God, and eventually Mother Nature herself – and it is probably precisely the return of this repressed opposition that threw his system into doubt in the late eighteenth century, when the entire aristocratic system and its culture of parasitic luxury was brought down by financial over-leveraging and the bankruptcy of a French monarchy that had become addicted to luxury consumption and the transgression of norms. There is no doubt that the socioeconomic luxury system was tame by comparison to what Sade imagined the project of criminal luxury was about. Lever (1993) explains that Sade even welcomed the revolution on the basis that it would open up a space of anomic normlessness that he could exploit in the name of his criminality. Upon his release from imprisonment in the wake of 1789, Sade imagined the emergence of a utopia of evil and satanic luxury but completely misunderstood the social and political situation. God was on His knees, there was no King, and Sade was next! Although the Marquis managed to survive the Terror by becoming Citoyen Sade, man of letters, his pornographic writing was too much for the virtuous Republic, and he ended up living out his days in Charenton asylum, where his criminal luxury was subject to treatment and explanation by the Enlightenment science set up to study precisely this type of psychological perversion – psychiatry.

The overall effect of the transition from a feudal to a secular modern society upon the libertine was profound because it essentially started to erode the basis of his war upon constraint. As Elisabeth Roudinesco (2009) explains in her book on the history of perversion, the post-revolutionary 1810 French penal code completely transformed the understanding of sex and sexuality. There was now little or no restriction upon how consenting adults could behave in private, even though adultery remained an offence on the basis of its potential to undermine family and certainty around inheritance of property. In instances of perversion, however, the religious frame of understanding was replaced by scientific disciplines, including sexology, criminology, and psychoanalysis, and the space of the libertine was severely constrained simply because transgressive behaviour was now subject to the kinds of normalising practice Foucault (1977, 2003, 2006a, 2006b) would explain in his work on the psychiatric power, the asylum, clinic, and prison. Although Sade was largely forgotten for much of the nineteenth and early twentieth centuries, it was primarily in opposition to this process of normalisation that he re-emerged in post-revolutionary, modern, capitalist France, finding a home in the works of the surrealists and radicals who saw that the new capitalist society was far less free than it claimed was the case. In the 1940s and 1950s Sade's work was picked up by Klossowski (1991) and Bataille (1991), who developed the theory of Sadean economics I have sought to explain in this chapter, where the norm-based restricted economy contains the seeds of a more base, primitive, general economy geared towards excess, luxury, and the destruction of regulation. On the basis of this reading and his theory of the libertine, Sade became a kind of counter-cultural hero through the 1960s up to 1968, when radicals sought to oppose the normalised, capitalist system in the name of everything prohibited and restricted.

In this way the principle of criminal luxury, as opposed to pseudo-luxury contained within the normal economic system, made a comeback through the 1960s, inspiring Deleuze and Guattari's radical *Anti-Oedipus* (1983), which was influenced by Klossowski's (2017) theory of libidinal economy developed in his reading of Sade. In Klossowski's theory, outlined in 'Living Currency' and 'Sade and Fourier', it is a mistake to understand economy in terms of the rational exchange of goods. In his view, economy is driven by impulsive, libidinal energy that attaches to phantasms or fantasy objects, which are then repressed into simulacra, or in Marxist terms, commodities, which can be industrially produced. This is why, from Klossowski's perspective, the economy is always highly sexually charged and functions on the basis of a repressed drive to obtain luxurious pleasure. If sex was purely instrumental and constrained by the natural need to reproduce, there would be limits to the dynamism of this system. But Klossowski explains that the real luxury of sexuality, and centrally for the purposes of the chapter the potential for criminal luxury, resides in the excessive – or what he calls the voluptuous – aspect of sex that is always about more than reproduction. The moment sex becomes about voluptuousness, rather than simply procreation, then Klossowski says that everything is potentially a phantasm, and later a simulacrum, or representation of sexual pleasure and the luxurious escape from the norm of utility. Now pleasure and luxury are everywhere, and everything can become a phantasmatic object. However, despite the infinite dynamism of this new consumption-based system, Klossowski is very clear that everything leads back to the body, which remains the essential (living) currency, simply because the primary energy behind the dynamic system is still libidinal, sexual energy. In this way the body of the other *remains* the ultimate luxury object.

In the move from a liberal to neoliberal capitalist ideology, the neoliberals therefore adopted both sides of the Sadean economic system, comprising both individual freedom as libertine transgression *and* the apathetic reduction of everything to the level of base objectivity capable of quantification, commodification, and traffic through the capitalist system. Since nothing was now beyond the system, and the entire economic machine was premised on the dynamism of the libidinal energy of the libertine, where the body is the ultimate commodity based upon its potential sexual luxury value, the new neoliberal version of capitalism would produce a strange effect where everybody becomes simultaneously master, libertine, and absolutely free, *but* also victim, object, and endlessly humiliated in their reduction to the level of a thing constantly in circulation in a highly sexualised system. Moreover, since this system was modelled upon meeting the creative, luxurious desires of the libertines of 1968 who transformed Sade into a hero of their own movement to break every rule, it also seemed to be infinitely dynamic and have no exterior, with the result that available luxurious pleasure seemed endlessly lacking or in the process of dissipating. The reason for this is clear.

Given that luxury relies on transgression, and the neoliberal system ended up having no limits, the only luxury available in this total system is a tame form of pseudo-luxury that never really satisfies or offers the neoliberal libertine (who is now coincidentally everybody, everywhere – the late capitalist individual) the criminal luxury he really desires in order to demonstrate his 'special liberty', his absolute individual freedom. Luxury joins violence as another domesticated and commodified libidinal form in the pseudo-pacification process's fold. Thus we approach the nightmarish situation narrated by the contemporary French author Michel Houellebecq, who specifically writes of the Sadean system in his novel *Atomised* (2001). Here the horror of the neoliberal individual resides in a position caught inside a system that casts him in the role of libertine, insists upon his isolation from others, and objectifies him in order to throw him into circulation. The system then takes away the possibility of criminal luxury which always kept the Sadean libertine alive by normalising it as a value degraded by its inability to transgress boundaries that have become infinitely elastic.

Houellebecq's materialist horror

In line with the normalisation, democractisation, and endless extension of the Sadean system, it can be argued that Houellebecq explores the contemporary nightmare of libertine culture caused by an unholy ideological mix of radical individualism, total objectification, absolute disenchantment, and the incorporation of criminal luxury into an economic model where the pursuit of pseudo-luxury is essential to survival. Where Sade wanted to keep the truth of the capitalist economy – that it is premised on the trade in bodies – confined to his secret Society of the Friends of Crime, leaving normal society to seek out pleasure and luxury in debased or simulated forms, the post-1968 neoliberal version of capitalism incorporated the demand for sexual freedom into the commodity system and in this way generalised the Sadean machine. One might imagine that the result of this generalisation of the Sadean economy would be the creation of a world characterised by sexual satisfaction and complete luxury, but Houellebecq's work shows that the opposite is actually the case simply because of the radical democratic context where everybody is supposed to play the role of both master *and* victim. Of course, Sade's sleight of hand was to suggest a society of communistic universal prostitution, where everybody could use everybody else, but to pursue something far more exclusive on the basis of his assumptions about his own feudal superiority, which meant that his universalistic vision was never serious.

Against the radical communistic vision, Sade's feudalism meant that he was always certain that he would occupy the position of the master and that the neighbour would serve his desires in the role of the victim. But in the neoliberal capitalist system the very opposite is the case. Here, everybody is supposed to be a radical individual, a luxurious master free of limitation and so on, but the reality of the constraints of the system, where there is no transgression but only ever pseudo-luxurious escape, means that everybody is thrown back upon their essential objectivity and subjection to the system, which is the true perverse master. This is, I think, precisely what Houellebecq's fiction illustrates. The key problem for his everyday libertines, and these characters appear everywhere in his novels, is that the normalisation of luxury and the absolute commodification of sex under conditions of neoliberal culture means that every attempt to find pleasure and achieve Sadean mastery only confirms the opposite state: the horror of objectification. The result of this miserable situation is that the search for pleasure, escape, and luxury becomes ever more desperate, a kind of addiction that only makes the inevitable failure of the drive for some kind of luxurious state of peace and satisfaction even harder to take. In this way we can argue that Houellebecq's novels re-stage Adorno and Horkheimer's (1997) culture industry thesis for a hypersexualised society that is completely open about the identity of the commodity and the body that it is possible to exploit in the name of the extraction of luxury value.

Although Boltanski and Chiapello (2006) identified the new spirit of capitalism with high-tech creative work, the other darker side of this new version of economy is the hyper-sexual system Carole Sweeney (2013) writes about in terms of the total objectification, commodification, and marketisation of the body. Of course, the irony of talking about this situation in terms of a new spirit of capitalism is that there is no real idealism here beyond the kind of porno fantasy-world that Houellebecq often sketches out in his representations of sex. Despite being criticised for his lack of realism in these scenes, which jar with the grey, miserable realism of his wider vision of human life under late capitalism, in my reading Houellebecq's fantastical depiction of sex makes perfect sense representing exactly what the failed libertine *imagines* sex will achieve – that is the luxurious escape from the horror of his pure objectivity, servitude, and subjection where there is no spirit, but only total meaningless materiality. From this point of view we might argue that Houellebecq picks up and runs with the Sadean element already contained in Adorno and Horkheimer's work, and specifically the chapter devoted to Sade in *Dialectic of Enlightenment* (1997). This is in a sense precisely what he achieves in his depictions of life under neoliberal capitalism. Adorno and Horkheimer never push the sexual dimension of their analysis, because in the pre-1968 version of capitalism they were engaged with, sexuality remained sublimated *within* commodities. But in Houellebecq's post-1968 universe sex is everywhere, and the late-capitalist worker is *supposed* to engage in sexual excess, transgression, enjoyment, and luxurious immersion in pleasure. This is the new Sadean normal, where criminal luxury becomes pseudo-luxury, and the dark castle of Silling is on endless porno websites catering to every kind of fetish and perversion.

Writing on the industrialisation of sex in the Sadean system, Henaff (1999) explains that the Marquis invented a kind of sexual Stakhanovism, and this is exactly what Houellebecq's characters must endure. In much the same way that the real Soviet worker could never measure up or match the achievements of the mythical figure of Stakhanov, who the Stalinist system used as a role model to push workers ever harder, Houellebecq's characters find that the pure luxury of the libertine, the ecstasy of sexual freedom, and sexual satisfaction are always out of reach. These characters never measure up, they are always failures, debased objects, in a world where somebody else is always the master, enjoying what they never can. According to Sweeney (2013) this is why what she calls *le monde Houellebecquien* is such a dark place. There is nothing here but the endless, depressive injunction to enjoy, to wallow in sexual luxury, to escape the horror of everyday life where everybody is an object, *and* the dawning realisation that it is impossible to execute or satisfy this command because there can be no sexual luxury in a system where everybody is already objectified and estranged from themselves. This is, in a sense, why it would be better to support Sweeney's discussion of Boltanski and Chiapello's new spirit of capitalism, which she refers to in order to explain the emergence of Houellebecq's society, through reference to Bernard Stiegler's (2014) lost spirit of capitalism, where radical disenchantment reigns because there is no real spirit about Houellebecq's Sadean world, but only a stupid, unthinking, process and a desperate desire for something else imagined in pornographic fantasy.

But the problem with this fantasy, which is admittedly wearing extremely thin today when the limits of sexual freedom are becoming ever more apparent, is neatly explained by Sweeney (2013) in her discussion of Anthony Giddens' early 1990s utopia developed in his book *The Transformation of Intimacy* (1993). For Sweeney the problem with Giddens' pure relationship, where sex and love are free and without obligation, is that it implies a kind of objective distance or separation between partners that means that sex and intimacy will never coincide, and sex will always degrade towards a kind of base materialism. Sade's libertine was, of course, never intimate, but he was a master by virtue of his position in philo-Feudal society, which meant that his neighbour was always his victim. What happens, however, in Giddens' fantasy of the pure relationship in the radical democratic society underwritten by capitalism where all that matters is the circulation of commodities, is that everybody becomes the object for everybody else. Surely this is less a utopia and more a sexual dystopia where absolutely everybody is fucked!

Under these miserable conditions, which Louis Betty (2016) writes about in terms of materialist horror, everybody loses and only survives by hanging onto the fantasy that the pure relationship is somehow possible. Giddens' (1993) utopia is, therefore, comparable to Sade's vision of universal prostitution and universal objectivity realised in the language of pseudo, rather than the Sadean form of criminal luxury. As we have seen, Sade knew that this would never really be possible (there could be no universal, communistic sexual system), which is precisely why he retreated towards the power relation of the criminal fraternity, the Society of the Friends of Crime, where the libertine elite would exploit the debased neighbour, but it is precisely this democratisation of criminal luxury that the radicals of 1968 sought to realise, that Giddens wrote out in his book on the pure relationship, and that Houellebecq reveals in its true horror across his novels *Whatever* (1999), *Atomised* (2001), *Platform* (2003), and *The Possibility of an Island* (2005).

Beyond setting out the problem of the Sadean system realised, perhaps the key issue Houellebecq raises is exactly what one would do about this situation politically. As Sweeney (2013) points out, Houellebecq sketches out a vision of a 'fallen France', and I would extend this to say 'fallen society' on the basis of the way his books speak to the situation in other advanced late-capitalist nations (the UK or US for example). However, the apathy, indifference, and resignation in his work never really suggest an obvious response to the dystopian condition he sets out. Or at least the suggestions Houellebecq makes often seem completely unsatisfactory and perhaps even more dystopian than the sexual, pseudo-luxurious dystopia he paints across his novels. Thus Sweeney (2013) notes that Houellebecq seems to appeal to both the political left, who would bemoan the commodification of everything, *and* at the same time the far right, who suggest that what is needed is a conservative revolution in order to return to pre-1968 norms and values, but also neither side, because of on the one hand his potential sexism and racism and on the other hand his refusal to completely reject the normalised libertine culture that is the legacy of 1968.

Although Houellebecq continually suggests that 1968 failed, leaving the neoliberal subject marooned somewhere between the endless pursuit of luxury and the crushing, desperate failure to ever escape his own objectivity into pleasure, he seems to have no utopia of his own. This is why Ben Jeffery (2011) writes of Houellebecq's depressive realism, where life is stripped bare of every illusion and we are left to contemplate a world of total isolation and bottomless unhappiness. Since we are all Sadean libertines now, the only answer we have to this situation is to pursue ever more criminal luxury in order to try to escape our subjection to utility into the freedom of pleasure, but this is a fatal strategy because there is no space for criminal luxury in an ideological universe where the only rule is the rule to transgress rules. As a result, the best we can ever hope to achieve is pseudo-luxury, which is luxury inside the economic system, that is no kind of escape into freedom, but only confirmation of the inescapable fact of subjection.

No wonder Houellebecq's characters are depressed! They are libertines without anything to rage against. They are, in Sweeney's (2013) words, 'botched subjects', failures in a society of libertines, where the passion for luxury has taken on the form of a Darwinian struggle. This is precisely the story Hoellebecq tells in his most famous work *Atomised* (2001) where brothers Bruno and Michel separate in their response to the neoliberal nightmare. Where Bruno takes up the challenge and seeks escape into sexual luxury and pleasure, Michel withdraws into the contemplation of science, physics, and the properties of atomic particles. Although Bruno imagines sex will save him, he soon runs up against the terrible truth of his lack, noting that the biological fact of his penis size means he will never make it in the world of the democratic libertine. Every woman looks at him with disappointment, and he realises that the possibility of luxury, of escape into pleasure, is always likely to be thwarted by the brutal fact of his objectivity. He's simply not big enough.

However, upon recognising the horror of materiality, Bruno makes no effort to take a different path. During a visit to a sex club, his partner, the ageing 68er Christiane, suffers a catastrophic spinal injury. Bruno abandons her, leaving her to suffer her fate, because she is no use to him in her crippled state. A similarly depressing situation leads Bruno's brother Michel towards science. In this instance his partner Annabelle contracts cancer and takes her own life to escape a future of pain, suffering, and the impossibility of living out a life of libertine luxury. Following this episode, which Betty (2016) says highlights Houellebecq's vision of the ultimate injustice of matter, Michel gives up on fleshy bodies and retreats into science. He recognises that he is on his own and decides to try to solve the problem of the impossibility of Sadean luxury through scientific manipulation.

As Sweeney (2013) points out, everything in Houellebecq's work tends to rest upon this separation between, on the one hand, Bruno and the fatal participation in libertine culture, and, on the other hand, Michel and complete withdrawal from the sexual-economic system. In *Platform* (2003) the libertine strategy characterised by the pursuit of criminal luxury takes the form of the normalisation of sex tourism in Thailand. In this book the main character Michel seeks escape from base materialism through Thai prostitutes, who he thinks are more authentic than their western counterparts. Unlike sex workers in the west who tend to reinforce the horror of materialism through their objective approach to their trade, which simply emphasises the reduction of criminal luxury to pseudo-luxury, Michel believes that Thai prostitutes are actually engaged in their work on a far deeper level. This means he can take more enjoyment or luxury value from them as they provide him with some kind of escape from the misery of his existence, precisely what Betty (2016) claims is the essential issue Houellebecq addresses in his work. Where Sweeney focuses on the place of the economy in his work, Betty explains that the core problem of Houellebecq is really the Sadean one. What happens after the death of God? As we have seen, even though he professed to be an atheist, Sade kept his luxury system going by raging against God. But what happens when there is nothing beyond materiality? What happens when there is no meaning and reality is a dark abyss? For Douglas Morrey (2013), Houellebecq's response is to say that humanity is finished, and some kind of post-humanity is necessary.

This is, of course, precisely what the Sadean system ended up suggesting by virtue of its extreme mechanisation, and Houellebecq outlines towards the end of *Atomised* (2001) and then in a more developed form in *The Possibility of an Island* (2005), where the escape into science leads to the invention of the neo-human who no longer feels desire, the drive for criminal luxury that could confirm mastery, or the disappointment of pseudo-luxury that only reinforces the reality of base materialism. In *The Possibility of an Island* the main character Daniel finds luxurious escape from his very human condition in the youthful sexual libertine Esther (he explains that he finds happiness inside her) even though he knows she will leave him in the end. His worst fears are eventually realised when he finds Esther engaged in a threesome that simply confirms his view that there is nothing in the world beyond the kind of brutal, natural materialism Sade confronted in his work. Fast forward into the future – Daniel's clone Daniel 25 no longer suffers, no longer desires, and no longer wants for anything.

Similarly, the neo-humans are no longer compelled to suffer decay and the collapse of the body. There are no old neo-humans, because they refuse to tolerate the injustice of matter by choosing suicide over decrepitude, but even here Houellebecq imagines unhappiness creeping back into the picture. Akin to Borges' (2000) immortals, who turn into beasts because they have no sense of finitude to structure their lives, Daniel 25 ends up envying the pain and suffering of Daniel 1 on the basis that *it* mattered to him. In world where nothing else carried meaning, Daniel 1 suffered and this meant something. From the point of view of Daniel 25, who no longer suffers in this way, this suffering *was* Daniel 1's luxury and precisely what he wants to find when he leaves the secure space of the neo-humans in search of the birthplace of the clones – Lanzarote. Of course, Daniel 25 never finds home and we are left to contemplate what seems to be Houellebecq's ultimate message contained in his book on the American writer, H. P. Lovecraft (2008). We inhabit a Lovecraftian universe of boundless darkness, and real luxury resides in understanding our non-place in this black sea of infinity.

According to Houellebecq's cosmic pessimism there is no escape from this situation. If Sade's criminal luxury led anywhere it was never to mastery, but rather to a recognition that there is nothing beyond negation, the abyss, and suffering. Although we can look up into the darkness and lose ourselves in the void of outer space every night, I think the key point of both Sade and Houellebecq is that the void is also inside of us, a black hole of suffering which we try to fill with luxurious escape. Where Sade sought to do this through criminal luxury which could make him a master, Houellebecq realises that this strategy is no longer available in neoliberal society where more or less everything is part of a pseudo-luxury system that tantalises us with the possibility of satisfaction. Although there is no obvious utopia in Houellebecq, which is why Jeffery (2011) writes of his depressive realism, I think that there is the possibility of escape in his focus upon the experience of suffering. For Houellebecq there is paradoxically a kind of nobility, a kind of freedom, a kind of luxury in suffering, which we should not try to escape, but rather must confront and embrace as the essence of what it means to be human. This is in a way where he departs from Sade, who ironically wanted to escape his own suffering by enjoying the suffering of the other who he could never escape in the name of his own desire for mastery. By contrast, I think the key message of Houellebecq is that the embrace of suffering is the very ground of the connection to the inescapable neighbour who we can never really know beyond his or her own suffering in the abyss of space. This is, I would suggest, Houellebecq's vision of the common luxury of suffering beyond the world of the libertine and criminal luxury.

References

Adorno, T.W. and Horkheimer, M. (1997) *Dialectic of Enlightenment*, London: Verso.
Bataille, G. (1991) *The Accursed Share: Volume I: Consumption*, New York: Zone.
Betty, L. (2016) *Without God: Michel Houellebecq and Materialist Horror*, University Park, PA: Pennsylvania State University Press.
Blanchot, M. (2004) *Lautreamont and Sade*, Redwood, CA: Stanford University Press.
Boltanski, L. and Chiapello, E. (2006) *The New Spirit of Capitalism*, London: Verso.
Borges, J.L. (2000) *Labyrinths: Selected Stories and Other Writings*, London: Penguin.
De Sade, M. (2016) *120 Days of Sodom*, London: Penguin.
Deleuze, G. and Guattari, F. (1983) *Anti-Oedipus: Capitalism and Schizophrenia: Volume I*, Minneapolis: University of Minnesota Press.
Foucault, M. (1977) *Discipline and Punish: The Birth of the Prison*, London: Penguin.
Foucault, M. (2003) *The Birth of the Clinic: An Archaeology of Medical Perception*, London: Routledge.
Foucault, M. (2006a) *Psychiatric Power: Lectures at College De France: 1973–1974*, Basingstoke: Palgrave.
Foucault, M. (2006b) *History of Madness*, London: Routledge.
Freud, S. (2003) *Beyond the Pleasure Principle: And Other Writings*, London: Penguin.
Giddens, A. (1993) *The Transformation of Intimacy: Sexuality, Love and Eroticism in Modern Society*, Cambridge: Polity Press.
Hall, S. (2012) *Theorizing Crime and Deviance: A New Perspective*, London: Sage.
Henaff, M. (1999) *Sade: The Invention of the Libertine Body*, Minneapolis: University of Minnesota Press.
Houellebecq, M. (1999) *Whatever*, London: Serpent's Tail.
Houellebecq, M. (2001) *Atomised*, London: Vintage.
Houellebecq, M. (2003) *Platform*, London: Vintage.
Houellebecq, M. (2005) *The Possibility of an Island*, London: Weidenfeld and Nicolson.
Houellebecq, M. (2008) *H. P. Lovecraft: Against the World, Against Life*, London: Gollancz.
Jeffery, B. (2011) *Anti-Matter: Michel Houellebecq and Depressive Realism*, Alresford, Hants: Zero Books.
Klossowski, P. (1991) *Sade, My Neighbor*, Evanston, IL: Northwestern University Press.
Klossowski, P. (1998) *Nietzsche and the Vicious Circle*, Chicago: University of Chicago Press.
Klossowski, P. (2017) *Living Currency*, London: Bloomsbury.
Le Brun, A. (1990) *Sade: A Sudden Abyss*, San Francisco: City Light Books.
Lever, M. (1993) *Marquis de Sade: A Biography*, London: HarperCollins.
Macpherson, C.B. (2010) *The Political Theory of Possessive Individualism: Hobbes to Locke*, Oxford: Oxford University Press.
Morrey, D. (2013) *Michel Houellebecq: Humanity and Its Aftermath*, Liverpool: Liverpool University Press.
Roudinesco, E. (2009) *Our Dark Side: A History of Perversion*, Cambridge: Polity Press.
Stiegler, B. (2014) *The Lost Spirit of Capitalism: Disbelief and Discredit: Volume III*, Cambridge: Polity Press.
Sweeney, C. (2013) *Michel Houellebecq and the Literature of Despair*, London: Bloomsbury.

3 The commodification of abstinence

Justin Kotzé

Introduction

In his introduction to Noam Chomsky's book *Profit Over People*, McChesney (1999: 8) describes neoliberalism as 'capitalism with the gloves off', a more selfish and predatory iteration that has become 'the defining political economic paradigm of our time' (McChesney, 1999: 7; see also James, 2008). Geared towards the sacralisation of wealth-creation the effects of this domination are profound and by no means benign. Indeed, the costs of neoliberalism are becoming increasingly visible: accelerated ecological degradation and habitat destruction (Smaligo, 2014), climate migration and conflict (Dupuy, 2013), and growing inequality as the gap between the rich and the poor continues to widen (Winlow and Hall, 2019). Moreover, alongside rising rates of mental ill-health (James, 2008; Fisher, 2009), a lack of meaningful employment, and the solidification of harmful working conditions and practices (Lloyd, 2018a), widespread poverty and homelessness have become endemic features of the twenty-first century (Taylor, 2013). What is more, neoliberalism has injected into every facet of the social body a deep sense of aggressive competition and symbolic violence (Taylor, 2013; Žižek, 2009a) which not only reproduces a competitive egoistic individualism but serves to militate against any sense of collectivism or ethical obligation to each other (Whitehead, 2018).

Any collectivist conception of morality or vestigial commitment to the social has now been thoroughly eroded by a neoliberal orthodoxy that favours moral relativism and encourages the privileging of 'consumer tastes and desires as a form of "freedom" and liberal self-expression' (Smith and Raymen, 2018: 67). Contemporary life is now well and truly organised around consumption (Bauman, 2012), and it is hardly contentious to state that consumer culture is now both pervasive and invasive (Kotzé and Antonopoulos, 2019). Perhaps so much so that many of us dare not risk sacrificing even the smallest facet of our consumer lifestyle to intervene in the world, to act now to ameliorate the suffering of others (Atkinson et al., 2017). There is quite simply, as Winlow et al. (2015: 14) point out, 'no significant popular desire for revolution, or even serious social democratic reform of the system's economic core'.

This is emblematic of what Fisher (2009) calls *capitalist realism*, the negative ideology that contends not only that capitalism is the only game in town but that it is impossible to even imagine anything different. But have there not been a number of significant protests against the system, particularly since the economic crash of 2008? Are there not a plethora of subversive acts happening every day that go against the grain of capitalism? Have you not seen the growth in the conscious consumption of sustainable and fairly sourced goods that hold a big stop sign up to capitalist exploitation? Yes, but our concern should not be with the presence of these gestures of ostensible resistance but rather with their *absence*. Indeed, this chapter aims to demonstrate how common acts of 'resistance' become commodified and assimilated into the circuitry of contemporary capitalism and therefore secure rather than threaten its existence. The chapter therefore makes a case for participating in a gesture of refusal to partake in micro-resistance and stresses the need for an enlightened catastrophism.

Welcome to the 'Resistance'

As previously alluded to, there is little doubt that the neoliberal order 'disadvantages and damages the mass of humanity' (Taylor, 2013: 22). Against this backdrop the liberal myth of perpetual incremental progress cannot be sustained (Kotzé, 2019; Winlow and Hall, 2019). Yet there is hope we are told, 'eddies of resistance' remain to combat the torrent of capitalism's excess; rest assured, 'in a grotesquely unequal society, resistance is always present' (Young, 2007: 77). Perhaps the English riots of August 2011 demonstrate pricelessly this. Some initial reactions were certainly quick to imbue the disorder of those taking part with the flavour of oppositional politics and protest (Hayward and Smith, 2017). However, as Treadwell et al. (2013) note, the rioters displayed no discernible political orientation and did not oppose the ruling ideology but were instead animated by it. This was not the action of individuals excluded from society's value system but of those thoroughly incorporated into capitalism's consumer culture. That is to say, 'rather than seeking to challenge the established political orthodoxy, the rioters (in the main) illustrated a deep commitment to the ideology of consumer capitalism' (Hayward and Smith, 2017: 318). Indeed, the anger and frustration on display was not directed towards the system but rather towards themselves for their perceived failure to get ahead *within the system* (Winlow et al., 2015).

Taking place in the same year, the Occupy movement certainly looked and felt a bit more anti-capitalist than the riots. Yet whilst it can perhaps be argued that Occupy was 'anti-capitalist *in practice*' (Smaligo, 2014: 115; original emphasis), this ostensible 'crack' in capitalist rule assumed more of an individualist spread of supposedly anti-capitalist practices intended to undermine the system. However, this was instrumental to its failure as it contributed to its inability to establish a political dissensus (Hayward and Schuilenburg, 2014). Indeed, the movement could not construct and popularise a discernible alternative to the present system and failed to engage and galvanise the support of an 'individualised, consumerised and depoliticised public' (Winlow et al., 2015: 155). Content, for the most part, to watch events unfold through their TV screens, those who Occupy failed to mobilise certainly wanted something different, something that would represent their interests. But it turns out that they also wanted that something different to fit into the existing political framework and not require more sacrifice than the ink used to potentially mark a ballot paper (Winlow et al., 2015).

Occupy undoubtedly opened up cracks in the system, yet far from serving to combat capitalist realism as Smaligo (2014) suggests, such cracks help perpetuate the system. In fact, as Lloyd (2017: 276) points out, 'capitalism endures because it "allows" resistance to take place'. Rather than being threatened by acts of resistance, capitalism has the uncanny ability 'to incorporate every attack by integrating the attack into the system' (McGowan, 2016: 12). It does this by taking the seemingly revolutionary practice and transforming it into a marketable commodity. Occupy was no exception. Any quick Internet search will reveal a litany of merchandise one can purchase to demonstrate their discontent, from t-shirts, coffee cups, badges, and bumper stickers to comfy sweatpants that allow you to display your activism from home. Far from serving to inspire or mobilise the masses, such commodities are purchased precisely so that one need *not* get involved. The commodity's slogans readily convey one's anger and abrupt designs clearly convey one's discontent, thus the commodity itself is *already acting* on one's behalf. As we shall see, this *interpassivity* (Žižek, 2006) is now a common feature of much of what passes for contemporary resistance, much of which has followed a more atomised and individualistic template (Hayward and Schuilenburg, 2014).

This new template is perhaps one of the most enduring 'products' of the counterculture. For Heath and Potter (2006: 69) 'the idea of a counterculture is ultimately based on a mistake'. Far from constituting any revolutionary doctrine, countercultural 'politics' have been a major driving force propelling consumer capitalism forward. Indeed, there was no real tension between the ideological requirements of capitalism and the ideas of the counterculture (Heath and Potter, 2006). Both endorse a commitment to competitive hyper-individualism, conspicuous consumption (Buccellato and Reid, 2014), the aggressive display of consumer items, the cultivation of envy (Raymen and Smith, 2016), social distinction, narcissistic hedonism, and instant gratification (Hall et al., 2008). Accordingly, countercultural movements fall very short of the mark in resisting anything; in fact it is more useful to think of them as *hyper-conforming* to the values and drives of contemporary consumer capitalism. Moreover, not only are they by no means anti-capitalist, but they actually negate the potential for political change in two very significant ways. First, the strong emphasis placed upon self-expression and self-fulfilment, and the commensurate erosion of collective politics, ensure that agitated energies are channelled in depoliticised and safely commodified ways (Hayward and Schuilenburg, 2014; Buccellato and Reid, 2014). Second, the frenetic *false activity* provides the appearance of change so that nothing has to change (Žižek, 2006), 'Look! The system is being held to account' (Winlow, 2013: 30) – no need to make personal sacrifices beyond the costs of consuming commodified symbols of 'resistance'.

What this ultimately equates to is the transformation of hedonism into a revolutionary doctrine (Heath and Potter, 2006). Various forms of dramatic gestures are lauded as rebellious resistance that in reality constitute nothing more than pseudo-activity succeeding only in providing marketable entertainment for the rebels (Heath and Potter, 2006). The literature is replete with a litany of examples of what passes for resistance these days. For instance, Hayward and Schuilenburg (2014: 23) note how even the Ibiza club and drug scene has been regarded as resistance despite it obviously being 'in rather short supply in these environments' (see also Ellis et al., 2018). Moreover, Hollander and Einwohner (2004) note how bodybuilding has been construed as resistance yet, as Kotzé and Antonopoulos (2019) have shown, it is more fruitful to view this as hyper-conformity. Various forms of deviant leisure have also been considered to be intrinsically transgressive and deeply political. Indeed, Kindynis (2017) notes how the practice of urban exploration is often thought of as an inherently transgressive and subversive act geared towards taking back one's rights to the restricted city-space. Such ideas have already emerged as a dominant narrative throughout much of the research literature; however, Kindynis quite rightly contests this.

Contra claims to its revolutionary potential, Kindynis (2017: 989) argues that 'the subculture arguably mirrors the hedonism, egotism and competitive individualism of a late capitalist culture of narcissism'. Whilst the practice of urban exploration, and its various offshoots such as 'rooftopping', may transgress liberal-capitalism's technical law they are hyper-conforming to its Symbolic Law (Hall and Winlow, 2015). Its practitioners' thrill-seeking, risk-taking, and egoistic competitiveness are precisely those attitudes and behaviours favoured by market capitalism (Kindynis, 2017; see also Kotzé and Antonopoulos, 2019) – not to mention the entrepreneurial ethic associated with various forms of urban exploration which have 'unhesitatingly aligned themselves with a hegemonic culture of spectacular consumption' as they become increasingly commodified and mainstreamed (Kindynis, 2017: 992). Similarly, Raymen (2019a) notes that there is a popular tendency to view parkour as anti-capitalist resistance because its practitioners reclaim their right to the city, re-appropriating the physical environment and performing a rich form of spatial politics by 'resisting' the hyper-regulated urban space of consumer capitalism. Taking an Ultra-Realist perspective, Raymen (2019a) provides an important corrective to this optimistic narrative. Like the urban explorers, there is no tension between their ideas, drives, and desires and those that capitalism endeavours to cultivate; nor is there any ' "tension" between rebellion and conformity in the commodification of parkour' (Raymen, 2019a: 57). In fact, it is argued that parkour has not simply been co-opted by consumerist forces but was 'pre-emptively shaped by consumer identities and logic', a pure product of *precorporation* (Raymen, 2019a: 58). Operating through its thinly veiled guise of *interpassive resistance* parkour is entirely conformist to mainstream values (Raymen, 2019a).

Evidently, 'resistance' is now seen everywhere and in everything, including the simplest forms of hedonistic indulgence. Certainly, there now exists a discernible lack of specificity and definitional consensus regarding the term (Hayward and Schuilenburg, 2014). However, what is becoming increasingly clear is that contemporary forms of resistance are more concerned with *feeling* good rather than *doing* good. This is a theme which I will explore further in a moment but suffice it to say for now that it constitutes a broad cultural current, one which certainly carries a seductive message: 'keep capitalism's destructive tendencies in check by enjoying and expressing yourself'. Yet despite the light hue of 'active' resistance granted to the previous examples, they remain unequivocally hyper-conformist. Their frenetic false activity is effortlessly absorbed by capitalism as it entertains our gestures of discontent; completely unthreatened it assimilates and commodifies these gestures and offers them back to us as evidence that the system is being held to account. This ultimately negates genuine political opposition by simply providing the appearance of incremental and progressive change (Winlow, 2013). Perhaps what is needed then is less 'active' and more 'passive' forms of resistance capable of subverting capitalism behind its back.

Redeemed consumers and interpassive resistance

We now occupy an Anthropocene age in which humankind rather than nature causes most of the negative effects on the world. We have been the architects of many disasters from wars, environmental degradation and habitat destruction, enforced population migration to rapid deindustrialisation, and the destruction of livelihoods (Hall and Winlow, 2015). Criminological records show quite clearly that neoliberalism has played a leading role in precipitating such disasters. However, only more recently has our own anthropocentric complicity in actively soliciting and reproducing the very sociosymbolic order that produces such harms been highlighted (Hall and Winlow, 2015; Kotzé, 2019). Put simply, we have long been complicit in perpetuating both the structural conditions and ideological tenets that cause severe harm to the wider social and environmental body. Indeed Raymen (2016) drives the point home well by noting that neoliberal consumer capitalism has, over the past four decades, influenced and nurtured the development of self-interested, individualistic, and potentially harmful subjectivities. Any sense of collectivism and social solidarity has been crushed under the weight of free-market ideology, and in its place the culture of competitive individualism has taken front-and-centre stage of the new social order (Raymen, 2016). There is now a palpable preoccupation with the self and one's quest for personal freedom and pleasure taken 'right to the edge of morality's toxic core' (Hall et al., 2008: 106).

But who's to say what is 'moral', 'toxic', or 'harmful'? This is precisely the questioning that liberal-postmodern subjects feel justified in posing as they guard against any suspected attempt to curtail their pursuit of self-interest (Raymen, 2019b). Yet our enamoured pursuit of this freedom to reject any adjudicating authority and define our own conception of what is good has been costly. We have been untethered from any sense of symbolic efficiency as we refuse to subscribe to the collective fib of the big Other, no longer adhering to the communal network of social institutions, customs, and laws into which we were once socialised (Myers, 2003; Kotzé, 2019). Instead, we have subscribed to the doctrine of emotivism. For MacIntyre, (2011: 13, original emphasis) this philosophical theory dismisses all evaluative and moral judgments as '*nothing* but expressions of preference, expressions of attitude or feeling'. Evaluative utterances then seemingly have no appeal to impersonal criteria, for there apparently are none, but are simply the expression of one's own attitudes and feelings set against those of others. Conceptions of morality and the good are rendered hopelessly relativistic as emotivism becomes more deeply embodied in our culture (MacIntyre, 2011). Accordingly, in the absence of any shared conception of the good, there are 'only manipulatively won battles of private interests and preferences' (Raymen, 2019b: 141).

Against this backdrop, active citizenship takes the form of a narcissistic pursuit for self-distinction and personal gratification, ultimately turning protest into an individualised project to be enacted within the orbit of obedient rule-following (Hall et al., 2008; Raymen, 2019b). 'Everyday resistance', intended to mitigate the excesses of, and fallout caused by, appropriating classes (Hollander and Einwohner, 2004), descends into various forms of 'consumer redemption' (Žižek, 2009b). One endeavours to mitigate the damage done to the environment and local communities by buying Rainforest Alliance Certified™ chocolate; various noble causes can be aided by simply buying a Starbucks® coffee (Žižek, 2009b); cancer can be beaten sooner by buying a Tesco bag emblazoned with a rallying message that 'this is beating cancer'; developing countries can be helped to 'develop a little quicker' by our engagement in volunteer tourism; and one can support those who suffer with mental ill-health by sharing or re-posting supportive messages on Facebook. Unfortunately, however, these acts are not combating capitalism's deluge of destruction or resisting its exploitative tendencies, nor is it subverting capitalism behind its back. Quite the opposite in fact; they feed directly into capitalism's self-critique, which provides only the appearance of change precisely so the existing order continues *unchanged* (Winlow, 2013).

Effortlessly converting potential attacks into opportunities for further commodification and thus expansion, late capitalism has imbued consumption with a narrative of repair and conservation so that redemption is infused within the very act of consumption itself (Igoe, 2013). So, one feels she is doing her part by buying a cancer-busting Tesco bag despite the fact that we remain complicit in producing the human-made carcinogens that cause cancer (Chernomas and Hudson, 2007). We feel, as a recent Tesco advert averred, as if we are 'doing our bit' to help farmers and protect the rainforest by simply buying and eating suitably branded chocolate. Yet deforestation is intimately connected to the fossil-fuelled consumer culture so extolled in the global north (Igoe, 2013). Similarly, one feels vindicated from the co-responsibility for the situation of the 'underdeveloped' by engaging in various forms of charity (Žižek, 2009a), and increasingly 'volunteer tourism' (Mostafanezhad, 2014). In this particular 'empathetic gesture of commoditized concern' (Mostafanezhad, 2014: 112), volunteers pay to participate in development or conservationist projects. However, demanding that friends 'Take my photo!' as one picks up the nearest child to capture an image that can almost immediately be made the next Facebook profile picture not only aestheticises deprivation but reinforces the individuation of political action and depoliticises global economic inequality (Mostafanezhad, 2014: 111). Finally, despite rising levels of mental-ill health being a direct consequence of the neoliberal order that we remain complicit in perpetuating (Taylor, 2013; James, 2008), many of us feel pardoned by the simple act of sharing or reposting supportive messages on Facebook. This is not unlike the good conscience gained by the committed clicktivist who, incidentally, also derives a sense of pleasure from signing online petitions (Kuldova, 2018).

This is commodified *interpassive resistance par excellence*, the outsourcing of one's 'politics' to commodified signifiers that grant the individual symbolic capital whilst simultaneously reinforcing the capitalist system and maintaining the status quo (Raymen, 2019a). The chocolate, the coffee, the bag, and the Facebook pictures and messages act on our behalf, performing our anti-capitalism for us so that we can continue to consume with impunity (Fisher, 2009). As Winlow (2013: 30) points out, 'interpassivity encourages us to rest easy, safe in the knowledge that a critique of the present is being waged daily on our behalf'. But hang on a second – surely, we are not ideological dupes? We are, as Lloyd (2017: 275–276) explains, 'too knowing to be duped by ideology'. Certainly, we know that participating in micro-rebellions or individualised acts of consumer redemption will not shake the foundations of the capitalist system. But here is the rub: we continue to act *as if* we did not know this, engaging in what Žižek (2008: 12) calls 'fetishistic disavowal' – *I know very well that this is the case but cannot bring myself to really believe and therefore act as if I do not know*. By maintaining a cynical distance individuals feel content that, at least at the level of knowledge, they have not been conned by the system whilst continuing to participate in the capitalist rituals of everyday life (Kotzé, 2019). However, these individuals remain pure subjects of ideology, for as Žižek (2008) reminds us, ideology works at the point of *doing* rather than *knowing*. Therefore, whilst we may believe that we know about capitalism's exploitative and oppressive practices we continue to participate, acting *as if* we do not know (Lloyd, 2017).

Taylor (2013: 102) argues that this prevailing form of cynicism 'is the perverted psychological resistance of the modern individual', one who refuses to believe in the efficacy of government or their politics but who refuses to do anything about it. Within this contemporary neoliberal condition, expressions of discontent remain little more than muted grumblings expressed harmlessly through bad jokes, 'edgy' t-shirt logos, and Facebook posts, all of which capitalism effortlessly absorbs. It is not that we have given up belief in fighting the system, but in acknowledging its difficulty we have deferred our agency and delegated our belief to various commodities that appear as the true believer in our stead (Kuldova, 2018). Moreover, individuals derive a sense of pleasure from the act of interpassivity and the fetishistic disavowal that sustains it because critique is served here on a plate of commodified enjoyment (Kuldova, 2018). Indeed, despite knowing that the interpassive object fails to 'act appropriately', and that such objects are themselves often produced in harmful and exploitative conditions, we consume and enjoy them nonetheless (Kuldova, 2018). To help make a bit more sense of this it is instructive here to briefly explore the contemporary reorientation of the super-ego. Rather than feeling guilty for desiring too much and overindulging, the super-ego now demands that we enjoy, making us 'feel guilty if we miss a single opportunity to indulge ourselves' (Winlow and Hall, 2018: 99).

Accordingly, we are, at a deep psychosocial level, far more committed to *feeling* good than *doing* good. Set against the backdrop of emotivism discussed previously and the generalised lack of agreement as to what constitutes both human and social good – with such matters left to the private discretion of the sovereign individual – (MacIntyre, 2011; Raymen, 2019b), interpassive gestures of commodified 'resistance' are not only enough to make us feel good (Žižek, 2011), but are mobilised *precisely because* they make us feel so. Indeed, Grant and Sonnentag (2010) suggest that doing good buffers against feeling bad. More specifically, they argue that perceived prosocial impact buffers against negative self-evaluations and thus emotional exhaustion. Engaging in actions perceived as being beneficial to others not only helps alleviate the psychologically aversive state of affective fatigue, a condition quite common in the neoliberal era (Taylor, 2013), but engenders feelings of joy and happiness (Grant and Sonnentag, 2010). Thus, despite their inefficiency, interpassive and reactive gestures of resistance are pursued *as* sources of pleasure and enjoyed just the same as any consumer product. Again, even in more passive forms of resistance we see commodified hedonism transformed into a revolutionary doctrine (Heath and Potter, 2006).

Since capitalism is so well-versed in co-optation and precorporation resulting in what appears to be the complete commodification of resistance, whilst at the same time encouraging the "rebels" to feel good about ' "saving the world" through consumption' (Mostafanezhad, 2014: 113), perhaps the answer to effective resistance lies in strategies of ascetic withdrawal (Barber, 2007).

The commodification of abstinence

There is undoubtedly a deep underlying violence that underpins consumer culture (Smith and Raymen, 2018). For instance, consider Morrison's (2014) analysis of *Unwatchable: Is your phone rape free?*, a viral video made on behalf of the Save the Congo NGO. Released in 2011, the video depicts scenes of systematic mass raping and extreme brutality driven by the trade in conflict minerals used in the production of mobile phones amongst other high-tech electrical devices. However, rather than capturing the actual story of Congolese victims, the film is framed in England and portrays the destruction of a white middle-class family. The reason for this is quite simple, Morrison (2014: 193) contends: 'we are "Africa'd out" '. Such atrocities have, he argues, become overdetermined (see also Žižek, 2009a). Accordingly, by locating the film in England the makers of the video attempted to 'shock Western consumers into ethical accountability in the trade in conflict minerals and, . . . the mass rapes and extreme brutality it fuels' (Morrison, 2014: 192).

Since our incessant consumption of various iterations of mobile phones appears to be the driver for much of the harm these Congolese victims experience should this not prompt an ascetic withdrawal, an abstinence from such commodities (Jameson, 2010)? Perhaps by going 'mobile free' for a month this gesture of abstinence could be used to protest against the use of conflict minerals. By resisting the commodified object forged in fields of violence we could demand ethical accountability and change. One could be forgiven for thinking that such a period of protest abstinence would be conducive to mobilising a concerted revolutionary force driven towards a collective duty to the other. However, as Barber (2007) reminds us, strategies of ascetic withdrawal are not very effective. This is because periods of commodity abstinence simply open up the space for different kinds of desire to emerge and be temporarily satiated by additional commodities that serve as intermittent replacements for the abstained object (Dean and Fisher, 2014). Indeed, such acts of withdrawal energise the capitalist system rather than inhibit its productivity, it capitalises upon such refusals actualising the potential value by transforming it into a site of immense production so that the initial refusal leads precisely to 'the privileging of a whole new commodity' (McGowan, 2016: 168).

Accordingly, as Bauman (2005) notes, even attempts to escape the grip of commodified consumerism turn into consumer commodities. It is within this context that we encounter the *commodification of abstinence*. If we continue with the example of going 'mobile free' for a month, this period of abstinence becomes yet another micro-rebellion that simply represents a new opportunity *for* commodification. Besides the inevitable flurry of suitably edgy t-shirts, badges, and bumper stickers, popular providers such as PlayStation, XBOX, or Nintendo might offer to alleviate the burden of giving up one's mobile phone by supplying great deals on the latest games – after all, this is dividualism's increasing leisure pursuit (Taylor, 2013). Going 'mobile free'? Why not binge-watch a series on Netflix? The ease with which these commodities replace the abstained object is intimately connected to the difficulty we experience in relinquishing 'the compensatory desires and intoxications we have developed in order to make the present liveable' (Jameson, 2010: 384). Indeed, with the reworking of the super-ego and its contemporary injunction to enjoy, any commitment to asceticism is incredibly difficult for 'the absence of pleasure weighs heavy upon the psyche' (Ellis et al., 2018: 4). In the current milieu, a period of abstinence from one's mobile would prove particularly weighty. As Fisher (2009: 24) aptly points out, 'to be denied, for a moment, the constant flow of sugary gratification on demand' is to court boredom, for the smartphone serves to plug the gaps where this contemporary malady would otherwise fervently grow (Dean and Fisher, 2014).

The period of protest abstinence is therefore likely to be short. A fleeting gesture curtailed further by the modern cynic's disbelief in the value of their action or its political efficacy. Commitment to collective fatalism endures as meaningful change is branded impossible and the masses to be mobilised instead defer decision-making and action to others, or other 'things', in the hope that they will act on their behalf (Taylor, 2013). In an act of pure sociosymbolic interpassivity the new 'thing' replacing the abstained object allows politically passive subjects to imagine themselves as rebellious and virtuous heroes. What is more, the commodified replacement – often produced under harmful conditions in developing countries (Ellis et al., 2018) and distributed by companies that operate 'beyond the pale in terms of working conditions and management practices' (Lloyd, 2018b: 246) – is enjoyed just the same as any other consumer product or experience. Then, once the brief period of protest abstinence is over and the replacement object takes its place amongst the 'discarded fashions, fads and trends in an ever-shortening life cycle of commodities' (Smith and Raymen, 2018: 72), one can return to the sanctity of the smartphone and its sensation-stimulus matrix (Fisher, 2009).

Let the posting and sharing commence. All the 'edgy' and rebellious gaming and Netflix-watching can now be shared via social media with incessant 'hashtagging': #game/series, #SavetheCongo, #donemybit, #timetodoyours. Watch the likes roll in as one's symbolic capital is elevated whilst simultaneously contributing to the further marketing of consumer products using the very phone one abstained from, the one produced with conflict minerals. The inevitable upload to social media is important, not because it possesses any revolutionary potential (Crary, 2013), but because it functions as a form of symbolic ratification of having 'done good' thereby allowing one to feel good. Social media, then, operates as a kind of big Other verifying the virtuous act (Myers, 2003), not as interpassive resistance but as anti-capitalism *proper*. However, the validation of this imaginary resistance does nothing to ameliorate the real harms precipitated by our current social arrangements. Rather, its ostensible appearance of change only serves to negate real change as we convince ourselves that it is sufficient to band-aid the fallout of neoliberalism through commodified gestures of 'intervention' (Mostafanezhad, 2014).

We know the band-aid is hopelessly insufficient, but we fetishistically disavow this knowledge and continue to act *as if* we do not know. Moreover, when such disavowal is momentarily threatened, as we are confronted with capitalism's obscene Real, we simply remind ourselves that 'at least we tried'. Kuldova (2018) makes the point well by noting that ignorance is not the problem. Efforts to de-fetishise commodities by revealing the truth behind their production fail precisely because most people *already know* (Kuldova, 2018). Destructive consumer behaviour continues because the majority of consumers maintain a cynical distance; they know very well the truth behind the exploitative, brutal, and harmful production of commodities. Far from foreclosing one's consumption it gives it a moral licence, people can continue to consume so long as they do not buy into the marketing discourse that tries to hide capitalism's destructive and exploitative nature. Therefore, we consume not despite this knowledge but precisely *because* of it. Moreover, this 'revolutionary knowledge' itself is further commodified (Kuldova, 2018). In the context of the aforementioned example of protest abstinence, the various replacements for the abstained object are not only sold to provide psychic relief but are marketed with a degree of symbolic capital in that they now constitute the object of interpassive resistance. Simultaneously the replacement assuages feelings of loss, acts on one's behalf as the rebellious hero, and displays one's enlightened and moral superiority (Kuldova, 2018).

There can be little doubt that we are complicit in perpetuating systemic and subjective violence both domestically and abroad (Žižek, 2009a). Yet our focus, in the instance of going mobile free, on the subjective violence occurring throughout the eastern Congo distracts our attention from the systemic violence of global consumer capitalism (Žižek, 2009a). A violence sustained on behalf of our incessant consumerism as we continue to acquire the symbols of a life deemed worth living through the harm inflicted on others (Smith and Raymen, 2018). Perhaps this is the tacit meaning behind the filming of *Unwatchable* in England. It brings the true locus of trouble back home, i.e. the west, as a significant driver of the systemic violence that precipitates the very subjective forms that capture our attention.

Ultimately, strategies of ascetic withdrawal are not only ineffective but counterproductive as the act of abstinence itself easily becomes commodified and assimilated into capitalism's self-critique adding yet another false indication of change. Cynically aware as we may be, we dare not vocalise it too loudly for the capitalist system has imposed upon us a compulsory refusal to refuse (Winlow and Hall, 2016). Our deep-seated commitment to consumer culture and the sociosymbolic significance attached to consumer objects as the source of identity and distinction means that any attempt at negation has already been negated by the system (Winlow and Hall, 2016). Morality and desire have been so thoroughly disconnected that contemporary calls for change demand that we act against our self-interest and desires, yet faced with the daunting scale of change required and berated by the super-ego's injunction to enjoy 'there is no incentive to act against one's sovereign desires' (Raymen, 2019b: 147). Indeed, as Raymen (2019a: 51, original emphasis) notes, 'we are not *naturally* resistant subjects who seek to continuously disrupt the status quo'. The only natural resistance is to resist re-assimilation back into the Real of our pre-symbolic biological being (Winlow and Hall, 2013). In lieu of a clear, alternative sociosymbolic order we are forced to either risk an encounter with the terrifying indeterminate void of the Real or continue to fetishistically disavow the destructive nature of consumer capitalism (Raymen, 2019b; Winlow and Hall, 2013). Against this backdrop it is easy to explain our penchant for passive, or more accurately interpassive, forms of resistance. As we have seen, such acts of resistance shore up rather than shake the foundations of the capitalist system and thus ensure its survival. This incessant 'tinkering at the edges' (Whitehead, 2018: 92) makes it look as though *something* is being done, as though the system is being held to account and its worst effects mitigated, making the aforementioned choice far easier: 'no need to risk an encounter with the Real, capitalism is being humanised by various acts of micro-resistance'.

Evidently then, the issue lies not in our doing nothing but precisely the opposite. Our prolific pseudo-activity helps capitalism run more smoothly by offering the appearance of positive change so that no change actually needs to occur (Žižek, 2006, 2009a). The first step towards real change thus necessitates that we take a step back and refuse to participate in micro-revolutions.

Towards a gesture of refusal and enlightened catastrophism

What I am advocating here is our participation in a gesture of refusal to being absorbed into various micro-revolutions of simulated transgression that offer nothing other than the appearance of change. Unlike strategies of ascetic withdrawal, or attempts to 'opt out' of competitive consumption, which simply open up the space for the commodification of abstinence, refusing to be forced along the path of simulated rebellion is the only true resistance in consumer capitalism (Hall et al., 2008). In the same way that charity acts as 'the humanitarian mask hiding the face of economic exploitation' (Žižek, 2009a: 19), the pseudo-activity of micro-resistance functions to 'mask the nothingness of what goes on' (Žižek, 2009a: 183). All the acts of ostensible resistance reviewed here endeavour to immerse us in the promise of the future and thus mirror rather than depart from the foundation of the capitalist structure. Indeed, the very act of investing in such promise means that we have 'already succumbed to the fundamental logic of capitalism' (McGowan, 2016: 13). McGowan (2016: 12) further drives the point home by stating that 'this is the problem with the insistence on revolutionary hope: it partakes of the logic that it tries to contest. Revolutionary hope represents an investment in the structure of the promise that defines capitalism'.

Perplexing as it may sound, we must refuse to participate in acts of micro-resistance that espouse the possibility of change and the promise of a better future. Whilst the latter weds us firmly to the logic of capitalism, the former is evoked to guarantee that it will not be acted upon so that no change actually takes place (Žižek, 2017). Accordingly, these hyper-conformist pseudo-struggles function not as a revolutionary spark, but as an extinguisher negating the explosion of true change. The possibility they evoke and the appearance of change they present stand in the way of actual change and thus constitute the very source of capitalism's continuation (Žižek, 2017). Difficult as it may be, we must dispense of the idea that doing *something* is better than nothing, that capitalism can be humanised or made less destructive and exploitative by piecemeal adjustments (Whitehead, 2018). Investment in the promise of something better offered by various anti-capitalist movements must be abandoned (McGowan, 2016). Rather than commit ourselves to discourses that promote baseless and incautious optimism (Kotzé, 2019), we have to confront a zero-point of hopelessness because 'it is only when we despair and don't know any more what to do that change can be enacted' (Žižek, 2017: x).

Enlightened catastrophism (Winlow, 2017), or what Dupuy (2013: 28) calls 'enlightened doomsaying', offers us a means of confronting this zero-point. Its radical move lies not in a promise of a better future but in its guarantee that there will be *no* future if we carry on as we are. It invites us to take an imaginative leap, projecting ourselves into the moment following catastrophe – the complete and total destruction of our socio-ecological terrain by the neoliberal forces we sustain – and then, casting our gaze back to the present, to see this catastrophe as our *fate* (Dupuy, 2013). Believing that it can be avoided, that science and technology will come to our aid, or that political leaders will eventually act on our behalf to do what is needed to avert the coming calamity is to believe that the impending catastrophe does not really threaten us. Only by believing and accepting that this fate will come to pass can we mobilise ourselves to prevent it from happening, to accept this fate as one that we may yet choose to avoid (Dupuy, 2013). As Winlow (2017: 191) points out 'the shock of recognition and conscious acceptance must compel us to begin to do what needs to be done', to think through the coordinates to set us on a different course. Enlightened catastrophism, then, succeeds in achieving that which the preceding doctrines of resistance have so far been unable to. It frees an honest appraisal and the subsequent critique of our current condition from the promise of a better future (McGowan, 2016).

To fully realise this commitment to the courage of hopelessness and enlightened catastrophism first requires our *absence* from, rather than presence in, the various forms of pseudo-activity discussed previously. The ultra-realist interpretation of absence as having a probabilistic causal influence is instructive here (Lloyd, 2018b). From this perspective it is not only the presence of something that can produce negative consequences but the absence of something, such as 'when things could and perhaps should be present, but remain absent, there is an effect' (Winlow, 2017: 180). However, absence can also be *transformative* (Winlow and Hall, 2016). In the current context, this transformative absence is realised by *not* participating in various micro-revolutions that serve only to negate real change by offering the appearance of change. By *refusing* to participate in forms of interpassive resistance that allow the system to run more smoothly. By abstaining from, rather than engaging in, frenetic activity that masks the destructive logic of consumer capitalism and the inefficiency of the nothingness that passes for contemporary progressivism. It is tempting to view various forms of resistance as opening up cracks in the system that may constitute a point of weakness ripe for revolutionary potential. Nevertheless, as has been demonstrated here, such cracks work *for* rather than against the system by providing the space within which ascetic abstinence can be commodified and incorporated into capitalism's self-critique.

Augmenting slightly Fisher's contention that direct action is required to precipitate systemic change (Dean and Fisher, 2014), this chapter contends that both inaction *and* action are required to achieve this end. They must, however, be put to work in a crucial order. First, we must participate in a gesture of refusal to partake in various acts of micro-resistance and refuse to enjoy the comforting myths we have created for ourselves (Kotzé, 2019). Second, having rid ourselves of discourses that promote baseless and incautious optimism we can take a good look at the world *as it is* and confront, through the medium of enlightened catastrophism, an honest appraisal of our current condition. Finally, by confronting a zero-point of hopelessness we can 'fashion the forms of intervention that can arrest our slow descent into the chaos of the future' (Winlow, 2017: 191). Do not be fooled by the *promise* of incremental change towards a better future or be tempted to participate in acts of 'resistance' intended to secure it. Do not heed the altruistic calls of charity that simply allow the system to run more smoothly. To act to the contrary ultimately prevents the carrying out of the only realist solution to our contemporary condition, the complete reconstruction of global society (Žižek, 2016).

References

Atkinson, R., McKenzie, L. and Winlow, S. (2017) Who Would Not Be for Society? In R. Atkinson, L. McKenzie and S. Winlow (eds.) *Building Better Societies: Promoting Social Justice in a World Falling Apart*, Bristol: Policy Press, 1–11.

Barber, B.R. (2007) *Consumed: How Markets Corrupt Children, Infantilize Adults, and Swallow Citizens Whole*, London: W.W. Norton and Company.

Bauman, Z. (2005) *Liquid Life*, Cambridge: Polity Press.

Bauman, Z. (2012) *Liquid Modernity*, Cambridge: Polity Press.

Buccellato, J.A. and Reid, I.D. (2014) Obscene Remainders: Neoliberalism and the Gang Crisis Narrative. *Journal of Theoretical and Philosophical Criminology*, 6, 2: 129–44.

Chernomas, R. and Hudson, I. (2007) *Social Murder and Other Shortcomings of Conservative Economics*, Winnipeg: Arbeiter Ring Publishing.

Crary, J. (2013) *24/7: Late Capitalism and the Ends of Sleep*, London: Verso.

Dean, J. and Fisher, M. (2014) We Can't Afford to Be Realists: A Conversation. In A. Shonkwiler and L. La Berge (eds.) *Reading Capitalist Realism*, Iowa City, IA: University of Iowa Press, 26–38.

Dupuy, J.P. (2013) *The Mark of the Sacred*, Palo Alto, CA: Stanford University Press.

Ellis, A., Briggs, D., Winlow, S., Esquinas, A.S., Verdugo, R.C. and Suárez, J.R.P. (2018) Liberalism, Lack and Living the Dream: Re-Considering Youth, Consumer Sovereignty and the Attractions of Night-Time Leisure in Magaluf. *Journal of Extreme Anthropology*, 2, 2: 1–19.

Fisher, M. (2009) *Capitalist Realism: Is There No Alternative?* Winchester: Zero Books.

Grant, A.M. and Sonnentag, S. (2010) Doing Good Buffers Against Feeling Bad: Prosocial Impact Compensates for Negative Task and Self-Evaluations. *Organizational Behaviour and Human Decision Processes*, 111, 1: 13–22.

Hall, S. and Winlow, S. (2015) *Revitalizing Criminological Theory: Towards a New Ultra-Realism*, London: Routledge.

Hall, S., Winlow, S. and Ancrum, C. (2008) *Criminal Identities and Consumer Culture*, Cullompton: Willan.

Hayward, K. and Schuilenburg, M. (2014) To Resist = To Create? Some Thoughts on the Concept of Resistance in Cultural Criminology. *Tijdschrift Over Cultuur and Criminaliteit*, 4, 1: 22–36.

Hayward, K. and Smith, O. (2017) Crime and Consumer Culture. In A. Liebling, S. Maruna and L. McAra (eds.) *The Oxford Handbook of Criminology*, 6th edn., Oxford: Oxford University Press, 306–28.

Heath, J. and Potter, A. (2006) *The Rebel Sell: How the Counterculture Became Consumer Culture*, Chichester: Capstone Publishing.

Hollander, J.A. and Einwohner, R.L. (2004) Conceptualizing Resistance. *Sociological Forum*, 19, 4: 533–54.

Igoe, J. (2013) Consume, Connect, Conserve: Consumer Spectacle and the Technical Mediation of Neoliberal Conservation's Aesthetic of Redemption and Repair. *Human Geography*, 6, 1: 16–28.

James, O. (2008) *The Selfish Capitalist: Origins of Affluenza*, London: Vermilion.

Jameson, F. (2010) *Valences of the Dialectic*, London: Verso.

Kindynis, T. (2017) Urban Exploration: From Subterranea to Spectacle. *British Journal of Criminology*, 57, 4: 982–1001.

Kotzé, J. (2019) *The Myth of the 'Crime Decline': Exploring Change and Continuity in Crime and Harm*, London: Routledge.

Kotzé, J. and Antonopoulos, G.A. (2019) Boosting Bodily Capital: Maintaining Masculinity, Aesthetic Pleasure and Instrumental Utility Through the Consumption of Steroids. *Journal of Consumer Culture*. Available at: https://journals.sagepub.com/doi/abs/10.1177/1469540519846196

Kuldova, T. (2018) Interpassive Phenomena in Times of Economic Subordination. *Continental Thought and Theory*, 2, 1: 32–49.

Lloyd, A. (2017) Ideology at Work: Reconsidering Ideology, the Labour Process and Workplace Resistance. *International Journal of Sociology and Social Policy*, 37, 5/6: 266–79.

Lloyd, A. (2018a) *The Harms of Work: An Ultra-Realist Account of the Service Economy*, Bristol: Bristol University Press.
Lloyd, A. (2018b) Serving Up Harm: Systemic Violence, Transitions to Adulthood and the Service Economy. In A. Boukli and J. Kotzé (eds.) *Zemiology: Reconnecting Crime and Social Harm*, Cham: Palgrave Macmillan, 245–64.
MacIntyre, A. (2011) *After Virtue: A Study in Moral Theory*, London: Bloomsbury.
McChesney, R.W. (1999) Introduction. In N. Chomsky (ed.) *Profit Over People: Neoliberalism and Global Order*, New York: Seven Stories Press, 7–16.
McGowan, T. (2016) *Capitalism and Desire: The Psychic Cost of Free Markets*, New York: Columbia University Press.
Morrison, W. (2014) War and Normative Visibility: Interactions in the Nomos. In P. Davies, P. Francis and T. Wyatt (eds.) *Invisible Crimes and Social Harms*, Basingstoke: Palgrave Macmillan, 178–98.
Mostafanezhad, M. (2014) Volunteer Tourism and the Popular Humanitarian Gaze. *Geoforum*, 54: 111–18.
Myers, T. (2003) *Slavoj Žižek*, London: Routledge.
Raymen, T. (2016) Designing-in Crime by Designing-out the Social? Situational Crime Prevention and the Intensification of Harmful Subjectivities. *British Journal of Criminology*, 56, 3: 497–514.
Raymen, T. (2019a) *Parkour, Deviance and Leisure in the Late-Capitalist City: An Ethnography*, Bingley: Emerald Publishing.
Raymen, T. (2019b) The Enigma of Social Harm and the Barrier of Liberalism: Why Zemiology Needs a Theory of the Good. *Justice, Power and Resistance*, 3, 1: 133–62.
Raymen, T. and Smith, O. (2016) What's Deviance Got to Do with It? Black Friday Sales, Violence and Hyper-Conformity. *British Journal of Criminology*, 56, 2: 389–405.
Smaligo, N. (2014) *The Occupy Movement Explained: From Corporate Control to Democracy*, Chicago: Open Court Publishing.
Smith, O. and Raymen, T. (2018) Deviant Leisure: A Criminological Perspective. *Theoretical Criminology*, 22, 1: 63–82.
Taylor, J.D. (2013) *Negative Capitalism: Cynicism in the Neoliberal Era*, Winchester: Zero Books.
Treadwell, J., Briggs, D., Winlow, S. and Hall, S. (2013) Shopocalypse Now: Consumer Culture and the English Riots of 2011. *British Journal of Criminology*, 53, 1: 1–17.
Whitehead, P. (2018) *Demonising the Other: The Criminalisation of Morality*, Bristol: Policy Press.
Winlow, S. (2013) Is It OK to Talk About Capitalism Again? Or, Why Criminology Must Take a Leap of Faith. In S. Winlow and R. Atkinson (eds.) *New Directions in Crime and Deviancy*, London: Routledge, 21–39.
Winlow, S. (2017) The Uses of Catastrophism. In R. Atkinson, L. McKenzie and S. Winlow (eds.) *Building Better Societies: Promoting Social Justice in a World Falling Apart*, Bristol: Policy Press, 179–92.
Winlow, S. and Hall, S. (2013) *Rethinking Social Exclusion: The End of the Social?* London: Sage.
Winlow, S. and Hall, S. (2016) Realist Criminology and Its Discontents. *International Journal for Crime, Justice and Social Democracy*, 5, 3: 80–94.
Winlow, S. and Hall, S. (2018) Criminology and Consumerism. In P. Carlen and L.A. Franca (eds.) *Alternative Criminologies*, London: Routledge, 92–109.
Winlow, S. and Hall, S. (2019) Shock and Awe: On Progressive Minimalism and Retreatism, and the New Ultra-Realism. *Critical Criminology*. doi.org/10.1007/s10612-019-09431-1

Winlow, S., Hall, S., Treadwell, J. and Briggs, D. (2015) *Riots and Political Protest: Notes from the Post-Political Present*, London: Routledge.
Young, J. (2007) *The Vertigo of Late Modernity*, London: Sage.
Žižek, S. (2006) *How to Read Lacan*, London: Granta Books.
Žižek, S. (2008) *The Sublime Object of Ideology*, London: Verso.
Žižek, S. (2009a) *Violence: Six Sideways Reflections*, London: Profile Books.
Žižek, S. (2009b) *First as Tragedy, Then as Farce*, London: Verso.
Žižek, S. (2011) Don't Fall in Love with Yourselves. In A. Taylor, K. Gessen and editors from n+1, Dissent, Triple Canopy, and The New Inquiry (eds.) *Occupy! Scenes from Occupied America*, London: Verso, 66–69.
Žižek, S. (2016) *Against the Double Blackmail: Refugees, Terror and Other Troubles with the Neighbours*, London: Allen Lane.
Žižek, S. (2017) *The Courage of Hopelessness: Chronicles of a Year of Acting Dangerously*, London: Allen Lane.

Part 2

Contexts and case studies

4 Mass indebtedness and the luxury of payment means

Mark Horsley and Anthony Lloyd

Introduction

One of the most remarkable things about late capitalism is that it seems, at least in part, to have disconnected consumer markets from the material prosperity of host societies. In the context of a persistent decline in the rate of economic growth driven, as much as anything, by international competition and resource scarcity it has adopted a distinctly extractive approach to social structuration in which it concentrates wealth upwards, dividing the population of Britain, America, and elsewhere into increasingly distinct and unsympathetic camps of 'winners' and 'losers'. Whilst an increasingly distant and disinterested elite inhabit an orbital, footloose realm of extraordinary luxury, the rest of us have lived through an era of growing uncertainty, impermanence, stagnation, and decline in which life and livelihood have fallen into a downward spiral of collapsing incomes, precarious employment, and growing resentment and yet the latter continues to consume, apparently a growing rate.

What we have, in other words, is something of a contradiction. On the one hand, we live within a fragile and dysfunctional economic form that has long conspired to reduce the proceeds of traditional capital distribution mechanisms such as wages and welfare, eroding the payment means available to the general population. On the other, a sequence of relatively healthy consumer markets that continue to grow year-on-year, albeit at a relatively slow rate, despite the deflationary pressures swirling around them. It's clear that large parts of the general population are finding it increasingly difficult to maintain meaningful, self-supporting lifestyles amidst a proliferation of insecure, poorly-paid employment practices but that vast majority, as Streeck (2016: 3) notes, nonetheless remain relatively confident consumers, 'happily discharging their consumerist . . . obligations in the face of the fundamental uncertainty of labour markets and employment'.

In this chapter, we want to explore the mechanism by which this has happened, using elements of our combined datasets (see Horsley, 2015; Lloyd, 2013, 2018) to explore the role of 'mass indebtedness' in the sustainability of late-modern consumer economies as they rely, perhaps increasingly, on the continued proliferation of lending practices to generate and distribute means of payment. We will suggest that this process has allowed late capitalism to go some way to transcending its material circumstances, maintaining participation by nominalising and dematerialising value, attaching it, given the events of 2008, to ineffectively risk-managed and overly optimistic assumptions about a future in which we will all somehow discover a capacity to repay our debts. In making this argument, we will explore the use of lending mechanisms to draw payment means from uncertain futures, how this might feed through into late capitalism's cultural imperatives and, finally, the effect it has on the lives of consumers.

The futurity of credit

Until recently, the accepted wisdom on the substantive origins of consumer credit held that banking institutions, as proximate or ultimate lenders, play little or no active role in creating credit. Instead, the largest and most influential parts of modern economics tend to see banks as intermediaries, investing deposits from one subset of their customers by transferring them into loans for another. In Paul Krugman's (2012: 147) terms, for instance,

> when debt is rising, it's not the economy as a whole borrowing more money. It is . . . a case of less patient people – people who for whatever reason want to spend sooner rather than later – borrowing from more patient people.

This relatively simple idea has been echoing throughout mainstream economics for decades, gracing most of the major work on banking, money, and consumer finance. It rears its head in Bernanke's (1993) assertion that credit boils down to making savings available for investment and consumption. It appears again in Allen and Santomero's (2001: 272) observation that 'financial systems perform the function of reallocating the resources of economic units with surplus funds (savers) to economic units with funding needs (borrowers)'. Time and again, from mass-market publications (see, for example, Ferguson, 2012) to highly specialised research literature (Allen and Gale, 2004; Fecht et al., 2008), students of economics are reminded that extending a line of credit is a process of allocation rather than creation.

Although this intermediary thesis has faced relatively little contest since the 1960s, it was once subject to healthy conceptual debate juxtaposed with the mutually exclusive assertion that consumer lending, rather than fulfilling a redistributive function, effectively creates money. This too is a relatively old idea, tracing back to the latter decades of the nineteenth century with early reflections in Marx's (1991 [1894]) concept of 'fictitious capital' and Macleod's (2012 [1891]) use of a factory analogy to describe the capacity to manufacture payment means. Discounted during the interwar years for separating banking from the rest of the economy by giving it a special status exempt from the sanctity of monetary value along with the utopian connotations of an unlimited money supply, the resultant 'credit creation thesis' nonetheless appeared in a swath of European economic theory (see, for example, Pettifor, 2017). The apotheosis of this position, however, can be found in Schumpeter's (2008 [1934]: 107) *Theory of Economic Development*:

> The kernel of the credit phenomenon . . . is essentially the creation of purchasing power . . . not simply the transfer of existing purchasing power. . . . By credit, entrepreneurs are given access to the social stream of goods before they have acquired the normal claim to it. It temporarily substitutes . . . a fiction of this claim for the claim itself.

The act of making a loan, in other words, might be less a recirculation of existing funds than a purposeful creation of payment means where none might otherwise exist. While Schumpeter's focus on the entrepreneur perhaps dates his work to a time before Keynesian demand management and our consequent focus on the consumer, the assertion that credit is created at the point of application in order to fulfil a request for payment still stands in irreconcilable opposition to the intermediary principle.

Taking these ideas as his starting point, Richard Werner (2014) recently set out to empirically test the credit creation thesis. Partnering up with a Bavarian bank, he agreed to take out a sizeable loan whilst monitoring their balance sheet for any corresponding movement of funds. If the bank worked on intermediary principles, there should have been some kind of traceable shifting of money from one account to the next but instead it simply appeared with no identifiable movement elsewhere within sight of the organisation. The money for his loan, it seems, magically appeared out of thin air allowing him to conclude:

> Thus it can now be said with confidence . . . it has been empirically demonstrated that each individual bank creates credit and money out of nothing, when it extends what is called a 'bank loan'. The bank does not loan any existing money, but instead creates new money. The money supply is created as 'fairy dust' produced by the banks out of thin air.
>
> (Werner, 2014: 16)

The difference between these two positions, barring the growing empirical evidence for the latter, is one of perspective and often one of ideology. The recent dominance of the 'intermediary thesis' comes out of an academic discipline that has overwhelmingly crystalised around a single approach to the social world, stalling its own dialectic in favour of an ever-closer relationship between 'neoclassical' ideas, 'neoliberal' policies and the growth of the global financial system (Nesvetailova, 2013; Earle et al., 2016). As part of this relationship, the intermediary principle perhaps works to minimise the 'link between lending and the amount of money in the economy' (Keen, 2017: 76), emphasising the independence of the two and thus sustaining the assertion that banking is a sober, risk-averse, and ultimately rather conservative profession (see Ryan-Collins et al., 2015). When it comes to actually explaining why our economy seems to readily inflate asset price bubbles and/or periodically fall into recessionary financial crises, intermediation removes banking from the equation by recapitulating the household analogy – the common assertion that national and international economies can and should be managed in much the same way as a household budget – for the credit industry through the assertion that only existing assets are transferred into payment means.

On the other hand, if the money for consumer lending is conjured into existence through the credit creation process, the value of the resultant assets remains notional and speculative until each loan matures. When a loan is made the financial industry creates payment means but, instead of attaching them to any existing resources, the lender almost literally reaches forward into the future staking a claim on the prospective value of a debtor's future income, transferring this into a contractual promise of payment, which, for the lender, represents actual corporate value in the present (Langley, 2009). Credit amounts to a promise to pay 'in a more or less distant and unpredictable future . . . requir[ing] one to estimate that which is inestimable – future behaviour and events – and to expose oneself to the uncertainty of time' (Lazzarato, 2012: 45) introducing an element of temporal expectation and of risk into the day-to-day life of the consumer. The result, however, is a monetary system that allows us to exceed the present by capitalising the future, separating participation from its 'anchoring in any objective measure of value', replacing it with 'a world of nominal value' (Palan, 2015: 381) attached to a black box of temporal uncertainty, which, due to the impossibility of long-term risk management in a system driven by accumulative euphoria, tends to spur capitalism's cyclical crises.

This inherent futurity enhances consumptive potential, at least in the near term, bridging the gap between increasingly unpredictable incomes and consumer capitalism's proliferation of desirable symbolic objects to facilitate spending beyond immediately accessible payment means. It accelerates our access to the social stream of goods and experiences, adding liquidity to the system by drawing prospective earnings out of the future to stimulate spending in the present. When that future rolls around, however, credit-fuelled consumption and the rising level of outstanding personal debt, particularly for the thirty-five or so per cent of the population that carry a longstanding balance (ONS, 2016), tends to accentuate the underlying decline of incomes. As outstanding debt increases so does the cost of servicing it with the effect that a larger share of declining incomes quickly works its way into the welcoming arms of the financial industry, further eroding the payment means available for other purposes.

The following pages will explore the possibility that plucking payment means out of the ether as contractual claims on an idealised future might affect the monetary and psychosocial dynamics of consumer culture, particularly when it comes to the seductive promises common to late capitalism.

Seductive promises

Were it not for the proliferation of speculative, future-facing credit instruments over the last few decades, western capitalism would almost certainly have faced a steep and potentially terminal decline beginning in the early 1970s as the relative abundance of post-war industrialism ran into conditions of scarcity by way of supply shocks, increased international competition, and massive industrial unrest. Without the capacity to artificially manufacture all but unlimited payment means, to supplement material models of circulation (wages and welfare, for example) with immaterial and unknowable futurities, it is almost inconceivable that post-industrial capitalism could have maintained the vibrant and multifaceted consumer markets of the last fifty years.

What we are looking at, we might suggest, is a substantial pro-consumptive augmentation of economy and society, a constant and growing infusion of outstanding credit that allows us to run through existing resources and push on into a realm of potentiality, papering over a growing shortfall of payment means by placing a speculative lien on prospective futures. One of the most remarkable socioeconomic trends of recent decades, the ascent of modern Britain's personal debt to GDP ratio, rising from '60 per cent . . . in the late 1970s to 127 per cent . . . by 1991, and then a peak level of 197 per cent . . . in mid-2009' (Keen, 2017: 92), is deeply illustrative of a social form increasingly reliant on the futurity of credit creation, harnessing and depleting the future ahead of itself in anticipation of repayments that might never materialise.

Although the largest share of aggregate demand does still trace back to material productivity (Stockhammer and Wildauer, 2016), the capacity to bolster capital circulation with regular infusions of the immaterial goes a long way to sustaining current relations of accumulation and exchange against the decline of prevailing socioeconomic contingencies. We live within a contradiction, a fissure between income and expenditure spanned by a speculative relation to the future in which, as recent OECD data (see *FT*, 2017a) attests, the British effectively lead the world in juxtaposing economic growth with falling wages. Whilst most of our national peers, the USA included, combine the two, modern Britain has largely succeeded in dropping the latter out of the equation, eroding the availability of material payment means whilst nonetheless maintaining a relatively healthy consumer sector and a relatively muted year-on-year record of aggregate growth.

Much of our 'consumer society' along with the cultures, values, and ideologies it sustains, in other words, might seem to be increasingly 'debt-driven', reliant on funds drawn from prospective futures on the strength of contractual payment obligations. At every level of consumer markets, debt is ever-present. It affords us a degree of day-to-day leeway, sustaining base-line economic participation as large and growing sections of the population resort to a range of short-term, high-interest, borrowing mechanisms to meet unexpected expenses, engage in public festivals, or simply make it to payday. Many of the milestones in our lives are similarly inextricable from the lending mechanisms that make them possible, often to an extent that might well have been unimaginable for previous generations. Whatever we do, just about any major or minor purchase comes with an array of finance options as a wide array of lenders from banks to supermarkets debt-generate payment means to enhance and maintain the immediate viability of all manner of consumer revenue streams in the face of declining incomes.

We might even suggest that financing cultures of consumption, under prevailing conditions of material productivity, would be all but impossible without the direct, immaterial stimulus of mass indebtedness. It's difficult to overstate the extent to which cultures of consumption have come to rely on borrowing and lending, embedding the socioethical spirit of capitalism into our lives by funding desires and aspirations, to take risks and cultivate relationships by buying, selling, using, disposing, and replacing a wealth of commodities and experiences. Debt provides us with the raw pecuniary building materials for fleeting, makeshift lifestyles constructed from the ritualised pursuit of satiety and satisfaction amidst a wondrous variety of socially cultivated desires (Barber, 2007; Hall et al., 2008).

Taking on debt allows the otherwise dislocated subject of late-modernity to live up to late capitalism's fundamental fantasy of autonomous subjectivity (Žižek, 2006; Johnston, 2008; Fisher, 2009), offering us a means of being and a means of becoming by lubricating our access to the social stream of goods, experiences, and accreditations. As such, the credit creation process is perhaps ideally suited to otherwise stagnating consumer economies precisely because a system that reproduces itself by harnessing our libidinal energies, beguiling us with dreams 'of freedom, of how your success depends on yourself, of the run of luck that is just around the corner, of unconstrained pleasures' (Žižek, 2009: 26), risks its own demise if we cannot be provided with means of payment.

In this way, Lazzarato (2012: 46) argues, debt subjectivises capitalism, integrating it into everyday life by tying the future into the present, 'reducing the future and its possibilities to current power relations' and to the promise of payment between creditor and debtor. It follows that a highly indebted society contains an implicit injunction toward a degree of post-hoc economic pragmatism, making the debtor 'accountable and guilty' (Lazzarato, 2012: 49) before capital and so limiting the horizon of the thinkable to spirals of consumption and repayment. For Lazzarato (2012; see also 2015), it seems, indebtedness provides capitalism with a control mechanism, a means of enforcing the prevailing accumulation regime that funnels the totality and complexity of social relations into the dualistic and potentially opposed camps of creditor and debtor.

McGowan (2016), on the other hand, suggests a slightly different direction. The fundamental relation of late-modern political economy, he argues, is far less reliant on power and control than on the tempting and seductive possibility of realising our desires within what Slavoj Žižek (see, for example, 1999, 2006) has repeatedly called a 'cultural injunction to enjoy'. For McGowan (2016: 11–12),

> The fundamental gesture of capitalism is the promise, and the promise functions as the basis for capitalist ideology. One invests money with the promise of future returns; one starts a new job with the promise of a higher salary; one takes a cruise with the promise of untold pleasure in the tropics; one buys the newest piece of electronics with the promise of easier access to what one wants. In every case, the future embodies a type of satisfaction foreclosed to the present and dependent on one's investment in the capitalist system. The promise ensures a sense of dissatisfaction with the present in relation to the future.

One of the most remarkable things about late capitalism is its ability to neutralise critique and survive its periodic crises by adopting our frustrations as its own, tempting us back into the fold by seducing us with a renewed promise of the future. Amid falling incomes and growing social divisions, however, credit increasingly provides the basic pecuniary means of that seduction, and, perhaps even more so, a condition of its possibility.

The crux of the credit phenomenon, in other words, rests on late capitalism's capacity to internalise this revolutionary ideal through our hopes for more and better. Through the advancement of debt-generated payment means we maintain our allegiance to the ritualised illusion that goods, property, experiences, and accreditations will finally satisfy our desires. Access to credit sustains the individualised promise of improved conditions allowing us to maintain the rotating transcendence of our dissatisfaction attached to consumer economies against the general decline of incomes. It thus ensures that we remain, as Pfaller (2014: 67) puts it, 'situated within the narrative' because mass indebtedness furnishes capitalism with the pecuniary means to redouble its mystification of social reality, transcending its limitations – in this context, the decline of incomes and rise of personal debt as claims on unknowable futures in otherwise stagnant and illiquid economies – in order to further inscribe 'the fetishist illusion . . . into our social practice' (Žižek, 2017: 190).

Incomes might well be in decline but instead of eroding the possibility of profit and investment by trapping the system and its subjects within internally reproduced deficiencies, debt affords us a return to the marketplace and an outlet for our frustrations, allowing us to take solace in the promise of tomorrow by capitalising prospective futures. Where other, more immutable and doctrinaire modes of production might ultimately crash into the limits of their closed reproductive cycles, personal debt represents capitalism's mobilisation of a revolutionary dynamic in order to escape the contradictions of a pre-existing accumulation regime and uncover profitable avenues for further expansion.

The reproduction of debt-financed payment means provides the pecuniary wherewithal for capitalism to transcend dissatisfaction and maintain the fetishised promise of a better, more prosperous future both of which are near constant features of our combined datasets. Between us, we have spoken at length to upwards of a hundred people about their debts, their experiences of trying to earn a living from post-industrial service economies and, more generally, about the monetary aspects of their lives. While there is, inevitably, a lot of variation in such a sample – some people have no discernable debts or manage to pay them off through luck, judgement, or third party assistance, others owe thousands and carry a long term and, in some cases, growing balance – perhaps one of the most remarkable commonalities is the extent to which our 'lifestyle projects' are enmeshed within and structured by our capacity to borrow on the potential but ultimately unknowable yield of prospective futures.

We turn first to Katie, a thirty-year-old woman from Middlesbrough, whose attempts to build a reasonably fulfilling career have been financed by access to credit, allowing her to move on each time her plans, in one way or another, were overwhelmed by dissatisfaction. When we met she was onto the fourth major iteration of her working life. The first came out of her time at university, financed by student loans, studying graphic design with the intention of starting a career in the field. After her graduation, however, she struggled to find work beyond a six-month placement and a few other fixed term contracts, eventually realising that she would have to move to either Manchester or London if she was to secure interesting and fulfilling work. Otherwise she would be stuck in the North East 'designing take away menus':

> I still was at that point . . . for that first six months and then it just became apparent that I would have had to move away to get a decent design job . . . uni[versity] is . . . tailored more towards if you worked for a big company in London. . . . [In] the northeast unless you set yourself up by yourself as a specific sort of illustrator or . . . something like that you would just end up designing takeaway leaflets and it would just bore me to death. And I kind of just thought . . . 'I need to do something else'.

She gave up on the idea of a career in graphic design and, having done some driving work between the end of university and the start of her placement, fell back into working as a courier. After two years, she left to set up as a driving instructor, franchised to a national company:

> I became . . . frustrated and fed up with DHL because there was . . . it was clear there was going to be no progression and I was like right I need . . . to earn some more money. I'm never going to get a house and all that sort of stuff . . . the only way to do that is obviously to progress and all the sort of supervisors and managers were fairly young and it was like I can't see any of them moving on any time soon so I'm going to have to move. I'm going to have to find something else.

In fairly short order she seems to have come to the decision that, for her ends, working as a courier was more of a stopgap measure providing very little prospect of reaching toward the seductive promise of property ownership and 'all that sort of stuff'. The driving school, on the other hand, enticed her with the prospect of a £36,000 salary and the flexibility of setting her own hours. She paid £3,000 for the training but the company went into administration and was bought out by another that promptly closed the local office removing one of her sources of clients.

> I was beginning to get less and less work, obviously the pupils I'd had at the beginning were passing their tests and it was like right they're not getting replaced. Um . . . yeah it went on and it was just less and less people and I was like it's not actually viable for me to continue. . . . I just thought . . . I need to get out because I'm nearly bankrupt. I'm earning no money; I'd actually moved out of home at that point. For six months I was renting a place with

> two friends and my mam was paying my rent for me. . . . I was near enough bankrupt; I was living off credit cards and yeah gave it up.

When her third career as a self-employed driving instructor tailed off in less than a year due to the terminal decline of her client base she owed the franchise holder nearly £2500 in unpaid management fees, her parents had been paying her rent for the better part of six months and most of her living expenses, along with petrol and a foreign holiday or two, had driven her outstanding balance across two credit cards to something like £5500, leaving her deeply in the red and potentially facing the prospect of some form of insolvency. When we met, however, she had gone back to working as a courier after a period in sports retail, bringing her to the fifth major iteration of her working life as her credit-fuelled pursuit of 'success' repeatedly culminated in failure. Nevertheless, she had paid off most of her original creditors using compensation from a car accident and a loan secured by her parents to allow her to escape mounting debts and keep plugging away at her attempts to realise capitalism's promise:

> The only way I got rid of that [her debts] . . . I'd moved back home, unemployed and then I'd started my job at [sports shop] so I was . . . like managing to pay some back . . . but I actually had to get my parents to get me a loan out. . . . I got them to get me a £7,000 loan . . . that paid off the credit cards and . . . left me with £1,500 to get a car . . . because I'd sold the one I had . . . so it was £1,500 to get a car, tax and insured and all that.

Whilst the specifics of this short vignette are entirely peculiar to Katie, the general trajectory is fairly common amongst those involved in our overlapping research. As we venture into the marketplace to chase goals and pursue desires, means of payment flood out of the credit industry sustaining as the progressive escalation of outstanding debt sustains our ritualised cultural allegiance to McGowan's (2016) 'fundamental gesture'. At each juncture, access to credit functions as a condition of possibility, allowing us to sidestep limits of material circumstance and continue to pursue satisfactions that might otherwise remain tantalisingly but frustratingly out of reach.

In place of any notion of objective value, the indebted society offers a form of speculation, a means of gambling on financial futures both personal and collective, that dematerialises or negates limits in order to sustain the cultural imperative that lies in our capacity to engage with and fulfil desires, to enjoy ourselves and strive for more. Debt-financed payment means provide a vital shot in the arm for our otherwise ailing economy, propelling consumption beyond the immediate into a realm of financial potentiality that stimulates and energises culture, economy and society. As such, we might suggest, there is perhaps something faintly 'luxurious' about the credit industry and its capacity to create and dispose of payment means as a way of transcending constraints. It's to this possibility that we now turn our attention.

The luxury of payment

What we have here, we might suggest, are two mutually reinforcing and economically productive relations to the future within the context of a finance-dominated accumulation regime that seems to be rapidly eroding traditional modes of capital distribution whilst replacing them with lending mechanisms. On the one hand we have a seductive and solicitous form of capitalism that cultivates rotating participation on the strength of a revolutionary promise only to point the way out of any such impasse with another round of economy-sustaining debt-financed consumption. On the other, a credit creation process that goes some way to helping us transcend our circumstances by plucking payment means out of the ether as contractual claims on prospective earnings, adding to the proliferation of outstanding debt, placing greater pressure on increasingly constrained incomes and so all but necessitating further infusions of credit.

Just like the debtor relation, cultures and economies of consumption appear to be future-oriented to the extent that they rest on the perpetually recycled promise of more and better. They captivate and enchant their subjects, cultivating fantasies of pleasure and beauty, autonomy and self-fulfilment, in order to harness the libidinal energy generated by their expression (see Hall, 2012, 2014). It is a system built on desire, on never having enough, on yearning for gratification and always keeping one eye on the next thing, seducing its subjects with the 'idea of accumulation and the promise of an ultimate satisfaction' (McGowan, 2016: 21). In so doing, it solicits recurrent financial investment, running through available resources and heading out into a realm of potentiality by deploying lending mechanisms to supply means of payment over and above the marginal productivity of post-industrial economies.

The process of credit creation thus allows late capitalism to supersede material constraints and rely instead on a kind of transgressive largesse that steps over impediments to capital circulation in favour of runaway borrowing and lending that lavishes payment means on consumers in the service of 'greater opportunities for being and doing' (Boltanski and Chiapello, 2005: 437). While this pretty much inevitably increases the level of outstanding debt, particularly in conditions of scarcity, it does so by breaking through barriers of materiality. The prevalence of borrowing opportunities, in other words, has expanded the division between means of payment and physical value to the point that something like ninety-six per cent of the total money supply exists in no other form than electronic bank deposits created as credit (see BoE, 2017).

Much of our social order, in effect, rests on a warped, slightly panglossian faith in the future, a kind of negative optimism in which we are – individually and collectively – speculating on the possibility that the current form of capitalism will miraculously come good, allowing us to repay our debts. This despite daily write-offs of at least £6 million across the banking sector (*Money Charity*, 2017), a prevailing expectation that as much as two-thirds of the student loan book will never be repaid (at current figures this amounts to something like £66 billion) and potentially unsustainable levels of credit risk associated with PCP loans used in the purchase of new cars (see, for instance, *FT*, 2017b; *The Guardian*, 2017). More than that, the number of county court judgements appended to unpaid debts rose thirty-five per cent in the year to April 2017 (*Registry Trust*, 2017) whilst the average value of debts requiring such arbitration fell to a historic low of £1495 (in 2008, for comparison, this figure was a shade over £3600). Taken together, this perhaps suggests that a greater number of people are struggling to pay smaller debts in a context of stagnating wages, price inflation, and a governmental austerity programme rapidly approaching its first decade.

In this context, there is undoubtedly an aspect of mass indebtedness in which it works to facilitate material luxury, enabling individual access to the booming consumer economies of the last few decades. It's entirely possible, as many have argued (see, for instance, Clayton, 1999; Calder, 1999; Manning, 2000; Ritzer, 2001; Burton, 2007; Marron, 2009), that credit is the essence of a consumer society, the seedbed of the 'American Dream' or the price of affordable luxury to the extent that consumers continue to finance their desires 'largely by reduced savings and increased debt' (Frank, 1999: 45). At this level, credit aids the diffusion of pleasing and desirable goods throughout the social body, providing an entry point to the playful, enjoyment-centred culture of late capitalism based on assessments of credit-worthiness, status-related interest rates and so on.

What's more, this is very much borne out by our data. Many of our interviewees spoke of an expensive something or an otherwise out of reach indulgence financed by a bank loan or some other form of credit. For Katie, this manifested as using credit cards to escape to foreign climes at the height of her financial troubles. Another of our interviewees, a solidly middle class professional named Alice, explained how she built up five-figure debts over about two years, dealing with frustrations in her life by

> [buying] something that gave me an instant buzz and then got hidden at the back of a cupboard. I'd spend a fortune on stuff for the kids, clothes, toys, the latest electrical gadgets, handbags, shoes – the normal female things . . . my problem is that I can justify anything. I can justify going out and spending £400 on a credit card or whatever when I know I haven't got the money . . . when I started sorting myself out the number of things I sold on eBay with labels still attached . . . I'd just bought them for the buzz, the feel-good-factor that you get before you get it home.

Further down the earnings scale, Rachel – a 22-year-old student from Middlesbrough – worked part-time in clothing retail taking home about £600 per month and spoke at some length about what she experienced as a perpetual tension between her attempts to save money and consumer habits that often carried her in the opposite direction. In her estimation she was relatively good with money, but her low income and unpredictable working hours meant that a few small indulgences could seriously erode her efforts, culminating in relatively significant debts on her employee's store card:

> if there's overtime . . . I put £200 into my savings every month, well I try to . . . but some months I'll have to dip back into them and bring it back out . . . it's just stupid things like food and clothes, I go out for tea a lot when I don't really need to. And I buy things I don't need. . . . I've got a credit card . . . they offered me one at the bank to get rid of my staff card, I was in debt on that by about £200 so they were like you could transfer the balance over so you're not paying the ridiculous interest on that but it didn't end up working.

In each case, there is a self-acknowledged element of material acquisition beyond need in which the capacity to borrow money works to facilitate and diffuse access to a relative degree of luxury consumption. For Katie, Alice, Rachel and many of our other interviewees, borrowing money comes with the possibility of pushing beyond what they can reasonably afford towards a succession of partial objects attached to socially cultivated desires.

Although the idea of luxury is often deployed in this explicitly material sense, Armitage and Roberts' (2016; see also 2017) concept of the 'spirit of luxury', drawing on Sombart's (1967 [1913]) *Luxury and Capitalism*, perhaps allows us to head in a slightly different direction. In their estimation,

> the spirit of luxury is neither economic nor materialistic but psychological, stimulating and energetic . . . it is a force that infuses industry, technology, culture, philosophy, and, above all, capitalism.
>
> (Armitage and Roberts, 2016: 11)

What they appear to be getting at is the possibility that the pursuit of luxury works as a kind of structural propellant, allowing the current form of capitalism to outlast the availability of material resources, lubricating the gears of commerce by eroding barriers to accumulation. Across of range of social fields, they argue, luxury seems to be an energising influence, cultivating activity that pushes the prevailing accumulation regime to new heights. In playing up a promise of more and better, for instance, late capitalism has largely succeeded in liberating desire from prohibitive moral sentiments, neutralising a psychosocial drag on the turnover of consumer markets. Similarly, in the combined fields of economy and technology, the all but unlimited capacity to generate means of payment by effectively buying IOUs from 'borrowers' (Mitchell et al., 2016) goes a long way toward circumventing monetary limits on processes of accumulation by creating liquidity as speculation on the future rather than as a reflection of pre-existing resources.

We might even see the reproduction of payment means beyond income as a sort of systemic luxury, an artifice of a self-referential system that seems to be 'rapidly losing its power to produce [or sustain] self-limiting rules' (Dupuy,

2014: 16), including restrictions on the money supply, because they ultimately represent lost commercial opportunities. Whenever the process of accumulation is threatened late capitalism enters a self-emancipatory mode in which market forces campaign to divest themselves of rules and regulations seen to be inimical to continued expansion in order to create the scope for another round of profit and investment.

Over the last few decades, this has been the primary function of credit industry. Consumer lending, as Dupuy (2014: 36) puts it, has allowed the market to absorb and deplete prospective futures in order to achieve a degree of co-ordination and stability in the present, projecting 'itself forward by means of a virtual traction point [in this case, the nominal point of repayment] that comes into existence only in, and as a result of, the very same forward movement'. It is almost as if debt creates the momentum that prevents our social and economic contingencies from succumbing to entropy, providing the scope to keep plodding on, ritualistically going through the motions.

More than that, however, this propulsive analogy perfectly captures the ideological function of mass indebtedness and the 'systemic luxury' of payment means. Incomes might well be in decline, employment seems to be increasingly precarious, and outstanding debt is pretty clearly on the rise but the latter nonetheless serves to smooth things over, allowing us to act out the reproduction of established sociocultural provisions without ever fully subscribing to the associated belief system. Its apparent success in doing so entails an 'ethical gesture' that Slavoj Žižek (2008) has called 'fetishistic disavowal' in which we individually and collectively repress inconvenient or uncomfortable information within a kind of ideological cynicism. In Žižek's (2008: 46) terms, disavowal amounts to a tacit declaration that 'I know, but I'm doing it anyway' allowing us to overwhelm knowledge or suspicion with a cynical disposition in which we 'refuse to fully assume the consequences of this knowledge, so that . . . [we] can continue acting as if . . . [we] don't know it'.

Running up the level of outstanding debt, personally or collectively, is often an exercise in exactly this kind of disavowal because borrowed money allows us to sidestep the consequences of relative incapacity attached to late capitalism's declining rate of profit. We might know that an unexpected expense will carry us beyond our finances, that we cannot afford the next desirable something or that a change of circumstances will leave us struggling with repayments but credit allows us to push that knowledge to one side and press on down an economically and culturally productive path of least resistance. Where the alternative would probably amount to a more or less conscious withdrawal, credit offers a period of extra time in which we maintain our place in the existing order over a voluntary but extremely disruptive refusal running the risk of severed relationships and increased isolation.

For many of our interviewees, this was something they had faced at one time or another. Admit defeat and go without or take up late capitalism's speculative and potentially destructive solution. Tom, for instance, faced the possibility of being unable to afford Christmas presents for his children whilst living on unemployment benefit but instead took up the payment means offered by one of the UK's better-known doorstep lenders:

> I'm still on the dole and I haven't had the money to buy my kids presents so I say can I have the £300 [loan] and they give me a [loan] book . . . it's £562 to repay but . . . when it comes to this Christmas I'll be able to do it again . . . when I eventually get into work I'll just pay it off and forget about them . . . it's just, I'm paying double. It's an easy means and it's the only chance you've got unless you go to like someone on the street who'll lend you money but you pay a lot [meaning an unlicensed moneylender, a 'loan shark']. I've spent this year paying off Christmas a bit at a time, just to do it all again.

Although he clearly suspects that he's being exploited and admits that he's probably paying over the odds for the privilege, credit offers him a means of active participation, allowing him to live up to social and cultural expectations whilst giving his kids something he feels they deserve. As far as he's concerned, the relatively high repayments attached to the loan count for very little compared to the alternative and so he takes up the 'systemic luxury' of monetary sustenance, overcoming the fundamental lack at the heart of late capitalism's prevailing economic conditions.

Conclusion

We began this chapter with the suggestion that neoliberal political economy no longer seems to be especially interested in funding sequential improvements to everyday life through traditional mechanisms of capital distribution and has instead taken to concentrating wealth upwards into the hands of a small but socially distinct elite. What's remarkable about this situation, however, is that even as day-to-day life becomes perceptibly harder, consumer participation, measured as growth in spending, seems to be relatively buoyant, continuing to grow, albeit at a reduced rate, through the end of 2018 despite a range of partial barriers centred on the proliferation of insecure and poorly-paid employment, substantial price inflation, and the ongoing uncertainty of the United Kingdom's imminent (at time of writing) withdrawal from the European Union.

A good part of the reason for this, we suggested, was that a much of the British economy, mirroring others across the developed and developing world, relies on a speculative model of credit-based expansion in which the circulation of capital has shifted away from productive capacity and material resource toward placing contractual claims on prospective futures. In effect, western capitalism has sustained itself by cheating on its own material foundations, severing payment means from any objective measure of value in order to continue its inexorable expansion fuelled by nothing more than the speculative assumption that the future will magically produce enough surplus capital for us all to individually and collectively pay off our debts.

This kind of debt-financing, we argue, provides a vital shot in the arm for our otherwise ailing economy, allowing capitalism to avail itself of a 'systemic luxury' – an individual and collective neutralisation of limits to further expansion – that sustains the primary appeal of its endlessly recirculated, revolutionary promise of more and better. More than that, however, it represents a condition of possibility, stimulating and energising consumption by propelling it beyond the immediate into a prospective realm where even the unrealised promise of the future is absorbed and depleted ahead of time in order to sustain prevailing socio-structural contingencies.

It is almost as if capitalism has shed itself of material constraints, allowing the system and its inhabitants to rely instead on a kind of transgressive largesse, producing a wealth of payment means at the expense of outstanding debt. Where other, more immutable modes of production might ultimately run into the limits of relatively closed reproductive cycles, capitalism deploys its revolutionary spirit to power through them by pioneering new avenues of profit and investment. Its influence has spread so far and so wide that it no longer has to assume the consequences of its internal contradictions but in so doing it offloads them, at least in part, into the lives of individual borrowers, allowing them to sidestep relative incapacity in the present by speculatively advancing the payment means to fund continued participation.

References

Allen, F. and Gale, D. (2004) Financial Intermediaries and Markets. *Econometrica*, 72: 1023–61.

Allen, F. and Santomero, A. (2001) What Do Financial Intermediaries Do? *Journal of Banking and Finance*, 25: 271–94.

Armitage, J. and Roberts, J. (2016) The Spirit of Luxury. *Cultural Politics*, 12, 1: 1–22.

Armitage, J. and Roberts, J. (2017) Critical Luxury Studies: Defining a Field. In J. Armitage and J. Roberts (eds.) *Critical Luxury Studies: Art, Design, Media*, Edinburgh: Edinburgh University Press, 1–21.

Barber, B. (2007) *Consumed*, London: W.W. Norton and Company.

Bernanke, B. (1993, Spring) Credit in the Macroeconomy. *Federal Reserve Quarterly Review*, 50–70.

BoE [Bank of England]. (2017) Bankstats (Monetary and Financial Statistics) – April 2017. *Bank of England* [Online]. Available at: www.bankofengland.co.uk/statistics/Pages/bankstats/2017/apr.aspx (Accessed: 12 June 2017)

Boltanski, L. and Chiapello, E. (2005) *The New Spirit of Capitalism*, London: Verso.

Burton, D. (2007) *Credit and Consumer Society*, Abingdon: Routledge.

Calder, L. (1999) *Financing the American Dream*, Princeton, NJ: Princeton University Press.

Clayton, J. (1999) *The Global Debt Bomb*, London: Routledge.

Dupuy, J. (2014) *Economy and the Future: A Crisis of Faith*, trans. M. DeBevoise, East Lansing, MI: Michigan State University Press.

Earle, J., Moran, C. and Ward-Perkins, Z. (2016) *The Econocracy*, Manchester: Manchester University Press.

Fecht, F., Huang, K. and Martin, A. (2008) Financial Intermediaries, Markets and Growth. *Journal of Money, Credit and Banking*, 40, 4: 701–20.

Ferguson, N. (2012) *The Ascent of Money*, London: Penguin.

Fisher, M. (2009) *Capitalist Realism*, Winchester: Zero Books.

Frank, R. (1999) *Luxury Fever: Why Money Fails to Satisfy in an Era of Excess*, New York, NY: The Free Press.

FT [Financial Times] (2017a) How Wages Fell in the UK While the Economy Grew. Available at: www.ft.com/content/83e7e87e-fe64-11e6-96f8-3700c5664d30 (Accessed: 15 November 2017)

FT (2017b) Warning Signs Emerge in the UK Car Loan Market. Available at: www.ft.com/content/8b6607de-6304-11e7-91a7-502f7ee26895 (Accessed: 13 January 2018)

The Guardian (2017) Are Cheap Car Loans the Vehicle Taking Us to the Next Financial Crash. Available at: www.theguardian.com/business/2017/jun/10/car-loans-personal-contract-plans-vehicle-financial-crisis-pcp (Accessed: 13 January 2018)

Hall, S. (2012) *Theorizing Crime and Deviance*, London: Sage.

Hall, S. (2014) The Socioeconomic Function of Evil. In L. Ray and J. Kilby (eds.) *Violence and Society: Towards a New Sociology*, Chichester: Wiley, 13–31.

Hall, S., Winlow, S. and Ancrum, C. (2008) *Criminal Identities and Consumer Culture*, Cullompton: Willan.

Horsley, M. (2015) *The Dark Side of Prosperity*, Farnham: Ashgate.

Johnston, A. (2008) *Žižek's Ontology*, Evanston, IL: Northwestern University Press.

Keen, S. (2017) *Can We Avoid Another Financial Crisis?* Cambridge: Polity Press.

Krugman, P. (2012) *End This Depression Now!* London: W.W. Norton and Company.

Langley, P. (2009) *The Everyday Life of Global Finance*, Oxford: Oxford University Press.

Lazzarato, M. (2012) *The Making of Indebted Man*, Los Angeles, CA: Semiotext(e).

Lazzarato, M. (2015) *Governing by Debt*, Los Angeles, CA: Semiotext(e).

Lloyd, A. (2013) *Labour Markets and Identity on the Post-Industrial Assembly Line*, Farnham: Ashgate.

Lloyd, A. (2018) *The Harms of Work: An Ultra-Realist Account of the Service Economy*, Bristol: Policy Press.

Macleod, H. (2012 [1891]) *The Theory of Credit*, vol. 2, Charleston, SC: Nabu Press.

Manning, R. (2000) *Credit Card Nation*, New York: Basic Books.

Marron, D. (2009) *Consumer Credit in the United States*, New York: Palgrave MacMillan.

Marx, K. (1991 [1891]) *Capital*, vol. 3, trans. D. Fernbach, London: Penguin Classics.

McGowan, T. (2016) *Capitalism and Desire*, New York: Columbia University Press.

Mitchell, W., Wray, R.L. and Watts, M. (2016) *Modern Monetary Theory and Practice*, Callaghan, NSW: Centre for Full Employment and Equity.

Money Charity (2017) The Money Statistics, December 2017. Available at: http://themoneycharity.org.uk/media/December-2017-Money-Statistics.pdf (Accessed: 13 January 2018)

Nesvetailova, A. (2013) Money and Finance in a Globalised Economy. In R. Palan (ed.) *Global Political Economy*, 2nd edn., Abingdon: Routledge.

ONS [Office for National Statistics] (2016) Household Debt Inequalities. Available at: www.ons.gov.uk/peoplepopulationandcommunity/personalandhouseholdfinances/debt/articles/householddebtinequalities/2016-04-04 (Accessed: 11 November 2017)

Palan, R. (2015) Futurity, Pro-Cyclicality and Financial Crises. *New Political Economy*, 20, 3: 367–85.

Pettifor, A. (2017) *The Production of Money*, London: Verso.

Pfaller, R. (2014) *On the Pleasure Principle in Culture*, London: Verso.

Registry Trust (2017) Rise in CCJs Against Consumers. Available at: www.trustonline.org.uk/press?download=228:england-wales-consumer (Accessed: 13 January 2017)

Ritzer, G. (2001) *Explorations in the Sociology of Consumption: Fast Food, Credit Cards and Casinos*, London: Sage.

Ryan-Collins, J., Greenham, T. and Werner, R. (2015) *Where Does Money Come From?* 2nd edn., London: New Economics Foundation.

Schumpeter, J. (2008 [1934]) *The Theory of Economic Development*, trans. R. Opie, London: Transaction.

Sombart, W. (1967 [1913]) *Luxury and Capitalism*, trans. W. Dittmar, Ann Arbor: University of Michigan Press.

Stockhammer, E. and Wildauer, R. (2016) Debt Driven Growth? Wealth, Distribution and Demand in OECD Countries. *Cambridge Journal of Economics*, 40, 6: 1609–34.

Streeck, W. (2016) *How Will Capitalism End?* London: Verso.

Werner, R. (2014) Can Banks Individually Create Money out of Nothing? *International Review of Financial Analysis*, 36: 1–19.

Žižek, S. (1999) *The Ticklish Subject*, London: Verso.

Žižek, S. (2006) *The Parallax View*, London: MIT Press.

Žižek, S. (2008) *Violence*, London: Verso.

Žižek, S. (2009) *First as Tragedy, Then as Farce*, London: Verso.

Žižek, S. (2017) *Incontinence of the Void*, London: The MIT Press.

5 Luxury brands in the wrong hands

Of Harleys, harm, and sovereignty

Tereza Kuldova

Introduction

The 'young Marx', still concerned with 'alienation' (Althusser, 1969), observed that to the political economist, and the capitalist

> every *luxury* of the worker seems to be reprehensible, and everything that goes beyond the most abstract need – be it in the realm of passive enjoyment, or a manifestation of activity – seems to him a luxury. Political economy, this science of *wealth*, is therefore simultaneously the science of renunciation . . . the science of *asceticism*, and its true ideal is the *ascetic* but *extortionate* miser and the *ascetic* but *productive* slave.
>
> (Marx, 1959: 51, emphasis in the original)

Young Marx touches here upon two crucial points. Firstly, the image of the worker as an ascetic slave without any right to sovereign moments of joy – moments when life serves him, instead of him serving life (Bataille, 1993). Secondly, that it is not *luxury as such* that is considered morally reprehensible; instead, its condemnation as reprehensible depends on *who* possesses this luxury.

Catherine Killerby's analysis of the notorious Italian sumptuary laws during the Renaissance is revealing in this respect. She notes that 'no government in this period regarded luxury as evil in itself. It was the context of its use, by whom and to what purpose, that determined the approval or censure of luxury' (Killerby, 1994: 119). Those deemed to be illegitimately transgressing their social position by flashing luxurious dresses were not only fined but often also temporarily excommunicated from the church. We may no longer have sumptuary laws, but the Protestant ethic of capitalism ensures that luxurious offences continue to arouse condemnation *when perpetrated by the wrong sort of people* (Weber, 2005). In this respect, Harley Davidson events – typically policed – with their VIP lounges for sponsors and dealer miles selling anything from trinkets to luxury items, are revealing. All those routinely condemned for their deviant indulgences meet here: working class bikers, wealthy businessmen and millionaire sponsors, the occasional bourgeois weekend bikers playing bad boys, and members and supporters of outlaw motorcycle clubs, who add the 'criminal thrill' and a dose of 'authenticity' to the event. What they all share is a lack – a lack of 'cultural capital'. Irrespective of the amount of wealth that circulates at these events, to most outsiders these events appear *cheap*, low, vulgar, and immoral. (This applies also when the outsiders become keen bystanders, taking pleasure in the 'vulgar' at a distance (Kuldova, 2017b).)

Historically, the Protestant hostility towards material excess, bodily and erotic pleasures, demanded that any 'time "wasted" in festivities' was to be converted into 'productive labour' (Ehrenreich, 2008: 160) – at least when it came to certain people. This class ideology of the lower-ranking bourgeoisie – itself fearing declassation (and thus staging itself as morally superior) – managed to institute a moral split between the low and the high. The low has been cast as worthless and despicable, the high as spiritual and admirable (Kuldova, 2016a). This ideology facilitated the legitimisation of the superiority of these 'threatened' lower-ranking bourgeois subjects. Any indulgence and any likeness to those on the top had to be punished in order to maintain the hierarchical order. Within this framework, a luxuriating worker claiming his 'right to be lazy' (Lafargue, 1883) offends far more than a lazy rentier living in luxurious excess. Any critique of the latter amounts at most to mentions of luxury's effeminising and demoralising properties (Berry, 1994; Adams, 2012), the former, on the other hand, faces an outright condemnation and a charge of irresponsibility, inferiority, and social parasitism. When we talk of luxury, we must therefore consider in whose hands it appears as vulgar, and in whose as divine or sublime. Whether considered vulgar or sublime depends on perspective – a class perspective. A class ideology imposing the respective moral judgements is disproportionately hostile towards those at the social bottom who dare to celebrate, dance, waste, have sex in excess, fight, party, and indulge in unproductive and potentially self-destructive but ecstatic pleasures. The deviant leisure of these populations must be contained, criminalised, and punished. And yet, the exact same acts of those on the top are either celebrated, considered unproblematic, or simply ignored (with the exception of the occasional scandal that merely confirms the rule). The perpetual historical struggle between the puritan forces and the forces of ecstasy and collective joy has always also reflected a class struggle. Despite the temporary ecstatic eruptions of the 1960s, puritanism, moralism, and hostility towards pleasure have been historically winning (Ehrenreich, 2008). Paradoxically, consumer capitalism has been bombarding us with ever-new answers to its one and only injunction: Enjoy! (McGowan, 2004) – thus re-channelling the aggressive energies into sociosymbolic competition through consumption, serving capital accumulation (Hall, 2014). Not surprisingly then, the negative passions of today's public are also disproportionately aroused by *luxury brands in the wrong hands* rather than by *luxury per se*.

In this chapter, I explore the relation between harm, crime, and luxury (consumer culture) by thinking through the transformations of outlaw motorcycle clubs since the 1960s until now. Outlaw motorcycle clubs have evolved from a wild counterculture into transnational organisations, labelled by law enforcement agencies worldwide as 'organized crime' (Barker, 2010; Kuldova and Sánchez-Jankowski, 2018). Their lifestyles, too, have changed considerably. The outlaw biker of the 1960s has become a commodified myth, consumed by the outlaw bikers themselves – seldom lived, but often staged for an audience (Kuldova, 2017b). Today's luxurious lifestyles of the Hells Angels' kingpins stand in direct opposition to the anti-consumerist old-school bikers. But first, let us think for a while longer about the ambiguities of luxury.

Vulgar luxury, sublime luxury, and the 'filthy sacred'

In contemporary imagination and social practice, there are two sorts of luxury: *vulgar luxury* and *sublime luxury*. The first category, an expanding one, is considered disgusting, harmful, despicable, deviant, ugly, crude, repulsive, cheap, and abhorrent. The latter category, a rapidly shrinking one, is wonderful, properous, desirable, classy, beautiful, even sublime. Sublime luxury presents itself to us precisely as the opposite of vulgarity. The first is reserved to the class impostors – the low, the latter to those 'truly classy' – the high. And yet, there is rarely a qualitative difference in the luxury objects *as such*. Instead, we are dealing with a *perspectival illusion*: not only is sublime luxury at its core no less vulgar, but it would not exist without vulgarity and harmfulness. Like smoking, luxury can either be perceived as terribly harmful or as sublime and glamorous (Klein, 1993). If it were robbed of the harmfulness at its core, of the inevitable human and environmental exploitation upon which it is based, it would lose its ability to provide us with pleasure. Or, as Klein puts it, 'if cigarettes were good for you, they would not be sublime' (Klein, 1993: 2), and we would not smoke them. We are dealing here with a form of pleasure that depends on *disavowal*. Stanley Cohen, in his famous *States of Denial*, was puzzled by people knowing, but acting as if they did not know and, as in the case of smoking, by what he understands as their inability to acknowledge the significance of the consequences of their actions even though they know (Cohen, 2001) – or else, the inability to take harm seriously enough to change one's behaviour. But Cohen misses the capacity of disavowal to produce pleasure (Pfaller, 2014) – and to provide people with a feeling of sovereignty. Disavowal of harm is at the core of many techniques of cultural pleasure. It is constitutive of the sovereign moments when we refuse to *submit* ourselves to the inevitable future consequences and act *as if* they were exempt from these (and from guilt). This is what allows people to put themselves on a level with their masters (Pieper, 1998).

Luxury belongs to the same order of objects as cigarettes, to the 'filthy sacred' (Pfaller, 2008). If luxury was not 'based on painful expropriations' (Calefato, 2014: 7), it would lose its lustre. *Ethical luxury* in this sense is an oxymoron (Kuldova, 2018a). Luxury is impossible without it being the very embodiment of harm and exploitation, without embodying the 'power over labour power', and without being vulgar to its core (Kuldova, 2016b) – 'the distance between diamonds and dung is not as great as you think' (Calefato, 2014: 21). If we accept that pleasure always, to lesser or greater degree, contains something harmful (Pfaller, 2008, 2009, 2014), we may have to accept that a world without harm would also mean a world without pleasure. In this sense, the plea for '*prosocial* leisure – leisure activities that have the potential to contribute to human flourishing, positively impact the natural environment and leave no identifiable traces of harm through their commission' (Smith and Raymen, 2016: 15) – may appear slightly naïve. Just because we see 'harm', we should not throw the baby out with the bathwater. Instead, we should consider the different possibilities of rendering the 'filthy sacred' sublime. We will never be able to rid ourselves of harm and filth; the question is what kinds of harm and filth can be sublimated into something prosocial and positive, and what remains merely destructive even in a sublimated form. The line of demarcation is fuzzy. But that does not mean that we should forsake this cultural resource and begin perceiving everything solely through the lens of harm. We may risk joy escaping through our fingers.

We are dealing with a cultural capacity to sublimate – to turn vulgar luxury into sublime luxury. Sublimation should not be imagined as a process by which, for instance, sex drives are converted into poetry, but rather as a process by which the *same* object or practice becomes transformed, or else: '*something which cannot always be unproblematically perceived as pleasurable – something obscene, awful, tasteless – is transformed into an agent of heightened pleasure precisely because of its problematic qualities*' (Pfaller, 2009; emphasis in original). However, there are three troubles with regards to this capacity to sublimate and transform something nasty into something wonderful: 1) it has been disappearing in the west with its puritan tendency to perceive everything primarily through the lens of harmfulness, 2) it has become progressively reserved to the few on the top, where once it was the masses capable of collective joy, transgression, and sublimation, and 3) it has been commodified, sublimation itself turned into an idea to be consumed along with a particular good. Even worse, all the leisure and the enjoyment we are today meant to indulge in is only permissible if it serves 'recharging our batteries' to work more and better, if it is a *means* to improve our own servility and not a leisure for its own sake (Pieper, 1998). As Weber would put it, with the increasing *disenchantment* of the world, we are left with pure barbarism of alienated individuals incapable of collective joy and thus of solidarity, and with it incapable of collectively producing genuine moments of sovereignty. Negative individual rituals won over collective positive rituals (Durkheim, 1965). And the last traces of positive rituals were commodified.

What we today perceive as vulgar luxury thus cannot be reduced to a matter of bad taste. Those deemed as vulgar in their luxury consumption are not only perceived as fundamentally incapable of sublimation, but also as *desecrating* luxury by their filthy desires. Sublimated luxury belongs to the realm of the sacred, to that which is set apart from the ordinary, that which transcends the normal order of things (Durkheim, 1965). Luxury brands put a lot of effort in creating *new rituals of sacralisation*, boundary making, and endowing their top-end products with heritage and other myths (Dion and Borraz, 2015; Belk et al., 1989). Consumer capitalism has effectively commodified even the sacred, turning consumption into the dominant and most advisable path to transcendence for its 'consumer citizens' (Lukose, 2009, Scammel, 2000).

Luxury goods as commodified sovereignty

Over centuries, luxury has been used to display sovereignty – the power to break law, to enforce a state of exception, and to transgress the realm of utility. Luxury being an *index* of sovereignty is precisely what makes it so desirable, especially to those at the bottom of society meant to serve and obey in the current world of 'total work' (Pieper, 1998). Marx clearly perceived this embargo on pleasure and on sovereignty imposed on the worker as an essential feature of capitalism:

> political economy – despite its worldly and voluptuous appearance – is a true moral science, the most moral of all the sciences. Self-renunciation, the renunciation of life and of all human needs, is its principal thesis. The less you eat, drink and buy books; the less you go to the theater, the dance hall, the public house; the less you think, love, theorize, sing, paint, fence, etc., the more you *save* – the *greater* becomes your treasure which neither moths nor rust will devour – your *capital*. The less you *are*, the less you express your own life, the more you *have*, i.e., the greater is your *alienated* life, the greater is the store of your estranged being.
>
> (Marx, 1959: 51)

However, this basic need and desire for sovereign life has become removed from the realm of *activity*, into the realm of *objects* – in particular, the *commodified luxury that appears as commodified sovereignty* – mere empty symbols of sovereignty desirable in their own right. And yet, unreal as they are, these objects are only ever capable of providing temporary relief. Not to mention that when even the smallest pleasures are costly, and the worker is able to afford only necessities in order to reproduce his bare life, they become incapable of quenching his thirst for sovereignty. Or as Bataille observes,

> the worker's wage enables him to drink a glass of wine: he may do so, as he says, to give him strength, but he really drinks in the hope of escaping the necessity that is the principle of labor. As I see it, if the worker treats himself to the drink, this is essentially because into the wine he swallows there enters a miraculous element of savor, which is precisely the essence of sovereignty. It's not much, but at least the glass of wine gives him, for a brief moment, the miraculous sensation of having the world at his disposal.
>
> (Bataille, 1993: 199)

Here we face a paradox: while a bravely *saving* worker still remains the theoretical ideal, the practical ideal is precisely the worker whose desire for sovereignty is quenched only by passionately throwing himself into *debt* and becoming a willing slave of capital (Lordon, 2014). The Real ideal hidden under the façade of protestant ethics is a worker 'confident to consume' beyond his means, the driver of the debt economy. It is no coincidence that one of the most popular reality TV shows across the Protestant Scandinavia is the *Luxury Trap*[1] featuring massively indebted individuals and families who took up consumer loans in order to afford not only luxury goods, but also quality food. These are cast as luxury addicts, and the audience is encouraged to condemn their wasteful and irrational habits, while taking pleasure in their failure to rationally manage their expenditures. Financial consultants preaching self-restraint enter to cure these addicts and show them how to spend only on that which is *necessary* and re-finance their loans. Their 'luxury addiction' is posited as the *real* problem, a perfectly treatable one, if only the addicts supress their irrational desire to spend and instead behave as good slaves. Debt-hoarding, which the system both desires and shames, is just the reverse side of crime aimed at acquisition of luxury goods. Both are a route towards quenching of the desire for sovereignty – the sole path to which within the capitalist consumerist society is the consumption of luxury. Luxury goods embodying an excess of labour provide a feeling of power and control over the world and over labour power *by proxy* even to those who do not belong to the capitalist class.

The transformation of the means of satisfaction of this desire for sovereignty can be observed through the lens of the evolution of the outlaw motorcycle subculture, epitomised by the notorious Hells Angels. The development of outlaw motorcycle clubs, from a wild and disorderly counterculture to a well-organised military-like transnational organisation that has commodified itself in order to grow (Kuldova, 2019), will tell us a great deal about the transformation of the ways of quenching the desire for sovereignty, and the place of luxury consumption within it, since the 1960s.

Outlaw bikers: from ecstatic transgressions to luxury consumption

Georges Bataille often remarked that it is among the outcasts, the marginalised, the revolutionaries but even the fascists, or else those leading a *heterogenous* existence, that we can best observe the nature of transgression of boundaries that opens a path to sovereignty. Outlaw motorcycle clubs are a subculture that emerged following the second world war in the US, only to spread across the whole world, promising not only a life of brotherly camaraderie on the margins of the polite society, but also meaning and the 'old world' values of honour. Today, it attracts predominantly those expelled by the capitalist system that has deemed them useless and redundant, but who aspire to the same satisfactions the system provides. Talking to outlaw bikers one quickly realises that their actions are often driven by a *philosophical act*, 'one which transcends the working world' (Pieper, 1998: 84), and a philosophical question par excellence: 'what is life worth living for' (Pfaller, 2011). Unlike a professional philosopher, rewarded for asking such questions, the type of man who becomes an outlaw biker, driven by the very same question, is not meant to question, nor to transcend the realm of utility. This does not mean we should suddenly become sympathetic to the practical answers he finds to this question, but we must recognise that it is this very question and the desire to transcend the realm of work and utility that drives his actions – and yet, for him, there is no reward in asking this question. Outlaw motorcycle subculture is just one of myriad of venues providing an answer to this desire. Bataille once noted that

> we have no real happiness except by spending to no purpose, and we always want to be sure of the uselessness of our expenditure, to feel as far away as possible from a serious world, where the increase of resources is the rule.
> (Bataille, 1993: 176)

It is this sentiment that resonates with the outlaw biker ideals; the brotherhood and crime may be one of the paths to achieve this happiness.

Since its inception, profound *resistance to servitude* has been at the core of the outlaw biker counterculture; a resistance to the boring middle-class life, to 8:00 to 5:00 jobs, to individualisation and consumerism. After all, the subculture drew on the same tropes as 'the beat – hippie subcultures of the 1955–1975 era eschewed the trappings of material wealth and popularized egalitarian camaraderie, and hedonistic sexual and drug activity' (Forsyth and Quinn, 2009: 245). But most importantly, it contained a promise of sovereign existence beyond the laws of utility and necessity. Jörg Schrat, a Harley biker, sums this promise perfectly in a foreword to Günter Brecht's yearbook about bikers in Germany in 1981 when he says the following:

> [T]oday, the pressure to perform is even stronger, each tries to steal the job of the other; each sees only his own advantage. Family now exists only in front of the television. Camaraderie is a worn out catch word. Honour is a lost something. Freedom – a statue in the harbour of New York . . . Sure, we have been expelled because we did not want to adjust to the ruling system. *We do not live in order to work, we work in order to live, in our own way!* . . . Outlaw bikers die like everyone else, but they live like no other!
> (Schrat, 1983: 7–8, transl. from German by author)

However, the subculture has transformed profoundly since its emergence. The old school bikers now nostalgically look back at their own past and talk of the need to purify the biker scene from the new 'entrepreneurs' (Kuldova and Quinn, 2018; Forsyth and Quinn, 2009; Quinn and Koch, 2003). The shift occurred around the late 1970s in the US, and around the mid-1980s and early 1990s in Europe and elsewhere, where the subculture arrived with a delay. The shift was a result of the organisational consolidation and transformation of the biggest clubs such as the Hells Angels into legal corporations with trademarked logos (Kuldova, 2017a). In the following, I will outline the paradigm shift that has occurred in respect to the forms of sublimation that outlaw motorcycle clubs offer to their members. The nature of this radical paradigm shift in the capacity to sublimate the filthy and attain pleasure has often been neglected, largely because crime has been taking precedence over thinking about any other aspects of the subculture. And yet, the case can tell us something about the commodification of pleasure (and thus also of transformation of harm) at large.

Ecstatic beginnings

'There is a raw animalistic, sexual quality to this milieu: The potential for sudden, lethal violence lurks in many of these taverns' restrooms and parking lots, alongside the promise of a promiscuous liaison' (Forsyth and Quinn, 2009: 246). Such was the portrayal of the 1960s outlaw biker milieu. Even a superficial visual analysis of the images from the initial days of the outlaw biker subculture shows us that there must have been a difference to what the subculture is today. It was a counterculture distinguished by *group ecstasy*, by *collective transgression* – violence, fights, dirt and filth, group sex, nakedness, collective dance, filthy initiation rites, excessive drinking, drugs – collective joy of transgressive 'deviant leisure', a *collective* sublimation. The counterculture, even if from the very beginning known for power struggles and violent brawls, was still primarily *hedonistic* and *egalitarian*; the early rallies were considered successful when enough people on bikes showed up, booze flowed as if limitless, sausages were juicy, rock music made people dance like there was no tomorrow, and it all culminated in stripping, sex, and passing out on the grass (Brecht, 1983). It was precisely this capacity for group ecstasy that offended the outsiders (i.e. the capacity to sublimate the dirty and the vulgar); it was not merely the crimes associated with the subculture, but rather the fact that the perpetrators appeared as 'thieves of our enjoyment' (Pfaller, 2017). The outlaw bikers revived a form of collective ecstasy that has always aroused the moral passions of the bourgeoisie. As Barbara Ehrenreich rightly observed,

> Group ecstasy was something 'others' experience – savages or lower-class Europeans. In fact, the capacity for abandonment, for self-loss in the rhythms and emotions of the group, was a defining feature of 'savagery' or otherness generally, signalling some fatal weakness of mind.
>
> (Ehrenreich, 2008: 9)

Ecstasy – the capacity for self-loss, disappearance in the group, dissolution of the precious *self* – has been perceived as particularly threatening due to its presumed irrationality (just think of Gustave Le Bon). And yet, it allows for a certain achievement of transcendence. While we are often led to think of ecstasy as a descent into barbarity, as something low, savage, and vulgar – the opposite may be the case. The real threat of ecstasy to the established order lies in its capacity to provide us with sovereign moments and to forge *solidarity*, and let us forget our little individual disagreements, and act in the name of a larger whole. Even if this act appears as a senseless expenditure, it may also be a moment of collective sovereignty.

While the counterculture drew on the myths of the American frontier, rugged individualism, and ideology of freedom, in practice it consisted of rebellious collective ecstatic practices directed against bourgeois morality. In this sense, it appeared primarily as a *carnivalesque* outburst (Ehrenreich, 2008), a symbolic inversion (Babcock, 1978) of the established hierarchy. In place of hierarchy, it posited a simple inside-outside dichotomy, where the outside is profane (the citizen) and the inside (the biker) sacred. The capacity to sublimate the filthy into a filthy sacred – something wonderful – has been most visible in the notorious rites of passage. As Hunter Thompson described the initiation rite in the 1960s:

> Every Angel recruit comes to his initiation wearing a new pair of Levis and a matching jacket with the sleeves cut off and a spotless emblem on the back. The ceremony varies from one chapter to another but the main feature is always the defiling of the initiate's new uniform. A bucket of dung and urine will be collected during the meeting, then poured on the newcomer's head in a solemn baptismal. Or he will take off his clothes and stand naked while the bucket of slop is poured over them and the others stomp it in.
>
> (Thompson, 2003: 26)

In 1981, Günter Brecht describes the baptism of five new members of the Knight Riders MC, a German-American biker club from Erlangen, a chapter of one of the oldest MCs in Germany, est. in 1969, as follows:

> Five naked men about to be baptized were allowed to watch as their still 'innocent' cuts lost all their purity in a beautiful mud hole. Mixed drinks, beer, ketchup, mustard, and mud broth were pressed into the cuts with the help of the wheels of the club motorcycles. Then, the prospects could dress in the jacket and then, otherwise naked, while releasing rustic screams, run and slide behind a bike, making an 'honourable round'.
>
> (Brecht, 1983: 99; transl. from German by author)

Some would argue that rather than challenging the system, any carnival or carnivalesque counterculture serves to maintain the status quo by effectively providing the very definition of (ab)normality (Stallybrass and White, 1986). But there is also an undeniable fear of transgressive subcultures and ecstasy. With the spread of Protestant culture, collective ecstatic events have been increasingly suppressed and controlled by the ruling classes. Or as E. P. Thompson argued, repression of festivities was a byproduct of capitalism (Thompson, 1974, 1993). Or rather, they have been *pseudo-pacified* (Hall, this volume). When presented at a safe distance, on the TV screens in our living rooms, they may appear as sublime. But in reality, they must be abolished (Burke, 1914; Kuldova, 2017b). Countless exploitation movies such as *Born Losers*, *Easy Rider*, *Hells Angels on Wheels*, *Savage Seven*, or *Werewolves on Wheels* testify to our desire to consume their imagined 'savagery' and vicariously participate in the filthy sacred (Kuldova, 2017b; Deis and Doyle, 2016; Osgerby, 2003). The bourgeoisie seized the moment and defined itself in opposition to what it perceived as savage behaviour; we can observe this in the smallest things: instead of dancing collectively to music, following the beat, we are meant to control ourselves, sit still in our chairs and become a mere audience. Any form of entertainment that involves *collective movement* is considered as lower. The cultural capacity of the bikers themselves to sublimate through rituals of *collective effervescence* (Olaveson, 2001; Durkheim, 1965) is not only looked down upon by the bourgeoisie, but utterly misunderstood and represented as a mere expression of savagery. It is both the reason for them to be fought and condemned as a menace, but also to make them into pop cultural heroes.

Through a trademarked transition into desire for luxury goods

The almost instant inclusion of the 'filthy' outlaw bikers into popular culture, their commodification for the consumption of the masses hungry for products embodying the spirit of transgression (Austin et al., 2010), also effectively purified the 'counterculture' itself. But the outlaw bikers were complicit – the moment they saw some bucks could be made out of their names and reputations, they jumped on the bandwagon of self-commodification. Clubs like the Hells Angels even consider themselves today 'one of the greatest American brands', as one member put it. In 1972, the Hells Angels trademarked their notorious 'death head' skull logo and turned themselves into Hells Angels Motorcycle Corporation. Other outlaw motorcycle clubs followed suit, and today most sell derivative support merchandise, from clothing and accessories via energy drinks to the outlaw biker 'experience' itself, while protecting the 'sacred patch' by restricting its use only to full-patch members (Kuldova, 2017a). The sublimated filthy sacred was thus transferred into the symbol – an object of desire in its own right. Along with trademarking and incorporation came the transnational expansion. As Wolfgang Haug rightly observed in his critique of the commodity aesthetics, marketing has been trying to commodify the sacred, in the process leaving very little that remains sacred (Haug, 1986). There are many outlaw motorcycle clubs across the world today, but irrespective of their individual mythologies and differences, their mystique derives from those who managed to monopolise the market and who continue to grow and swallow smaller clubs through patch-overs – the Hells Angels. Hells Angels, the 'elite of the elite' as they like to call themselves, are a form of monopoly, not unlike a famous luxury brand, in which the sacred of the subculture becomes condensed.

> The means of establishing this monopolistic situation is to elevate the commodity to the status of brand-name. All available aesthetic devices are employed to further this end. The decisive factor, however, is the concentration into one named character of all the aesthetic, visual and verbal communications contained in the styling of the commodity. The common language used for this purpose at most serves to name the manufacturers and to give them an air of prestige. While brand-named goods which are distributed locally seem laughable, like other local customs, names and dialects, the trans-regional brand-names of large companies impose themselves on to the public's experience and virtually assume the status of natural phenomena.
>
> (Haug, 1986: 26)

The marketing strategies of the Hells Angels are almost identical to those of luxury brands. Expensive and unique one-off luxury goods are limited and reserved for the carefully screened select few who have to wait for it for a considerable amount of time. Perfumes and other trinkets that amount to the majority of the business, on the other hand, are easily available to many consumers. Hells Angels have mirrored, consciously or not, the structure of the luxury brand in their self-commodification. Not unlike the luxury brand, they, too, are a perfect example of sublimation of the filthy and vulgar into something sacred – only here, the sacred, the trademarked and fetishised logo, is reserved to those initiated rather than those possessing enough capital and reputation. The entry requirements are different as are the demands of this 'greedy institution' (Coser, 1974) on its members, but the 'sacred' thus produced is structurally the same. This careful self-commodification that managed to preserve the 'sacred' for its core members, while offering consumer goods with derivative power mystique to the supporters, is precisely how the subculture managed to survive its own commodification. Self-commodification also meant effective reorganisation, hierarchisation (despite the one man one vote claims) of the clubs and the subculture at large: it led to growth and consolidation, but most importantly – *expulsion of uncontrolled forms of ecstasy* and *purification*. Instead – the carefully cultivated myth of the ecstatic transgressions has been channelled into the logo, its symbol, while the reality itself has been progressively purified of ecstasy and replaced with military order. While the sacred still remained dependent not only on the myth but also on the brotherhood, and on the 'chosen few', it was also at the same time effectively condensed into its derivative symbols destined for individualistic consumption.

Purification of the subculture can be observed in the material transformation of the clubhouses – from the 1960s trashed habitats into the secure, clean, and orderly fortresses with cameras with heavy metal gates. Outlaw bikers, too, are far away from the legendary filthy predecessors – they smell like newly washed clothes and perfume. Even the disorderly and wild rock music, though it is still breathing its last breaths, is being progressively replaced by gangsta hip hop produced by both club members and their friends, featuring heaps of cash, luxury cars, guns, and 'hookers'. But this progressive purification has been most visible in the transformation of the aforementioned filthy rites of passage. In the 1990s, the German *Biker News* magazine was regularly reporting on initiations of club members. But these initiations had little in common with those from the 1960s and even the 1980s. At most, new members received a couple of handshakes, hugs, and beers. Over time, even the prostitutes shared by the initiate and all the members, have mostly disappeared, replaced first by parties with Go-Go girls or even new silly rituals such as circling a couple of times on a pink children's roller around the clubhouse – a purified form of humiliation, followed by some grilling. If stripping occurs, it is no longer the men spontaneously showing off in the heat of the night and imitating guitar play on their penises but paid female professionals.

The separation between the performer and the audience, native to the bourgeois theatre, has been enforced even here. The outlaw bikers themselves have turned both into occasional performers, but also the most avid consumers of their own myths and their own legends, such as Sonny Barger. In Paris, during the celebrations of the sixtieth anniversary of the Oakland charter, members and fans alike lined up in a long queue to get their copy of the anniversary photo book *Sonny: 60 Years Hells Angels* signed by Sonny Barger, while others shopped for the Support 81 merchandise for their friends and families. The ordinary members have thus become both a myth embodied and the keenest consumers of this very myth.

Even the biker events at large have fundamentally changed. Most large biker events, such as the *European Bike Week* in Faaker See in Austria, organised by Harley Davidson and sponsored by brands like Jeep, Bacardi, or Michelin, have turned into luxury events of excess in their own right. With hundreds of exhibitors spread across many square kilometres around the idyllic lake, it is a pure consumer spectacle. Thousands arrive to check out the latest bikes, gadgets, clothes, cars, and to shop till they drop while showing off their customised Harleys, taking obscene amounts of selfies and videos, eating and drinking, and watching the concerts. It is more of a festival of excessive consumption than anything reminiscent of collective ecstasy. The different charters of Hells Angels have their own stands there, selling their support merchandise next to the notorious Jägermeister bar. The members and prospects who sell this support merchandise, however, still denounce this consumer spectacle and think of themselves as being there to promote the true sacred of the subculture that has been profaned by consumption excesses, turning away from *being* to *having*. They resent the hobby riders, the desperate consumers, the rich who shop for luxury commodities, as well as those who shop for second-hand patches from previous events only to put them on their jackets and pretend that they were around already twenty years ago. The resentment they feel is exactly the same as that felt against those indulging in 'vulgar luxury' we have described above – a resentment against those who *desecrate* the subculture. And yet, they themselves contribute to and live of this very desecration – a paradox through which they set themselves apart precisely as the 'elite of the elite' of the outlaw bikers. This is also why they are so extremely protective of their patches, where the sacred is condensed – pursuing those who infringe on them by legal means and those they meet on the street wearing knock-offs with violent retaliation. They have to protect the boundary else they risk to dissolve in the world of consumption as any other counterculture that has been commodified and thus lost itself and all its disruptive power in the 'conquest of the cool' (Heath and Potter, 2005; Frank, 1998). They know fully well that 'there is no better way to subvert a revolution than to enlist it in the service of moneymaking' (Ehrenreich, 2008: 223), and yet they participate in it. This is because they are not a counterculture, but a semblance of it, dependent on the system and necessary for its perpetuation – dependent for its own growth on a system that produces ever new disillusioned and hopeless individuals in search of meaning, recognition, community, and material security (Kuldova, 2019).

The outlaw bikers' sacred aura depends on producing those who desecrate it, on their profane enemies who do not live the lifestyle but only ride on the weekends, appropriating the outlaw power mystique. This has been the business model of Harley Davidson for a while – turning the low and vulgar into an object of luxury for the consumption of the bankers, dentists, and lawyers (a reason why mechanical skill and ability to customise is still posited as the line of demarcation between the true bikers and the wannabes). While there was a time when Harley Davidson believed that it needed to remove any association with the outlaws and produce its own narrative of purity for the law-abiding aspiring middle classes, it quickly realised that the 'low domains, apparently expelled as "Other", return as the object of nostalgia, longing and fascination' and 'symbolic contents of bourgeois desire' (Stallybrass and White, 1986: 191) and that there is money to be made out of turning the low into the luxurious.

The *collective* transgressive ecstasy has been progressively transformed into *individual* consumption of goods that promise sovereignty, but rather than providing it – they leave people with its sign: always unsatisfied, always wanting more (Tudor, 2018; Ellis et al., 2018). The capacity of ecstatic transgression to produce moments of sovereignty has thus been displaced onto the consumption of goods that package sovereign moments of rebellion and of the very life beyond utility. Even the subculture itself, no matter how much it tries, cannot escape this general tendency of capitalism to swallow the rebellious and originally anti-consumerist forces and turn them into just another object of consumption, like those Che Guevara tote bags (Kuldova, 2018b).

Progressively, the brotherhoods have transformed from being an end in themselves, and thus capable of producing sublime and sovereign moments, into *means* for some to acquire the very luxury goods that bear this promise of sovereignty, once the very promise the club itself bore. The patch itself is no longer enough. As Quinn and Forsyth observed:

> modern one percenters retain the traditional fascination with motorcycles, often well-accessorized and somewhat customized, generally kept in superb aesthetic and mechanical condition. However, an increasing proportion seem to prefer SUVs and luxury cars. These one percenters are among the most entrepreneurial and many of the chapters to which they belong lack the gang-like loyalty of the purist biker, focusing instead on acquiring underworld power.
>
> (Forsyth and Quinn, 2009: 249)

This has been mirrored in the rise of new heroes of the outlaw scene, very different from the anti-consumerist and hedonist old-school bikers who preferred to live in the here and now and enjoy life's simpler pleasures. A rise of entrepreneurs like the Hannover Angel Frank Hanebuth, who used the power of the club to become the king of the pimps in Hannover, stand for the new paradigm – something that is not free of internal conflicts between the old-school and the new entrepreneurs. The German media refer to him as the *ruler* of Steintorviertel, a new type of self-made aristocrat with a sovereign power to impose his rules in his neighbourhood. As one report in the Spiegel TV has it: 'it is his rules that apply here, drug addicts and thieves must stay away, under his rule the dirty quarter turned into a prosperous amusement business'.[2] Or else, where the state is unable to enforce its laws against petty crime, he is – nobody dares because of his reputation. Frank has acquired a celebrity status, his criminal charges, his luxury lifestyle, his 'welcome back to Hannover' party after his years in Mallorca, his birthdays or his wedding celebrations reported widely in the media. While his luxurious excesses become a sign of his power, to many new members it is the desire to have such things too, and quickly, that underlies their desire to become part of the brotherhood. New members, lacking other legitimate opportunities, often join the club in order to pursue their desire for luxury – they do not only want to feel like kings in the here and now, shitting on the rules of the polite society, but they also want to look like kings, like those who have arrived, like the new rich. For the old-school bikers, who see the subculture and the pleasure of living as a biker as a (collective) *end in itself* and who live for the moments of simple collective joy and transgressions, these young and ambitious brothers, often but not always of immigrant backgrounds, who use the club as (individual) *means to an end* and are filled with desire to show off often represent the vulgarisation and desecration of the subculture itself – even though both forms of pleasure are financed partially by crime. They complain of the 'times that have changed' but still insist that at least to the outsiders they have to look like a united force. To them, the young entrepreneurial brothers also represent 'luxury in the wrong hands' – they themselves are not unlike the old wealth, the aristocracy, about to be replaced by the new rich neo-aristocrats.

This is not to indulge in some form of nostalgia, but rather to show that there are different possibilities to the sublimation of the filthy – one on the side of collective joy, ecstasy, and transgression, or else *luxuriating*, and the other on the side of *luxury goods*, individual acquisition of symbols of sovereignty and transcendence – the latter dominating today at the cost of the erasure of the former. In practice, of course, both are present, the erasure being a matter of degree. This however does not mean that one paradigm has not replaced the other over the course of time as the dominant paradigm. This is also visible in the introduction of the split between 'vulgar luxury' and 'sublime luxury' within the subculture itself. This also goes to show that this split is not only native to a larger social class hierarchy but can occur even within a subculture which to the 'citizen'-outsider would simply appear to fall into the former.

Coda

There is an additional trouble we need to bear in mind. Often it is precisely certain *objects* through which we can experience sovereign moments. The feeling one has when riding a Harley with its wonderful roar is certainly a case in point. The danger it embodies, the threat of death of which one is reminded at biker funerals of those who died crashing, is something that only intensifies the sublime feeling. One thing that has not disappeared and that still provides the utmost pleasure to the biker is riding in a pack, far from being the same as riding alone – the danger increases in proportion. The synchronous, collective moment, offers a genuine feeling of sovereignty, similar to the one achieved through collective moment in dance or in military drill. There is a profound satisfaction in being 'incorporated into the community in a way far deeper than shared myth or common custom can achieve. In synchronous movement . . ., the petty rivalries and factional differences that might divide a group could be transmuted into harmless competition . . ., or forgotten' (Ehrenreich, 2008: 24). In *Keeping Together in Time*, McNeill thought in depth about this peculiar power of moving together, wherein 'a strange sense of personal enlargement; a sort of swelling out, becoming bigger than life, thanks to participation in collective ritual' (McNeill, 1995: 2) emerges. When such objects are *put into action*, they are capable of transforming the mundane and the dangerous into something extraordinary – hence the trouble with the ideal of immaterial harmless pleasures. But even here, more and more Harleys are becoming so preciously customised, so luxurious, that they are never ridden. They are exhibited and displayed – at a recent biker event I have attended, the winning customised Harley, judged on its beauty, could not even be started, the owner confessing that he would never ride it. Here we must not mistake the symbols of sovereignty for sovereign moments – the desire is for the latter, while its satisfaction is far often sought in the former, the necessary dissatisfaction a reason to repeat the same mistake and hoard the former. But one question beyond the scope of this text remains. Namely, how can we reconcile social equality with the need for sovereignty of individuals, and is it even possible?

Notes

1 For more on the Danish concept of the TV show, see: www.bump-productions.com/index.php?option=com_contentandview=articleandid=98:luxury-trap-r-luxury-debt-r-bump-productions-live-in-luxury-and-become-debt-free-in-one-evening-tv-format-andcatid=34:international-formatsandItemid=55 (Accessed: 10 January 2018).

2 www.youtube.com/watch?v=PvwYg3-n_k4

References

Adams, W.H. (2012) *On Luxury: A Cautionary Tale*, Washington, DC: Potomac Books.

Althusser, L. (1969) *For Marx*, London: The Penguin Press.

Austin, D.M., Gagne, P. and Orend, A. (2010) Commodification and Popular Imagery of the Biker in American Culture. *The Journal of Popular Culture*, 43, 5: 942–63.

Babcock, B.A. (1978) *The Reversible World: Symbolic Inversion in Art and Society*, Ithaca, NY and London: Cornell University Press.

Barker, T. (2010) *Biker Gangs and Organized Crime*, Newark, NJ: Elsevier Science.

Bataille, G. (1993) *The Accursed Share: Volumes II and III*, New York: Zone Books.

Belk, R.W., Wallendorf, M. and Sherry, J.F. (1989) The Sacred and the Profane in Consumer Behavior: Theodicy on the Odyssey. *Journal of Consumer Research*, 16, 1: 1–38.

Berry, C. (1994) *The Idea of Luxury: A Conceptual and Historical Investigation*, Cambridge: Cambridge University Press.

Brecht, G. (1983) *Rocker in Deutschland '81*, Heidelberg: Biker News and Kübler Verlag M. Akselrad.

Burke, E. (1914) *A Philosophical Inquiry into the Origins of Our Ideas of the Sublime and Beautiful*, New York: P.F. Collier and Son Company.

Calefato, P. (2014) *Luxury: Fashion, Lifestyle and Excess*, London: Bloomsbury.

Cohen, S. (2001) *States of Denial: Knowing About Atrocities and Suffering*, Cambridge: Polity Press.

Coser, L.A. (1974) *Greedy Institutions: Patterns of Undivided Commitment*, New York: The Free Press.

Deis, R. and Doyle, W. (2016) *Barbarians on Bikes: Bikers and Motorcycle Gangs*, New York: New Texture.

Dion, D. and Borraz, S. (2015) Managing Heritage Brands: A Study of the Sacralization of Heritage Stores in the Luxury Industry. *Journal of Retailing and Consumer Services*, 22, 1: 77–84.

Durkheim, É. (1965) *The Elementary Forms of the Religious Life*, New York: The Free Press.

Ehrenreich, B. (2008) *Dancing in the Streets: A History of Collective Joy*, London: Granta Books.

Ellis, A., Winlow, S., Briggs, D., Esquinas, A.S., Verdugo, R.C. and Suárez, J.R.P. (2018) Liberalism, Lack and Living the Dream: Re-Considering Youth, Consumer Sovereignty and the Attractions of Night-Time Leisure in Magaluf. *Journal of Extreme Anthropology*, 2, 2: 1–19.

Forsyth, C.J. and Quinn, J.F. (2009) Leathers and Rolexs: The Symbolism and Values of the Motorcycle Club. *Deviant Behavior*, 30, 3: 235–65.

Frank, T. (1998) *The Conquest of Cool: Business, Culture, Counterculture, and the Rise of Hip Consumerism*, Chicago: University of Chicago Press.

Hall, S. (2014) The Socioeconomic Function of Evil. *The Sociological Review*, 62, S2: 13–31.

Haug, W.F. (1986) *Critique of Commodity Aesthetics: Appearance, Sexuality and Advertising in Capitalist Society*, Cambridge: Polity Press.

Heath, J. and Potter, A. (2005) *The Rebel Sell: How the Counterculture Became Consumer Culture*, West Sussex: Capstone Publishing.

Killerby, C.K. (1994) Practical Problems in the Enforcement of Italian Sumptuary Law, 1200–1500. In T. Dean and K.J.P. Lowe (eds.) *Crime, Society and the Law in Renaissance Italy*, Cambridge: Cambridge University Press, 99–120.

Klein, R. (1993) *Cigarettes Are Sublime*, Durham and London: Duke University Press.

Kuldova, T. (2016a) Heads Against Hands and Hierarchies of Creativity: Indian Luxury Embroidery Between Craft, Fashion Design and Art. In M. Svašek and B. Meyer (eds.) *Creativity in Transition: Politics and Aesthetics of Circulating Images*, New York: Berghahn Books.

Kuldova, T. (2016b) *Luxury Indian Fashion: A Social Critique*, London: Bloomsbury.

Kuldova, T. (2017a) Hells Angels Motorcycle Corporation in Fashion Business: On the Fetishism of the Trademark Law. *Journal of Design History*, 30, 4: 389–407.

Kuldova, T. (2017b) The Sublime Splendour of Intimidation: On the Outlaw Biker Aesthetics of Power. *Visual Anthropology*, 30, 5: 379–402.

Kuldova, T. (2018a) The 'Ethical Sell' in the Indian Luxury Fashion Business. In V. Pouillard and R. Blaczczyk (eds.) *European Fashion: The Creation of a Global Industry*, Manchester: Manchester University Press, 263–82.

Kuldova, T. (2018b) Interpassive Phenomena in Times of Economic Subordination: From Self-Playing Games Via Cryptocurrency Mining to Dressing up in Subversion. *Continental Thought and Theory: A Journal of Intellectual Freedom*, 2, 1: 32–49.

Kuldova, T. (2019) *How Outlaws Win Friends and Influence People*, New York: Palgrave Macmillan.

Kuldova, T. and Quinn, J. (2018) Outlaw Motorcycle Clubs and Struggles Over Legitimization. In T. Kuldova and M. Sanchez-Jankowski (eds.) *Outlaw Motorcycle Clubs and Street Gangs: Scheming Legality, Resisting Criminalization*, New York: Palgrave Macmillan, 145–73.

Kuldova, T. and Sánchez-Jankowski, M. (2018) *Outlaw Motorcycle Clubs and Street Gangs: Scheming Legality, Resisting Criminalization*, New York: Palgrave Macmillan.

Lafargue, P. (1883) *The Right to Be Lazy*. Available at: www.marxists.org (first published: Charles Kerr and Co.)

Lordon, F. (2014) *Willing Slaves of Capital: Spinoza and Marx on Desire*, London: Verso.

Lukose, R.A. (2009) *Liberalization's Children: Gender, Youth, and Consumer Citizenship in Globalizing India*, Durham: Duke University Press.

Marx, K. (1959) *Economic and Philosophic Manuscripts of 1844*, Moscow: Progress Publishers.

McGowan, T. (2004) *The End of Dissatisfaction? Jacques Lacan and the Emerging Society of Enjoyment*, New York: SUNY Press.

McNeill, W.H. (1995) *Keeping Together in Time: Dance and Drill in Human History*, Cambridge, MA: Harvard University Press.

Olaveson, T. (2001) Collective Effervescence and Communitas: Processual Models of Ritual and Society in Emile Durkheim and Victor Turner. *Dialectical Anthropology*, 26: 89–124.

Osgerby, B. (2003) Sleazy Riders: Exploitation, 'Otherness', and Transgression in the 1960s Biker Movie. *Journal of Popular Film and Television*, 31, 3: 98–108.

Pfaller, R. (2008) *Das Schmutzige Heilige Und Die Reine Vernunft: Symptome Der Gegenwartskultur*, Frankfurt am Main: Fischer Taschenbuch Verlag.

Pfaller, R. (2009) Sublimation and 'Schweinerei': Theoretical Place and Cultural-Critical Function of Psychoanalytic Concept. *JEP*, 29, 2: 11–48.

Pfaller, R. (2011) *Wofür Es Sich Zu Leben Lohnt*, Frankfurt am Main: Fischer.

Pfaller, R. (2014) *On the Pleasure Principle in Culture: Illusions Without Owners*, London: Verso.

Pfaller, R. (2017) *Erwachsenensprache: Über Ihr Verschwinden Aus Politik Und Kultur*, Frankfurt am Main: Fischer.

Pieper, J. (1998) *Leisure: The Basis of Culture*, South Bend, IN: St. Augustine's Press.

Quinn, J. and Koch, D.S. (2003) The Nature of Criminality Within One-Percenter Motorcycle Clubs. *Deviant Behavior*, 24, 3: 281–305.

Scammel, M. (2000) The Internet and Civic Engagement: The Age of the Citizen-Consumer. *Political Communication*, 17, 4: 351–55.

Schrat, J. (1983) Vorwort: Rocker Heute. In G. Brecht (ed.) *Rocker in Deutschland '81*, Heidelberg: Biker News and Kübler Verlag M. Akselrad.

Smith, O. and Raymen, T. (2016) Deviant Leisure: A Criminological Perspective. *Theoretical Criminology*, 1–20.

Stallybrass, P. and White, A. (1986) *The Politics and Poetics of Transgression*, London: Methuen.

Thompson, E.P. (1974) Patrician Society, Plebeian Culture. *Journal of Social History*, 7, 4: 382–405.

Thompson, E.P. (1993) *Customs in Common: Studies in Traditional Popular Culture*, New York: New Press.
Thompson, H.S. (2003) *Hell's Angels*, London: Penguin Books.
Tudor, K. (2018) Toxic Sovereignty: Understanding Fraud as the Expression of Special Liberty Within Late-Capitalism. *Journal of Extreme Anthropology*, 2, 2: 1–15.
Weber, M. (2005) *The Protestant Ethic and the Spirit of Capitalism*, London: Routledge.

6 Substances

The luxurious, the sublime, and the harmful

Tammy Ayres

Introduction

The global luxury market is now worth nearly $1 trillion USD – one of the few markets to grow each year (Euromonitor International, 2018). In today's multi-mediated society, we are bombarded constantly with direct-to-consumer advertisements for substances that offer a quick-fix solution to any real or imagined ailment, imperfection, or illness (Singer and Baer, 2009). A plethora of creams, pills, potions, and tinctures promise to improve our appearance, make us happier, healthier, more muscular, smarter, or thinner (Evans-Brown et al., 2012). As this chapter shows, many of these luxurious substances reflect Žižek's (2008) 'chocolate laxative', where the problem is sold as the solution. The real problems and issues that underpin the harmful subjectivities characteristic of contemporary society and sustain the consumption of these substances – some of which contain toxins such as Botox, mercury, and lead – are constantly disavowed. Despite offering solutions to our problems, luxurious substances are just another part of the capitalist dynamic – sublime objects of ideology (Žižek, 1989).

Substances: the luxurious and the sublime

While substances have been consumed for many reasons throughout history, this chapter will focus on consumption linked to leisure and pleasure – particularly, the conspicuous, wasteful consumption of the leisure classes (Veblen, 1969). While much has been written about the 'control' function of substances and the hypocrisy of the upper classes' moralising and criminalising attitude to the poor, we now live in markedly different times. The command to enjoy has replaced the 'symbolic law of prohibition' as everyone searches for 'the mysterious and elusive X' via 'our compulsive consumption' (Žižek, 1999: 1). The compulsion to repeat is a powerful subjective force that drives capitalism forward, but it is also linked to substance use and addiction, which the 'commodified provocations to enjoy' push us toward (Žižek, 2006: 311). As ultra-realist criminologists argue (Hall, 2012; Hall and Winlow, 2015, 2019), the consumption of luxurious substances is symptomatic of the drives, structures, and processes inherent in capitalism.

Drug use and leisure have filled the gap left by deindustrialisation[1] and are now used to simultaneously stimulate and pacify the resultant subjectivities characteristic of neoliberal consumer capitalism (Ayres, 2017, 2019; Hall, 2019; Bauman, 1991; Smith, 2014). Industrialisation, economic growth, and mass production have turned once luxurious and exclusive substances into today's necessities, regardless of their harmfulness. Traditional structures and institutions have crumbled, and the social has disappeared, replaced by a fragmented and individualistic society where everyone is competing with each other to reach the imaginary top (Bauman, 1991; Hall et al., 2008; Smith, 2014). The traditional values of hard work, sacrifice, and deferred gratification have been largely displaced by a consumer culture that prioritises pleasure, desire, self-enhancement, fantasy, instant gratification, and competitive individualism (Bauman, 2001; Hall et al., 2008; Winlow and Hall, 2016). Neoliberalism's insecure and anxious subjects, lacking any traditional sources of identity, can be appeased only by the consumption of products, services, and substances available from the capitalist marketplace as everyone consumes themselves into being (Bauman, 2001; Winlow and Hall, 2016).

Symbolism is used to seduce consumers with increasingly luxurious substances that promise to address their physical and social deficiencies. In a society where representation has overtaken reality (Baudrillard, 1994) and an economy of deception operates (Bauman, 2007), conspicuous consumption of 'affordable luxury' items, lifestyles, and experiences has come to dominate the construction of the self. Buying their public persona and lifestyle from the marketplace, consumers frequent exclusive venues to consume luxurious substances to display personal images of success (Bauman, 2007; Hall et al., 2008; Smith, 2014, Žižek, 2014). The experience of extreme experiential luxury has been intensified by social media platforms, where experiences can be shared and disseminated, which can combine with tales of entrepreneurial success to act as 'symbolic props for storying the self' (Hayward and Smith, 2017: 307). Thus, the entrepreneurial and consuming self can be created, disseminated, and reinforced in a form of self-branding (Hearn, 2008).

The entrepreneurial consumer has become the role model of social subjectivity as individuals become entrepreneurs of themselves (Bröckling, 2015) and subjectivity becomes a 'commodity to be bought and sold in the market as beauty, cleanliness, sincerity and autonomy' (Bauman, 2007: 28). The carefully branded entrepreneurial self draws upon the processes, symbols, and market logic of the mainstream image-economy of the culture industries as they reconstruct and reproduce their own human capital (Hearn, 2008: 207). However, pleasure and enjoyment must be healthy and risk free in an era of 'spiritualised enlightened hedonism' (Žižek, 2014: 4), where only a controlled loss of control is tolerated (Hayward, 2004). However, this contradictory and sanitised injunction to enjoy drives us toward excessive enjoyment and nonrepressive hedonism as *jouissance* has been made obligatory (Žižek, 2006). The capitalist world of overproduction and myriad of consumer objects now relies on a tense combination of anxiety and excess – 'the more you have the more you feel the lack' (Žižek, 2017: 9).

Excess and wastefulness denote wealth and status, while the 'individual becomes ruthlessly narcissistic' in his pursuit of *jouissance* as 'the barbaric part of the split narcissist is basically competitive, warlike, wasteful and orientated towards personal rather than communal achievements' (Hall, 2012: 33). Here the entrepreneurial consumer self takes advantage of every opportunity to maximise enjoyment, driving the desire for and consumption of luxurious and often intoxicating and harmful substances to avoid the guilt attached to not enjoying properly and not enjoying enough (Dean, 2016).

The unrestrained consumption of intoxicating substances provides an escape and freedom from symbolic castration by providing 'a purely autistic *jouissance*, a *jouissance* accessible without the detour through the Other' (Žižek, 2006: 311); a *jouissance* that invades the body to induce an ephemeral 'feeling of completeness . . . of pure and full Being' (Bjerg, 2008: 10). Consuming drugs facilitates the transcendence of symbolic reality and desire, allowing people to imagine themselves freed from the rules and expectations of society, while simultaneously encouraging them to feel like conformity is their choice. Thus 'transgression' merely reinforces the rules, as the law 'solicits its own transgression' in a double-bind of guilt and desire as businesses rake in the profits (Žižek, 2006: 90). Whether it is drug testing at every stage of the criminal justice system, the implementation of alcohol and cannabis warnings/fines or the luxurious rehabs full of recovering celebrity addicts, transgression of the laws controlling the consumption of substances is big business. Here the luxurious and expensive substances of the bourgeoisie are prioritised, while those associated with the great unwashed are taxed and removed from the legitimate marketplace.[2] Politics thus revolves around the ideological manipulation of *jouissance*, which operates as an 'obscene underside of the law' (Žižek, 1989). Obedience is disguised as rebellion and radicality to avoid any authentic act that may actually challenge the dominant status quo and undermine the preservation of capital realism (Fisher, 2009).

Prioritising the superego and the promotion of *jouissance* normalises substance users as they obey the demands placed on them to prioritise enjoyment and consume to excess (Žižek, 2002). This sort of happiness through excessive consumption has become a moral obligation, which not only facilitates the transition from recreational to more problematic patterns of substance use, but actively encourages it, as pleasure is prioritised above anything else (Žižek, 2002). However, the *Jouisseaur Propre*, although a consumer par excellence, is unwelcome in society, despite being solicited by the very system that seeks to punish and control it (Žižek, 2014). Problems arise when the consumption of drugs is seen to complete the person by addressing his or her lack – of self-confidence, stamina, sociability, beauty, and so on – which results in a compulsion to repeat and the potential for more problematic patterns of substance use. As Burroughs (1972: 9) highlights 'junk is the ideal product . . . the ultimate merchandise. No sales talk necessary. The client will crawl through the sewer and beg to buy' making it a 'commodity par excellence' (Žižek, 2006: 311). However, addiction and dependence on substances is not welcomed by all in contemporary capitalism because it constitutes 'the product to end all products' and therefore 'implodes the desire for other products' (Bjerg, 2008: 16). Bar dependence on commodities and consumerism, there is no place for dependence in a neoliberal society (Bauman, 2000), despite once being the standard condition for most human beings and their communities (see Hall, this volume). Thus, the only way substance induced *jouissance* may be enjoyed is if it is not too excessive, thus in the Durkheimian sense functioning to mark out the boundaries of social order (Douglas, 1969) and acceptable consumption rather than the territory beyond them. Despite their harmfulness, only substances available from the legitimate marketplace are sanctioned (e.g. alcohol, medications, and beauty products) for consumption in allocated spaces (e.g. pubs, clubs, and salons) at dedicated times.

Drug prohibition focuses on excessive consumption and the minority of individuals that lose control and suffer addiction and loss of function as producers and consumers in the capitalist market. Where the people who have fallen foul of the consumer markets in substances are failures and a burden, other substance users, particularly those consuming luxurious substances, are 'enlightened hedonists' who 'carefully calculate their pleasure to prolong their fun and avoid getting hurt' (Žižek, 2014: 4). Thus, the control of *jouissance* and risky individuals emphasises the neoliberal focus on self-governance and individual responsibility, while ignoring capitalism's systemic violence manifested in its tendency to show contempt for 'losers'. Such an ideology conceals 'the underlying unbalanced, uncanny structure' (Žižek, 1997: 82) that relies on 'a crucial paradox' (Žižek, 2008: 15), a paradox that has been normalised and is reflected in the use and supply of substances. Despite its industrial promotion of excessive consumption, neoliberalism demands that pharmacological hedonism must not veer out of control, while circumventing dependent intoxication, which is the principal negative consequence of maintaining a desirable and competitive identity as a product of self-management (Hayward, 2004; Smith, 2014). However, the precarious subjectivities and cultural injunction to enjoy has led to a culture of determined intoxication and the pursuit of pharmacological oblivion that not only offers an escape from the constraints and drudgery of everyday life, but facilitates superficial personal relationships based on manufactured beauty, hyper-sexuality, and sexual encounters (Ayres and Treadwell, 2012; Featherstone, 1982; Hall et al., 2008; Ruggiero and South, 1995; Smith, 2014; Winlow and Hall, 2006).

The most luxurious product or experience is now 'the one that generates the most benefit to all involved in its production and trade' (Bendell and Kleanthous, 2007) as people endeavour to 'do something meaningful, show they care . . . and participate in a large collective project . . . [and] . . . in communal life' (Žižek, 2014: 7–8). Whether this means consuming Krug champagne in a VIP bar to feel part of an elite group (see Smith, 2014) or embarking on a luxurious *ayahuasca* retreat in search of spirituality, self-enlightenment, and alternative remedies for contemporary ailments, luxurious substances offer not only a solution, but an ethical, ecologically friendly and sustainable solution to our problems as capital's 'ruthless pursuit of profit is counteracted by charity' (Žižek, 2008: 22). Luxurious substances now need to be ecologically sound, healthy, ethical, and risk free; 'sustainability and social responsibility are no longer just nice to have, but are requirements for luxury brands' (Winston, 2016) that warrant a higher price tag and ease the conscience of the consumer.

Such marketing strategies are known as 'bluewashing' or 'greenwashing' (for a review see Brisman and South, 2016) and are rife in the luxurious substance market. From beauty products to alcohol and coffee there is no such thing as ethical consumption or a green product despite the marketer's attempts to convince consumers otherwise (Brisman and South, 2016; Kuldova, 2018). Instead these fantasies constitute 'reality in itself which is ready to be conceived as ideological', covering up the trauma of the symbolic order and the fact *jouissance* is not possible (Žižek, 2008: 16). The 'anti-consumerist sentiment' to do something is incorporated into the very thing being consumed, fetishistically disavowing the harms it perpetuates whilst offering people their own redemption for being nothing more than egotistical consumers in the market (Žižek, 2006, 2008). Thus, the luxurious substance is a sublime object with a fetishistic quality; a substance that embodies a sublimity it does not possess and therefore acts as a symbolic object in the overall ideological fantasy (Žižek, 1989).

Luxurious substances promise to address our imperfections and improve our competitiveness and our performance by offering to address our sense of lack; what we purchase reflects our innermost desires (Baudrillard, 1998) and the truth about the subject (Žižek, 1989). According to Appadurai (1986: 38) luxurious substances are 'incarnated signs' that promise to provide an escape from mundane necessity as a fleeting moment of bliss (Featherstone, 2016). However, they are sham objects that can bring happiness neither to the self nor others, but only increase the wealth and power of the plutocratic elite (Hall et al., 2008; Veblen, 1969). The consumer is consistently cheated by the symbolic object's deferred promise of fulfilment, which feeds back into the consumer and elicits the dissatisfaction that perpetuates further desire and consumption (Dean, 2009; Horkheimer and Adorno, 2002; Winlow and Hall, 2016; Žižek, 1997). However, the constant failure of the luxurious substance to make us complete and satisfied is constantly individualised while the impact of the systemic violence inherent in consumer capitalism is constantly disavowed. The individual's problems are never the fault of the system.

To maintain and reproduce its hyper-individualised hegemony, neoliberalism promotes a value system that prioritises self-interest, competition, and entrepreneurialism above what remains of our social values. Socioeconomic inequalities and harms are individualised and turned inwards as people blame themselves for their own misfortune; those who make bad choices 'deserve everything they get'. Freedom is thus an illusion, as both desire and choice are structured and controlled by capitalism's mass mediated ideology of individual choice and 'resilience'. The entrepreneurial self is in a constant state of becoming with no limits to self-improvement (Bröckling, 2015), but to prosper one must engage in risk, but not too much risk (Žižek, 2008, 2014) for fear of being excommunicated as a weak individual, a failed entrepreneur, and a flawed consumer unable to calculate risk and come out on top. Thus, the consumption of luxurious substances is integral to the purchasing of cultural experiences and lifestyles (Žižek, 2014) as well as constructing the perfect persona, both vital aspects of the sublime object of ideology, the fantasy of wholeness that can have no real existence in the post-modern world.

Consumption of substances: a sublime object of ideology

The society of the spectacle, wherein representation has overwhelmed reality, has encouraged a 'preoccupation with the self' (Lasch, 1979: 239), which has reconstituted need and turned desire towards an array of substances proffering a quick fix solution to every ailment or imperfection, no matter how trivial or serious (see Singer and Baer, 2009). Via symbolism the entrepreneurial subject is encouraged to preserve itself, to delay aging, look youthful, and keep healthy, by adopting instrumental strategies that emphasise the importance of aesthetics alongside the performance of the self (Featherstone, 1982). Luxurious substances are not only integral to leisure and pleasure (see Ayres, 2019) but are also aids in the construction of the perfect entrepreneurial and consuming self, which is never complete but a nervous passenger on a procession of identities that are 'adopted and discarded like a change of costume' (Lasch, 1985: 38). People are trying to make themselves more marketable and desirable as they are 'trapped in the narcissistic, self-surveillance world of images' (Featherstone, 1982: 22). It is in this world and to this end that an increasingly diverse array of substances has entered the marketplace offering the illusion of freedom, choice, and perfection; a quick-fix solution that, as we have seen, appeases insecurities while also being ecologically sound and ethical as 'life itself is turned into a commodity' and 'we become the consumers of our own lives' (Žižek, 2014: 5).

Normal everyday objects of necessity are no longer sufficient to satisfy our desires and meet our everyday needs. In their place the traditional capitalist marketplace continued ancient traditions to create a range of substances indicative of luxurious lifestyles that have come to dominate the construction of self in the contemporary culture of ornamental consumerism (Hall et al., 2008). These traditional luxurious substances seduce us into thinking they are superior and more effective because they contain other luxurious and desirable products such as gold and diamonds, while concealing the reality that these luxurious but inert ingredients provide no pharmacological or physical benefit to the consumer. To overcome this 'necessity deficit' in the age of personal health and well-being, the burgeoning market in substances has led to an array of new products purporting to be miracle cures, which not only improve our health and well-being but also denote a desirable healthy lifestyle and able to prevent some serious diseases. Beauty creams and serums such as JK7®, which cost anything up to $1,800 per ounce, promise to delay the signs of aging while combatting cancer (Huen, 2017). To meet consumer demands, the luxury market in substances has been flooded with aquaceuticals and cosmeceuticals, made from exotic combinations of organic and luxurious ingredients that are allegedly ethical and sustainable. Luxury products promote a healthy ecological lifestyle and allow consumers to show that they care, as they pay extra to participate in the collective projects of charity, social responsibility, and saving the planet by buying eco-friendly and fair-trade products designed to ease our guilt and disavow the exploitative realities and harms underpinning such products (Bendell and Kleanthous, 2007; Žižek, 2014). Despite the burgeoning market in dietary supplements, herbal remedies, and lifestyle drugs, these products have not only been scientifically analysed and identified as a waste of money (Jenkins et al., 2018; NHS, 2011; Pope et al., 2014), but also potentially harmful because little is known about some of the substances being ingested, let alone how they interact with each other or metabolise in the body, which is particularly problematic since most people consume several products together. This category of 'potentially harmful' includes concentrated doses of natural herbal antioxidants such as green tea, which have been shown to cause liver and kidney damage (EFSA Panel, 2018), and pharmaceuticals, natural dietary supplements[3] and luxurious beauty products such as lipstick[4] (Hall, 2019; Moore, 2011; Romanowski and Schueller, 2013; Singer and Baer, 2009; Tucker et al., 2018), which contain banned and harmful ingredients that negatively impact people's health and well-being. However, these harms are consistently and forcefully disavowed by suppliers and sellers in the market, perpetuating the illusion that only illegitimate drugs are bad because they create undeserving, unproductive, and immoral citizens. Thus, the prohibition of any product but their own is rationalised in their marketing strategies (Taylor et al., 2016). These potentially harmful but luxurious substances use clever marketing strategies based on wholesome concepts such as 'organic' and 'natural' to dupe consumers into thinking they are ecologically sound, healthier to the individual and contain no harmful ingredients. Promoting health, well-being, happiness, and beauty, these products relieve anxiety, signify altruism, and promise to address that which is lacking in both the individual consumer and the heart of the marketplace (Hall, 2019; Winlow and Hall, 2016).

Regardless of whether the product is licit or illicit, it is branded,[5] and the same marketing strategies are implemented (see Martin, 2014) as we are constantly reminded that there is room for improvement in all aspects of our lives (Featherstone, 1982) and the market can provide a substance to help us achieve a move towards perfection. However, those with insufficient money and from regions with inadequate and expensive healthcare systems are denied lifesaving medications (e.g. AIDS medication in some regions of Africa). The extortionate price of legitimate drugs is the outcome of a capitalist system that prioritises the creation of lucrative markets and the maximisation of profits rather than people's health needs. Under these conditions alternative medicines that also carry the promise of personal lifestyle enhancements have moved in to fill gaps in the market. Consumers now address a broad spectrum of ailments ranging from physical illnesses to psychological conditions by popping a privately obtained pill or paying for a luxurious retreat that may or may not involve consuming other luxurious substances such as exotic food, champagne, and *ayahuasca*. Consumption of these luxurious substances not only offers consumers a quick-fix solution to a wide variety of ailments, but also a competitive edge in the ability to display to others participation in a more exciting, healthy, and luxurious lifestyle. Thus, they hope they are perceived by others to be 'more attractive, flirty, young, ambitious, sexy, mature and smart' (Hudders et al., 2014: 571). Their assiduously displayed consumption elicits envy as others desire similar luxurious products and what their use symbolises, as enjoyment becomes concentrated in the hands of the other that might steal it from them (Žižek, 1997). The consumption of harmful but luxurious and sublime substances offers us beauty, perfection, youth and longevity, which, given that the desire of the other becomes the desire of the self, 'transform[s] us into objects of our own desire', which completes the circle and ensnares the subject in consumer culture's energy-trap (Hall, 2019: 9). Of course, these are superficial, fragile, and ephemeral objects with uncertain imaginary identities that are reliant on the constant procession of symbolic products and cannot endure or reproduce themselves over time (Appadurai, 1986; Dean, 2009). All the self-branded self (Hearn, 2008) can do is continue to adopt changes in lifestyle fashion and appease anxiety by displaying its serially renewed self on commodified hedonism's various public stages, such as social media platforms, the workplace, the holiday resort, or the night-time economy (Smith, 2014).

The consumption of luxurious substances is thus largely about aesthetics; constructing the perfect body image and the perfect lifestyle (Baudrillard, 1998) as products that are sold to produce returns for capitalist investors (Bauman, 2007). Postmodern consumer subjects consume luxurious substances and products that promise to appease their imperfections, ease their insecurities, improve their health, and increase their longevity, while also offering them the social status and envy that the perfect lifestyle can elicit. The market promises to fulfil every want and desire that is driven by the sense of lack that the ephemerality of its products' social value causes (Bauman, 2007; Hall, 2019; Winlow and Hall, 2016). The consumer subjects must compete with others as they search for happiness and success, while dutifully obeying the cultural injunction to enjoy (Žižek, 2002). However, they are continually cheated as we live in an 'aesthetic hallucination of reality' (Baudrillard, 1993: 94) or what Satre calls the 'derealization . . . of everyday reality' where representation (Simulcra) is prioritised over the real (Baudrillard, 1998). In this unstable and competitive realm, luxurious substances act as sublime objects of ideology, the symbols of the capitalist fantasy which, to save face, the subject must obtain to imagine himself in existence. However, often the only way those short of money can pay for luxurious substances and lifestyles is via debt or credit as most people consume beyond their means, taking out loans to pay for items that promise them perfection (Horsley, 2015). Those who wish to buy valued symbolic goods in these markets must become successful, highly paid workers or entrepreneurs or they must find other ways of funding their luxurious lifestyles and paying down their loans.

Criminal entrepreneurs: the supply of luxurious substances

Ruggiero and South (1995), Hall et al. (2008) and Hobbs (1995, 2013) have all identified the role entrepreneurs play in the supply of illicit or licit substances across the globe. The supply of these substances provides meaning, work, and status (see also Preble and Casey, 1969) alongside the financial means to buy the luxury items society tells us we not only want but need to make ourselves feel complete (Hall, 2019; Hall et al., 2008; Treadwell and Ayres, 2014). Throughout history the corporations and entrepreneurs, sometimes criminal, have implemented the same ruthless undertaking in the supply of luxurious substances, both legal and illegal, as they all compete in markets and justify their often harmful practices by bestowing on themselves the entrepreneurial entitlement of 'special liberty', a secularised, individualised, and post-social variant of 'divine right' (see Hall, 2012).

The neoliberal system of governance promotes the entrepreneurial values of competitiveness, self-interest, individual empowerment, and decentralisation, which encourage self-interested actors who embody the neoliberal ideal of market-orientated entrepreneurship (Hall, 2012). Individuals become criminal entrepreneurs as they are forced to 'deal with the ferocious financial world . . . dominated by hypocrisy and throat-cutting competition' (Ruggiero and South, 1995: 179), not only as a means to survive, but also to excel in an economy where many traditional skill sets are no longer functional or valued (Ayres and Treadwell, 2012; Hall et al., 2008; Hobbs, 2013; Treadwell and Ayres, 2014). Thus, drug supply can be seen to fulfil a number of functions in these criminal entrepreneurs' lives; it provides viable employment for some, and thus a dignified way of financing a luxurious lifestyle with its 'ornamental trinkets' (Hall et al., 2008: 77); for others it supplements a legitimate income or business to generate the surplus income required to purchase desirable luxury items; others shift in and out of illegal drug supply depending on their needs, wants, and desires (Daly and Hall, 2018; Treadwell and Ayres, 2014).

Drug supply must increasingly be seen against the backdrop of economic austerity and receding legitimate opportunities for increasingly diverse sections of the populace (Hall et al., 2008). Some involved in the supply of substances hold down jobs in the legitimate economy but supplement their income by selling drugs, along with doing other low-skill work such as debt collecting, security work, and driving. Many individuals become involved in drug supply not simply to make ends meet, but also to buy the luxury items we are all ideologically persuaded to want; the items that denote wealth, success and, ultimately, our sense of self and identity (Daly and Hall, 2018; Hall et al., 2008; Hobbs, 2013; Treadwell and Ayres, 2014; Treadwell et al., 2018). Selling drugs fuelled the luxurious lifestyle they all desired, without putting them into too much debt, and was seen as a solution to their problems, offering upward mobility, economic stability, and the social standing that elicited both envy and respect (Hall et al., 2008; Hobbs, 2013; Treadwell and Ayres, 2014).

Convinced these luxurious objects, substances, lifestyles, and experiences provide them with freedom and life satisfaction, they buy what they consider to be the best of things to show they have made it (Hall et al., 2008; Treadwell and Ayres, 2014). Drug dealing, particularly of cocaine, which has traditionally been seen as a rich man's drug, is not only demonstrative of a celebrity lifestyle but is also integral to the nocturnal economy (Ayres and Treadwell, 2012; Daly and Hall, 2018). Today, changes in the sale of cocaine have accompanied the changing culture of the night-time economies in many countries. The emergence of luxury bars and VIP clubs has provided favoured leisure spots for criminal entrepreneurs who have bought into the 'celebrity lifestyle' and seek out 'a celebrity-like status' (Daly and Hall, 2018: 1) at home and abroad, a lifestyle characterised principally by wasteful luxury consumption and excess, as they literally 'buy (the time of)' their own lives (Žižek, 2014: 5).

For others, however, drug supply is one of the few available ways of surviving, as they are systematically ejected from dying industrial economies in the west, which have shifted into service economies where their traditional skill sets are no longer valued. In this disappearing world most workers had little disposable income at the end of the week, but their lives had a rhythm and they had a firm identity and more stability, security, and social status. Now, under neoliberalism and thrust into service economies in a post-industrial, post-social world, the traditional threat of living in poverty has not disappeared but is now compounded by the threat of disappearing into an anthropological vortex of cultural insignificance, of becoming a nobody not just to capital but to all others (Hall et al., 2008). Drug supply provided a productive and profitable outlet for their defunct skill set no longer needed in the deindustrialised towns and cities where traditional forms of highly physical and masculine employment has dwindled (Hall, 1997; Hall et al., 2008; Hobbs, 2013; Treadwell and Ayres, 2014; Treadwell et al., 2018), and increasingly large swathes of the traditional working class are 'hanging on by their finger nails to the mainstream economy' with no hope of 'mainstream incorporation' (Hall, 1997: 476). Instead, for them, like many others, economic success is defined 'by the cool entrepreneurial individual's adroit performance' (Hall et al., 2008: 130) and displays of consumer symbols in a neoliberal society where individuals are expected to self-manage their own rise to positions of social security status. It is the responsibility of individual citizens to realise their personal life project; if they fail, they only have themselves to blame.

The supply of substances associated with luxury lifestyles has become so entwined with the legitimate global economy that it is difficult to disentangle. Thus, it is seen by some as a legitimate and preferable form of work and cultural life (Hall et al., 2008; Treadwell and Ayres, 2014). The democratisation of the drug market, alongside the democratisation of criminal opportunity more generally, has meant that more people from very diverse backgrounds have moved into the supply of luxurious substances, which has been facilitated and expanded by the growth of the Internet and other forms of technology (Hall and Antonopoulos, 2016; Treadwell et al., 2018). In today's 24-hour marketplace drug dealers are working around the clock to adapt and advance their supply methods and capitalise on new trading opportunities as they emerge (see Coomber and Moyles, 2018).

As Hall (2012: 205) argues, 'neoliberalism's zeitgeist is not about freeing but energising subjects with asocial and ruthless forms of ambition'. Drug dealers are no different. Like the early traders of opium, contemporary drug dealers participate in competitive and sometimes ruthless criminal undertaking, which means they 'get things done regardless of the harm inflicted on others'. Increasingly this means they will hurt, maim, and punish anyone who directly threatens their own personal interests. In what is now known as 'county lines drug dealing', urban drug dealers travel to out-of-town areas to sell drugs where there is less competition (see Coomber and Moyles, 2018) and new markets as subjects seek escape from drab existences with uncertain futures into the imaginary world of consumer symbolism. The ruthless undertaking – for instance physical violence, intimidation, the exploitation of vulnerable populations and their recruitment of children as both traffickers and consumers – exercised by drug dealers in these new markets (see Coomber and Moyles, 2018) is both a manifestation of and a reaction to the extreme systemic violence exercised on populations by the neoliberal market over the two hundred years of the capitalist project. The violent flashpoints associated with maintaining market share, debt collection, or taxing weaker drug dealers have become more frequent as the marketplace has been democratised, economic freedom prioritised, and ruthless competition augmented and normalised (see Treadwell et al., 2018).

As Hall, Winlow, and Ancrum showed in *Criminal Identities* (2008) and Hobbs (2013) showed in *Lush Life*, the pursuit of profit and its maximisation alongside the manipulation of markets and the acquisition of wealth is now the measure of both social value and occupational competency among criminals. What Hall (2012) calls 'criminal undertakers', those who are willing to do what it takes to ensure the success of business and the post-social elevation of the self, will inflict harm on others, if necessary, in order to ensure their prosperity and preserve their reputations (Daly and Hall, 2018; Treadwell and Ayres, 2014). The luxurious substances and the criminal undertakers operate together in the same socioeconomic space, as they 'perform the role of the pharmakon, threatening to poison the community at the same time as increasing its security and material prosperity and thus saving it from decline' (Hall, 2012: 218).

Conclusion

Luxurious substances are sublime objects of ideology imbued with fantasies, promising to make us healthier, prettier, more competitive, and successful in the eyes of others. Such substances enable consumers to create in their imaginations the near-perfect socially performing self, while they provide traders with the means to buy other luxurious products as they all strive for happiness, perfection, and a place in neoliberalism's sun. But in the fields of consumption and trading we can find numerous harms that range from addiction to intimidation and violence, which are selectively disavowed in public by liberalism's two political wings – by the right because making too much of them would be an impediment to business, and by the left because it would be a restriction of individual freedom. In late capitalism's consumer culture all 'forms of desire and identity are elicited so long as they are profitable' (McMillan, 2012: 104), and this principle applied in the market in substances opens up endless opportunities that can often result in exploitation, harm, and enslavement (Dean, 2016). If every desire is 'included in capitalism but never satisfied' (McMillan, 2012: 104), substances mundane and luxurious become sublime objects of ideology, functional to the maintenance of capitalism's core fantasy of freedom, progress, and perfection, yet enslaving as the post-industrial subject is recruited to a culture of obligatory enjoyment (Žižek, 2002) and an occupational life of obligatory enterprise.

Despite the injunction to excessive consumption, addiction and dependence on substances is not permissible in the harsh glare of a culture that commands the individual to be resilient and exercise choice in even the most abject circumstances. The individual should exercise the natural power of discernment and ensure that consumption is confined to the correct substances, which are tied to the internally logical demands of the capitalist market (see Hall, this volume) and the cultivation of a subjectivity that is simultaneously competitive and safe. If citizens consume luxurious substances in an attempt to feel better and address their sense of lack, they risk a variety of harms that pour more fuel on the demise of the social world that is the fundamental cause of that lack (Winlow and Hall, 2016).

In sum, luxurious substances, just like the drug-dealing entrepreneur, are Hall's (2012) pharmakon, both poison and antidote in a system that relies on dynamic tension. They are also Žižek's (2008) chocolate laxative, the palliative that deflect the subject's attention from the objective violence of capitalism and the actual problems facing its subjects as they traverse its post-social, post-political, world. Luxurious substances and their consuming and trading subjects embody the paradox of zombie capitalism, the condition of living yet not living in contemporary society (Althofer et al., 2018). Thus, luxurious substances are, as this chapter has shown, sublime objects of ideology.

Notes

1 The heroin epidemic of the 1980s filled the vacuum left by deindustrialisation, mass unemployment, political unrest, disinvestment, and poverty in Thatcherite Britain; the discarded working class youth that capitalism no longer had use for used heroin to create a 'euphoric oblivion' that blocked out the realities of living in 1980s Britain (Buchanan and Wyke, 1987) and the same is true today (see Ayres, 2017, 2019).

2 Cheap, high-strength varieties of alcohol have not only been subject to higher taxes, but they have also been removed from the shelves of many high-street shops to discourage crime, antisocial-behaviour, and street drinking (Ward, 2013).

3 Natural dietary supplements have been shown to contain banned and harmful ingredients (about 25%) and also contain more than one unapproved pharmaceutical ingredient, which are not always declared on the label (Tucker et al., 2018).

4 There is lead in 60% of lipsticks, particularly red lipsticks, with samples of lipsticks containing levels higher than USFDA guidelines of 0.1 ppm. The levels of lead varied from 0.03 to 0.65 parts per million (CSC, 2007).

5 From the early trade in opium to more contemporary ecstasy tablets and cocaine bricks stamped with legitimate luxury brands like Louis Vuitton, Ralph Lauren, Bugatti, and Gucci, drugs piggy-back on corporate designer brands as entrepreneurial suppliers' brand and market their products with symbols of wealth and luxury (Lopez, 2014; Payne, 2017; Ruggiero and South, 1995). Corporate designer and luxurious brands also piggy-back on illicit drugs (e.g. Calvin Klein's heroin chic) as transgression is packaged up, commodified, and sold back to us as 'cool' individualism (Hall et al., 2008).

References

Althofer, J. and Musgrove, B. (2018) 'A Ghost in Daylight': Drugs and the Horror of Modernity. *Palgrave Communications*, 4, 112: 1–11.

Appadurai, A. (1986) *The Social Life of Things*, Cambridge: Cambridge University Press.

Ayres, T.C. (2017, Winter) Drugs, Leisure, Consumption and Harm. *BSC Newsletter*, 20–26.

Ayres, T.C. (2019) Substance Use in the Night-Time Economy: Deviant Leisure? In O. Smith and T. Raymen (eds.) *Deviant Leisure and Social Harm*, London: Policy Press.

Ayres, T.C. and Treadwell, J. (2012) Bars, Drugs and Football Thugs: Cocaine Use Amongst English Football Firms. *Criminology and Criminal Justice*, 12, 1: 83–100.

Baudrillard, J. (1993) *Symbolic Exchange and Death*, London: Sage.

Baudrillard, J. (1994) *Simulcra and Simulation*, Michigan: University of Michigan Press.

Baudrillard, J. (1998) *Consumer Society: Myths and Structures*, London: Sage.

Bauman, Z. (1991) *Imitations of Postmodernity*, London: Routledge.

Bauman, Z. (2000) *Liquid Modernity*, Cambridge: Polity Press.

Bauman, Z. (2001) *The Individualized Society*, Cambridge: Polity Press.

Bauman, Z. (2007) *Consuming Life*, Cambridge: Polity Press.

Bendell, J. and Kleanthous, A. (2007) *Deeper Luxury*, Surrey: WWF-UK.

Bjerg, O. (2008) Drug Addiction to Capitalism: Too Close to the Body. *Body and Society*, 14, 2: 1–22.

Brisman, A. and South, N. (2016) Consumer Technologies, Crime and Environmental Implications. In M.R. McGuire and T.J. Holt (eds.) *The Routledge Handbook of Technology, Crime and Justice*, London: Routledge.

Bröckling, U. (2015) *The Entrepreneurial Self: Fabricating a New Type of Subject*, London: Sage.

Buchanan, J. and Wyke, G. (1987) Drug Abuse, Probation Practice and the Specialist Worker. *Probation Journal*, 34, 4: 123–26.

Burroughs, W. (1972) *Junkie*, Paris: Pierre-Belfond.

Campaign for Safe Cosmetics (CSC) (2007) *A Poison Kiss*, San Francisco: CSC.

Coomber, R. and Moyles, L. (2018) The Changing Shape of Street-Level Heroin and Crack Supply in England. *British Journal of Criminology*, 58, 6: 1323–42.

Daly, M. and Hall, A. (2018, March 20) Cocaine Is the Hidden Mixer in Newcastle's Economy. *Vice*. Available at: https://www.vice.com/en_uk/article/wj7qzb/cocaine-is-the-hidden-mixer-in-newcastles-economy

Dean, J. (2009) *Democracy and Other Neoliberal Fantasies*, Durham: Duke University Press.

Dean, J. (2016) Why Žižek for Political Theory? *International Journal of Žižek Studies*, 1, 1: 1–35.

Douglas, M. (1969) *Purity and Danger*, London: Routledge.

EFSA Panel et al. (2018) Scientific Opinion on the Safety of Green Tea Catechins. *EFSA Journal*, 16, 4: 1–89.

Euromonitor International (2018) *World Market for Luxury Goods*, London: EI.

Evans-Brown, M., McVeigh, J., Perkins, C. and Bellis, M.A. (2012) *Human Enhancement Drugs: The Emerging Challenges to Public Health*, Liverpool: Northwest Public Health Observatory.

Featherstone, M. (1982) The Body in Consumer Culture. *Theory, Culture and Society*, 1, 2: 18–33.

Featherstone, M. (2016) Luxus. *Cultural Politics*, 12, 1: 66–82.

Fisher, M. (2009) *Capitalist Realism*, Ropley: Zero-Books.

Hall, A. (2019) Lifestyle Drugs and Late Capitalism: A Topography of Harm. In O. Smith and T. Raymen (eds.) *Deviant Leisure and Social Harm*, London: Policy Press.

Hall, A. and Antonopoulos, G.A. (2016) *Fake Meds Online*, Basingstoke: Palgrave.

Hall, S. (1997) Visceral Cultures and Criminal Practices. *Theoretical Criminology*, 1, 4: 453–78.

Hall, S. (2012) *Theorizing Crime and Deviance*, London: Sage.

Hall, S. and Winlow, S. (2015) *Revitalizing Criminological Theory*, London: Routledge.

Hall, S. and Winlow, S. (2019) Ultra-Realism. In W. Dekeseredy and M. Dragiewicz (eds.) *Routledge Handbook of Critical Criminology*, London: Routledge.

Hall, S., Winlow, S. and Ancrum, C. (2008) *Criminal Identities and Consumer Culture: Crime, Exclusion and the New Culture of Narcissism*, Cullompton: Willan.

Hayward, K. (2004) *City Limits: Crime, Consumer Culture and the Urban Experience*, London: GlassHouse Press.

Hayward, K. and Smith, O. (2017) Crime and Consumer Culture. In A. Liebling, S. Marunna and L. McAra (eds.) *Oxford Handbook of Criminology*, Oxford: Oxford University Press.

Hearn, A. (2008) Meat, Mask, Burden: Probing the Contours of the Branded Self. *Journal of Consumer Culture*, 8: 197–217.

Hobbs, D. (1995) *Bad Business*, Oxford: Oxford University Press.

Hobbs, D. (2013) *Lush Life*, Oxford: Oxford University Press.

Horkheimer, M. and Adorno, T.W. (2002) *Dialectic of Enlightenment*, Stanford, CA: Stanford University Press.

Horsley, M. (2015) *The Dark Side of Prosperity: Late Capitalism's Culture of Indebtedness*, Farnham: Ashgate.

Hudders, L., De Backer, C., Fisher, M. and Vyncke, P. (2014) The Rival Wears Prada: Luxury Consumption as a Female Competition Strategy. *Evolutionary Psychology*, 12, 3: 570–87.

Huen, E. (2017, January 31) World's Most Expensive Anti-Aging Serum Costs $1,800 Per Ounce. *Forbes*. Available at: https://www.forbes.com/sites/eustaciahuen/2017/01/31/worlds-most-expensive-anti-aging-serum-costs-1800-per-ounce/#6724b5eb1bc5

Jenkins, D., Spence, J.D., Giovannucci, E.L., Kim, Y., Josse, R., Vieth, R., et al. (2018) Supplemental Vitamins and Minerals for CVD Prevention and Treatment. *Journal of the American Journal of Cardiology*, 71, 22: 2570–84.

Kuldova, T. (2018) The "Ethical Sell" in the Indian Luxury Fashion Business. In edited by V. Pouillard and R. Blaczczyk (eds.) *European Fashion: The Creation of a Global Industry*, Manchester: Manchester University Press, 263–282.

Lasch, C. (1979) *The Culture of Narcissism*, New York: W.W. Norton and Company.

Lasch, C. (1985) *The Minimal Self: Psychic Survival in Troubled Times*, New York: W.W. Norton and Company.

Lopez, J. (2014, October 4) Creative and Stylish: Branded Cocaine Seized in Costa Rica. *The Costa Rica Star*. Available at: https://news.co.cr/creative-and-stylish-branded-cocaine-seized-in-costa-rica/34120/

Martin, J. (2014, August 12) 'Fair Trade' Cocaine and 'Conflict-Free' Opium: The Future of Online Drug Marketing. *The Conversation*. Available at: https://theconversation.com/fair-trade-cocaine-and-conflict-free-opium-the-future-of-online-drug-marketing-30127

McMillan, C. (2012) *Žižek and Communist Strategy*, Edinburgh: Edinburgh University Press.

Moore, B. (2011) *Style Over Substance*, Manchester: Ethical Consumer.

NHS (2011) *Supplements: Who Needs Them?* London: NHS Choices.

Payne, M. (2017, March 23) Police Find More than a Ton of 'Lionel Messi'-Branded Cocaine in a Shipment of Giant Squid. *The Washington Post*. Available at: https://www.

washingtonpost.com/news/early-lead/wp/2017/03/23/police-find-more-than-a-ton-of-lionel-messi-branded-cocaine-in-a-shipment-of-giant-squid/

Pope, H.G., Wood, R.I., Rool, A., Nyberg, F., Bowers, L. and Bhasin, S. (2014) Adverse Health Consequences of Performance-Enhancing Drugs: An Endocrine Society Scientific Statement. *Endocrine Reviews*, 35, 3: 341–75.

Preble, E. and Casey, J. (1969) Taking Care of Business. *International Journal of Addiction*, 4: 1–24.

Romanowski, P. and Schueller, R. (2013) *It's OK to Have Lead in Your Lipstick*, Chicago: Brains.

Ruggiero, V. and South, N. (1995) *Eurodrugs*, London: UCL Press.

Singer, M. and Baer, H. (2009) *Killer Commodities: Public Health and the Corporate Production of Harm*, Lanham: AltaMira Press.

Smith, O. (2014) *Contemporary Adulthood and the Night Time Economy*, Basingstoke: Palgrave.

Taylor, S., Buchanan, J. and Ayres, T.C. (2016) Prohibition, Privilege and the Drug Apartheid. *Criminology and Criminal Justice*, 16, 4: 452–69.

Treadwell, J., Ancrum, C. and Kelly, C. (2018) Taxing Times: Inter-Criminal Victimisation and Drug Robbery Amongst the English Professional Criminal Milieu. *Deviant Behavior*, online first: 1–13.

Treadwell, J. and Ayres, T.C. (2014) Talking Prada and Powder: Cocaine Use and Supply Among the Football Hooligan Firm. In J. Treadwell and M. Hopkins (eds.) *Football Hooliganism, Crime and Crowd Control: Contemporary Themes in Relation to Research and Theory*, Basingstoke: Palgrave Macmillan.

Tucker, J., Fischer, T., Upjohn, L., Mazzera, D. and Kumar, M. (2018) Unapproved Pharmaceutical Ingredients Included in Dietary Supplements Associated with US Food and Drug Administration Warnings. *JAMA Open Network*, 1, 6: 1–11.

Veblen, T. (1969) *Theory of the Leisure Class*, London: Penguin Books.

Ward, V. (2013, April 4) Shop Ban on High-Strength Booze Cuts Street Drinking Crime by 50%. *The Telegraph*. Available at: https://www.telegraph.co.uk/finance/newsbysector/retailandconsumer/9971418/Shop-ban-on-high-strength-booze-cuts-street-drinking-crime-by-50.html

Winlow, S. and Hall, S. (2006) *Violent Night: Youth Identities and Violence in the Night-Time Economy*, Oxford: Berg.

Winlow, S. and Hall, S. (2016) Criminology and Consumerism. In P. Carlen (ed.) *Criminologias Alternativas*, Buenos Aries: IEA.

Winston, A. (2016, February 8) Luxury Brands Can No Longer Ignore Sustainability. *Harvard Business Review*. Available at: https://hbr.org/2016/02/luxury-brands-can-no-longer-ignore-sustainability.

Žižek, S. (1989) *Sublime Object of Ideology*, London: Verso.

Žižek, S. (1997) *Plague of Fantasies*, London: Verso.

Žižek, S. (1999, August 1) The Superego and the Act. *Zizek.UK*. Available at: https://zizek.uk/the-superego-and-the-act/

Žižek, S. (2002) *Welcome to the Desert of the Real*, London: Verso.

Žižek, S. (2006) *The Parallax View*, Cambridge: MIT Press.

Žižek, S. (2008) *Violence*, New York: Picador.

Žižek, S. (2014) The Impasses of Consumerism. In teNeus (ed.) *Prix Pictet 05: Consumption*, London: teNeus.

Žižek, S. (2017) The Varieties of Surplus. *Problemi International*, 1, 1: 7–32.

7 Gambling and harm in 24/7 capitalism

Reflections from the post-disciplinary present

Thomas Raymen and Oliver Smith

Introduction

The past decade has witnessed extraordinary growth in the gambling industry. While this has certainly been a global phenomenon, it has been particularly noticeable in the UK. The Gross Gambling Yield (GGY) – the total amount of money lost by UK gamblers – rose to £14.4bn in the 2017–18 financial year, an increase of 4.5% on the previous twelve months with consecutive year-on-year growth tracing back to 2011, aided by the democratisation of all-purpose, always-online, mobile computing technologies. Smartphones, laptops, tablets, and the like have transformed the way we live, work, socialise, travel, and, for the purposes of this chapter, gamble. Remote online gambling is now far and away the largest single aspect of the UK gambling industry (40% of overall GGY) with punters losing a total of £5.4bn during the 2017–18 financial year (Gambling Commission, 2018a). Online casinos constitute 70% of all casino gambling after surpassing the land-based portion of the sector more than a decade ago whilst online sports-betting also surpassed its physical counterpart in 2016–2017 and now accounts for 56% of all sports-betting (Gambling Commission, 2018b). Over the last 8 years, the online casino sector has grown by 203%, compared with 46% growth in their land-based counterpart while online sports-betting and bingo have grown by 211% and 278% respectively, compared with declines of 15% and 25% in their land-based format over the same time period. In the last twelve months alone, online gambling has grown by 11%, with 40% of its GGY generated through smartphone and tablet apps, a statistic forecast to rise to 50% by 2020 (Gambling Commission, 2018b).

Whilst this kind of rapid growth is genuinely staggering, especially within a wider economic form that can barely maintain 1.5%, it's also largely predicated upon the slow and pervasive spread of gambling-related familial, psychological, and financial harms. What's more, technological innovation has had a far great impact than simply expanding participation and industry profit, working in concert with post-industrialism's '24/7 capitalism' to fundamentally alter the *nature* of gambling practice in general and problem gambling in particular. Much contemporary gambling, as this chapter and other recent studies show (see, for example, Albarran-Torres, 2018; Raymen and Smith, 2017), has shifted away from the spatially fixed, fundamentally *separate* practice of extreme expenditure and high drama described by the seminal gambling texts of previous decades (Caillois, 1958; Geertz, 1973; Goffman, 1967). Gambling today is a far more spatially flexible practice embedded into daily life and typified by the kind of low stakes that encourage repeated, accelerative play within an affective state characterised by a sedentary, catatonic 'depressive hedonia' (Fisher, 2009). The growth of information technology has substantially transformed gambling, allowing its harms to bleed outwards from the fixed geography of casinos and bookmakers into day-to-day life, becoming far more pervasive and insidious even as gamblers, regulators, and industry insiders struggle to keep pace.

With a few notable exceptions (see Albarran-Torres, 2018; Raymen, 2019; Raymen and Smith, 2017), social-scientific conceptualisations also lag behind, cleaving to theoretical approaches conceived in a pre-digital age that arguably fail to capture the distributed, flexibilised realities of gambling policy and practice. In this context, this chapter begins at the nexus of mobile computing and late capitalism, locating the altered nature of contemporary gambling within a shift from the 'disciplinary societies' of the last century to the 'post-disciplinary societies' of 24/7 consumer capitalism. It then moves on to explore how the gambling industry has capitalised upon this sociostructural transformation, opening the way to a far more subtle but no less profitable form of 'problem gambling' that often flies under the radar of prevailing risk assessment tools. The chapter concludes with some reflections on current policy and legislative implications before suggesting that we require new and original accounts of individual subjectivity in order to truly grasp the impact of technological change on contemporary gambling.

A note on our participants

The data presented in this chapter comes from an ethnographic research project designed to explore the ins and outs of male sports-betting in the context of consumer capitalism, something we have elsewhere described as 'lifestyle gambling' (Raymen, 2019; Raymen and Smith, 2017), conducted over the course of 18 months and beginning in the winter of 2015. With the aid of successive generations of cheaper and more accessible mobile technologies the gambling industry, including sports betting, has changed markedly over the last decade or so, breaking free of its established spatial moorings to create a thoroughly socialised and identity-oriented culture of sports-betting by pushing its way further into the associated spheres of the masculine weekend leisure experience. All of the men we observed and interviewed (n=28) were fully embedded in such cultures and practices centred on a passionate commitment to football fandom. While far from being middle-class or particularly wealthy, these were all socially-included men with families, relationships, jobs, and mortgages – on the surface just normal, happy-go-lucky twenty- and thirty-somethings whose free time happened to include a bit of 'lifestyle gambling' of a kind not even remotely close to the vice-laden, degenerative stereotype of decades past.

Over time, however, as our research shifted out of its initial, observational disposition into more in-depth, one-on-one interviews, many of our participants began to reveal that there was rather more to their gambling, that the 'lifestyle' aspect actually accounted for a relatively small proportion of their expenditure. Whilst sports-betting was more or less confined to weekends along with the occasional midweek fixture, the secondary costs of beer, recreational drugs, and travel quickly became prohibitive, encouraging a shift into more mundane and isolated forms of gambling in online spaces. To a greater or lesser degree, most of our participants confessed to gambling almost every day, using a variety of gambling mediums including online poker, mobile casino apps, and/or 'gamble-play' stock-trading apps and games (Albarran-Torres, 2018). Moreover, these gambling practices took place in almost every imaginable time and location: at work, on the commute, lying in bed, on the toilet, at home, while looking after children, or during quiet evenings once their children and/or partner had gone to bed.

In every pocket and sphere of their daily lives, dispersed within and around familial commitments, professional responsibilities, and personal relationships was a low-stakes *perpetuity of gambling* comprised of momentary, fleeting betting instances of many different forms. While most of these individuals were only classified as 'moderate risk' gamblers on the Problem Gambling Severity Index (PGSI) – a standardised self-assessment measure of at-risk gambling – the combination of low stakes and immediate access had allowed them to develop pervasive and repetitive gambling behaviours that were well on their way to generating serious financial, psychological, and familial problems far in excess of what we might expect for 'moderate risk' gamblers.

What's more, most of our participants were not losing staggering sums of money in grand-gesture bets, just a slow but steady drip-feed of smaller amounts that had nonetheless become problematic as it had deepened their overdrafts, drained their credit cards, and added to their phone bills, accelerating their exposure to the culture of indebtedness that fuels the current model of late capitalism (see Horsley, 2015). Nevertheless, they kept returning to the marketplace on their commute, during work meetings and whilst half-watching their kids, not in pursuit of 'excitement', 'action', or even profit, but as Kenny, one of our participants, put it, 'just keep playing and pass the time. When you're gambling, you're never bored. It looks boring. But the time passes in a really pleasant way'. In an accelerated timeframe, the consequences of this 'not being bored' include strained personal relationships, family breakdown, and the proliferation of mental health issues such as alcohol abuse, depression, and anxiety and the use of prescription medications to stave off their symptoms. It is these harms, along with their connections to the cyclical nature of online gambling, that provide us with the focal point of this chapter as we turn our attention to the contextual mechanics of the gambling industry within the post-disciplinary society of 24/7 consumer capitalism.

Gambling in a post-disciplinary society

A great deal of the existing social-scientific research positions gambling as a distinct sphere of activity separate from everyday life, often describing it as '*a ritual which is strictly demarcated from the everyday world around it* and within which chance is deliberately courted as a mechanism which governs a redistribution of wealth among players as well as a commercial interest' (Reith, 1999b: 1; emphasis added). For the most part, gambling spaces are understood as separate 'magic circles' of play with different rules, rhythms, norms, and values (Barthelme and Barthelme, 1999; Huizinga, 1949). Gamblers are perceived as taking on temporary gambling identities and personas of action within these spaces, exciting substitute identities detached from otherwise humdrum lives (Caillois, 1958; Geertz, 1973; Goffman, 1967) in which gambling provides a 'temporal break', an escape from the emotional rhythms of everyday life (Cosgrave, 2006; Reith, 1999a, 1999b).

Most of these ideas rest on an explicitly 'disciplinary' understanding of society drawn from the work of Michel Foucault (1995), placing a great deal of emphasis on his assertion that day-to-day life is a more-or-less ordered and regimented affair structured by a series of closed institutions that shape social interaction through the meticulous segmentation of time and space. In this conceptualisation, individual life passes from the family, to school, to the military or the workplace constrained by the 'three great methods' of disciplinary power – established rhythms, behavioural routines, and cycles of repetition – and the resultant systems of subtle manipulation that tie its subjects into pervasive systems of 'control'. What much of the existing scholarship does, in other words, is to adopt a carceral analogy that positions enjoyment-pursuant behaviours like gambling as challenges to the prevailing order's capacity to manage the 'diffuse circulation' of warm bodies. The amassed organs of discipline and control, the story goes, are fundamentally opposed to people enjoying themselves, therefore their attempts to do so can be seen as 'magic circles' of play, expressions of autonomy, and freedom and the escape from repression.

Given the temporal origins of such work, it should perhaps come as no surprise that it has never quite captured the realities of the early twenty-first century, particularly the erosion of the system's capacity for discipline by the emergence of a technologically-advanced 24/7 capitalism in which the various spheres of public and private life have almost entirely collapsed in on one another. The way we live today is, according to Mark Fisher (2009: 23) more accurately characterised as a 'post-disciplinary society' in which 'the old segmentation of time is breaking down' as we experience a raft of competing pressures that lead us, for example, to work beyond contracted hours, checking emails from home in the middle of the night or as soon as we wake up (Cederström and Fleming, 2012; Crary, 2013). At the same time, the personal has bled into our working lives, many of us working in front of computers that allow us to divide our attention between email, social media, paperwork, music, YouTube, online banking, and/or retail purchases.

Instead of going to lunch or sitting down for a family meal, many of us eat at our desks or in front of the television. The idea of a family meal scheduled at the same time each night sounds entirely antiquated when faced with the seductive allure of the latest addition to Netflix. Laptops, smartphones, and tablets, as Nicholas Carr (2010) has remarked, are 'technologies of distraction', providing much of the material basis for a society that does everything at once rather than focusing upon one task at a time – the antithesis of the carefully segmented, concentrational logic of the Foucauldian disciplinary system. Even time spent on the toilet is not exclusively dedicated to performing bodily functions, a task often accomplished whist also scrolling social media, texting, playing Candy Crush, or, for our participants, gambling. Many of our interviewees joked with candour that they would rather not think about the amount of money they had lost gambling 'on the shitter'.

Of course, we should be careful not to mistake technology for the *cause* of this shift. As Marx pointed out in the *Grundrisse* (1993), capital refuses to abide any material limits to its incessant accumulation and further extraction of surplus value. The disciplinary segmentation of the social – while once functional for industrial capitalism – has since become a barrier for a post-industrial capitalism which requires the diffusion of consumption throughout time and space. The spatial and temporal limits of what last century's theorists described as a 'disciplinary society' were simply barriers to accumulation that have now been fully and completely circumvented by the advance of information technology and the emergence of the ubiquitous 24/7 capitalism that has rapidly penetrated almost every aspect of our daily lives (see Crary, 2013). What is perhaps even more significant, however, is that such technologies do not only permit us to work *or* consume *or* view marketing materials *or* communicate with friends but instead allow and encourage us to do *all of these things simultaneously*, all of the time. The emergence of this post-disciplinary digital culture has undeniably filtered down into the daily lives of our participants, allowing them to weave gambling into everyday rhythms and routines, at mundane times and during otherwise boring tasks. As Darren, an office worker, and Nick, a tradesman, describe:

DARREN: You can set your watch by my gambling during the week to be fair. I have an hour's commute there and back [to work] on the train every day. I get on, find my seat, scroll through Facebook . . . Instagram, check out the football. . . . That takes about 10–15 minutes. Then I tend to jump on [mobile casino app] and play a bit of roulette on there. I can get through God knows how many spins on there. It's so fast. That's what I tend to play as well. It's just easy bit of play innit? Don't have to think about it too much, which is why I like it. Once I'm on there, I kind of just zonk out a bit. . . . Depending on if I have to do work emails or whatever I tend to do the same thing on the way home. I used to sometimes do a little at work as well . . . I still do some days, if I'm in a boring meeting or something. . . . Problem with that though is that you get on your phone and start playing [gambling apps] and you look up and an hour has gone by. Then you have to do work when you get home.

NICK: [I gamble] everywhere mate. I don't have a routine for it really. But it's definitely more days than not. Sometimes when [colleague] picks me up in the van in the morning to go do a job. He's not very chatty in the early morning so I do it quite a bit then. During a lunch break maybe. Sitting on the bog [toilet]. If I'm waiting for a bus or a train or something, or if there's nothing decent on telly and it's just kind of on in the background. Me and the missus tend to just sit on our phones and ignore each other in the evening. Sometimes

> I do it in bed if I can't sleep. Just play slots or whatever. It's quite relaxing. So yeah. . . . Just kind of flit in and out of it really. Two or three times a day. Mostly casino slots and games like that. Play for 20 minutes, half hour if I'm bored. Sometimes longer. It depends.

Darren's and Nick's words are certainly illustrative of the kind of post-disciplinary capitalism in which the previously distinct space-times of work, domesticity, and leisure collapse in on one another. Their approach to gambling, however, also raises a number of interesting questions that go beyond the mere fact of its spatial flexibilisation, reflecting changing patterns in the *nature* of gambling and the affective states common to the digitalised world of late capitalism. What Darren and Nick describe is representative of the entire sample and also points us towards what Schüll (2012) has termed 'the rise of repeat play', an immensely profitable form of gambling typified by low-stakes, rotational game forms.

'Too wired to concentrate'

Schüll's (2012) study of machine gambling in Las Vegas observed a marked shift in the industry's focus away from high-rolling table gamblers who would stake large sums and lose quickly towards local players who sought a steadier, low-stakes repeat play oriented around video poker and slot machines. These machines began popping up around the city in the 1980s and 1990s, occupying bars, diners, supermarkets, and petrol stations, perhaps making it one of the earlier examples of post-disciplinary capitalism, expanding opportunities for accumulation by eroding the boundaries between different spheres of life. Interviewing machine gambling addicts, Schüll's research revealed a kind of repetitive, 'in the zone' mentality similar to Borrell's (2008) description of a state of 'suspended animation'.

When in this 'zone', repeat gambling takes on an affective dimension characterised by a trance, a numb, mindless synergetic fusion between self and machine that is experienced as an almost catatonic state of mentally undemanding mechanical repetition. When using these machines, gamblers appeared less concerned with winning or losing and more with extending the experience, of switching off and tuning out for as long as possible (Raymen and Smith, 2017; Reith, 1999b). These findings are reflected in our own, both in Darren's description of 'zonking out' and Nick's assertion that he finds mobile casino slots relaxing. Countless other participants used similar language in their paradoxical characterisations of their gambling in almost therapeutic terms, variously describing it as 'monging', 'chilling', or 'switching off', despite its damaging overall effects on their finances and mental health issues:

DAVE: It's just something easy to do. . . . That's why I'm not big on like live poker tournaments or anything because it takes too much brain power. . . . I'm more into slots or roulette. Just easy and mindless. Something to keep you occupied. It's like, you ever on YouTube or summin' and you just kind of get into those wormholes where you just watch one pointless video after another and you're not really interested, you just kind of watch and mong out and let it go onto the next video? It's a bit like that.

GLENN: I spend a shit-load of time on things like casino slot games and stuff. It's just like a game really, to switch off. That's the thing. You keep talking of it as *gambling*. But like, I *know* it is gambling, yeah? But I don't think of it in the same way as say when I've been to an actual casino and played blackjack or roulette. It's more just a game. I'm not living and dying on each spin. It's more like how I feel when I play Candy Crush. Just easy. Tap. Tap. Swipe.

MARK: In the week I just play those kinds of like mind-numbing games. I don't mind betting on the football and stuff when you're out with the lads and that because that's part of the fun. . . . But in the week like on the way home from work or something? Nah. I'm stressed out enough as it is with work and dealing with parents and that . . . if I do bet, it's more like games of chance where you don't have to think.

The gamblers of the early twenty-first century, in other words, appear to desire an affective state of borderline-catatonia that is a far cry from the conceptions of high drama, which, through the likes of Caillois (1958), Geertz (1973), and Goffman (1967) continue to dominate the gambling literature. With their gaze fixed firmly on roulette wheels, card tables, and cockfighting circles, these pre-digital accounts depict gambling as a symbolically meaningful practice through which people seek action, prestige, and the elevated status of *dramatis personae*. Many of our participants, in contrast, carried an expressed distaste for this kind of emotionally and functionally demanding gambling activity with a desire to avoid things like poker tournaments because it would require too much of them.

What is particularly striking about the earlier comments is how contemporary gambling has converged with and responded to broader trends in digital behaviour, establishing and building upon significant affective similarities with the experience derived from other non-gambling activities such as scrolling through social media or the simplicity of 'hyper-casual' games such as Candy Crush, Fire Balls 3D, or Rolly Vortex. Indeed, it is notable that upon entering the game of Candy Crush, the user is confronted with messages such as 'Chill and Unwind', ''Relax . . . and play Candy', 'Swipe the Stress Away', and 'Swipe. Match. Relax'. Such games are designed to induce a state of 'zoned out' numbness mimicked, arguably, by forms of repeat-play mobile gambling as a large and rapidly growing segment of the wider gambling industry. This lends credence to Albarran-Torres' (2018) recent theorisations of contemporary gambling not as a form of risk-laden profit-seeking organised around the sums of money won and lost, but as a form of 'gamble-play' geared toward achieving a distinct shift in the player's affective state.

The emergence of this form of intuitive, undemanding repeat-play, as it has filtered outwards through cyberspace, has allowed the gambling industry to cut itself free from fixed spatial moorings, converging with the wider technological subjectivities generated by a post-disciplinary consumer capitalism.

especially the affective state that Mark Fisher (2009) described as 'depressive hedonia'. Whilst depression, as Fisher notes, is usually associated with a state of 'anhedonia' – an inability to feel pleasure in anything – 'depressive hedonia' denotes an 'inability to do anything *except* pursue pleasure' (Fisher, 2009: 22) at any given moment, irrespective of activity or location. What he describes, in other words, is an edgy and agitated condition, a 'too wired to concentrate' state of affective readiness (Fisher, 2009: 24) in which we compulsively check and re-check mobile phones, repetitively scroll social media, play endless games of Candy Crush or, for our participants, gamble small stakes of little computerised light shows.

With the proliferation of smartphones and tablet devices as ever-present extensions of our physical selves, the gambling industry in the UK and further afield has been able to circumvent many of the challenges presented by earlier forms of machine gambling, no longer having to sufficiently 'hook' the player to keep them in situ. When the name of the game was to keep the player sat in a chair for hours on end, 'time on device' (Cummings, 1997) was always limited; sooner or later they would have to move to eat or relieve themselves (see Schüll, 2012), whereas modern forms of mobile gambling have pretty much neutralised or circumvented the otherwise obstructive demands of bodily functions and competing commitments. Mimicking the appearance and functionality of social media and instant messaging services, mobile gambling allows players to flit in and out, adopting an intermittent, spasmodic form of repeat-play dedicated to bridging interstitial moments of boredom and idleness within their daily routines:

NOSEY: [Mobile gambling] is just something to do to kill the time. That's the main thing. A bit like checking social media and that. Just something to do so you're not bored if you're waiting for someone, or sitting on a bus, or just have fuck all to do.

MARC: Boredom mainly. I get bored quite easily to be honest so I need to always be doing something. That's why I'm always on my phone. Can't be just sitting there doing nothing.

JORDY: I reckon most people would say boredom [when asked about gambling motivation]. Play a few games of something. Kills time dunnit? Kills too much time sometimes! Can't tell you the amount of times I've been sitting somewhere needing to leave for something in half hour or whatever, play a few spins, go on Facebook or whatever, or even just play a normal game on my phone like Candy Crush and before I know it I'm rushing out the door 'cos I'm late.

What was most notable across all of our participants, contrary to Banks' (2013) edgework-inspired analysis of 'advantage play' gambling, the negative motivation to avoid boredom was not accompanied by a *positive* motivation to *pursue* excitement, entertainment, or financial profit. In its place was the act of 'killing time', of preserving a perpetual state of low-level stimulation consistent with

Svendson's (2005) description of boredom as a 'tame longing without any particular object', Schüll's (2012) 'zoned out' affective state, and Fisher's (2009) depressive hedonia. In the late-modern world of endless, rotating 24/7 consumption the highest premium is placed upon activity for its own sake (see Boltanski and Chiapello, 2007; Crary, 2013), on maintaining a connection to the 'communication sensation-stimulus matrix' (Fisher, 2009: 24) by always doing something, always occupying our minds and our fingers.

With the end goal of creating such a close synergy between player and machine/game that the rest of the world might simply drop away, huge amounts of research time and monetary investment, as documented by the likes of Cummings (1997) and Schüll (2012), have gone into making the gambling experience as frictionless as possible. When it comes to mobile gambling, however, the established connection between the gambler and his phone provides a fertile seedbed for exactly this kind of economically-productive synergy, allowing the industry to attach its revenue streams to existing interactive frameworks by internalising transfer and payment techniques already common to banking industry apps and the online iterations of doorstep credit vendors. Having infiltrated smartphones, laptops and tablet devices, the gambling industry—operating alongside the advertising, banking and money-lending industries—has effectively created a closed loop of gambling through the provision of everything one would need for the indefinite continuation of play. The gambler is constantly exposed to industry advertising; has access to myriad gambling apps all synced seamlessly to their bank accounts; and can source additional funds through the ability to extended overdrafts and sign up for high-interest loans with a few taps and swipes.

Nevertheless, the industry continues to seek new and increasingly immediate ways of smoothing out and removing obstacles from the gambling process. In some of our later interviews, for example, participants reported using methods of pay-by-phone billing, which add their gambling outgoings to their monthly phone bill, effectively allowing them to gamble beyond existing bank deposits. While this was a relatively recent development at the time of our research, many of our participants were already moving over to the next innovation in the shape of Apple's Touch ID payment system, which uses fingerprint recognition to immediately add funds to a user account, cutting out any additional steps and allowing gamblers to stay in the zone. In the terms used by Apple Pay Casino's (2018) website, 'the disadvantages' of other more cumbersome payment methods 'disappear with one simple tap. . . . Now just one finger is all you need for everything to be taken care of: just place your finger on your device's Touch ID and it's all done, you've deposited at your favourite mobile casino. It's that simple'.

As we have already suggested, this kind of frictionless payment and the repeat play that it fosters came at a cost for many of our participants. Almost all had experienced intermittent but nonetheless significant financial difficulties as a result of their gambling, with many extending their overdrafts to cover losses, taking out multiple credit cards (with bills often going unpaid), or taking on small, high-interest loans to cover abnormal phone bills after failing to keep track of their losses. In some cases, this had contributed to some pretty serious strains on personal relationships as the isolated and embedded nature of gambling began to undermine the surface texture of our interviewees' lives. As Danny, a twenty-nine-year-old plasterer, explained:

DANNY: I need to rein it [gambling] in a bit. That girl I've been seeing, remember her? She's left me because of it. She doesn't know that, but it is why.

TR: How do you mean?

DANNY: Well like, obviously she doesn't know I gamble. It's not the kind of thing you tell people is it? Especially when you first start going out with them. And money has been a bit difficult recently [later revealed to be over £1,000 in debt], so like I've been trying to tighten the belt a bit. But of course, we just started going out a few months ago, so she's like wanting to be fun and going and doing this and that and actually go out and do stuff. And I'm always going like 'Nah, don't feel like it' or 'Ah, I've got a job this weekend' or something like that, just to make excuses. I'm not about to tell a new girlfriend 'Oh, I can't go out because I've got load of gambling debt'. Guess she got fed up in the end and chucked it in.

Danny's story was far from unique, with numerous other participants discussing relationships which were strained or failed as a result of their attempts to mask or otherwise conceal gambling expenditure. Others found themselves in need of medical help after the stress and anxiety of mounting losses began to take its toll, manifesting as a range of physical and mental illnesses from depression and alcohol abuse through to anger management issues all with a series of professional and domestic implications. In spite of this, few of our participants, with the notable exception of Danny, ever acknowledged that their gambling might be a problem, most insisting that the obvious ramifications of funnelling money into online gambling apps did not place them within the reprobate sphere of 'gambling addicts':

DEAN: I wouldn't say I have a gambling *problem*. Not at all. Yeah, I gamble too much, but I think that's just because I'm bad with money. I spend too much money in general mate – on clothes, food, booze, whatever. And it does land me in shit sometimes, having to borrow money or miss credit card payments or whatever. But I'm not a gambling addict. Like, I don't skip off work or call in sick to spend the whole day down the bookies or sit at home and play online poker.

TOM: I still manage to pick up [daughter's name] from her after-school clubs and take her to stuff like dance and gymnastics on the weekend. I'm not like some of these fucking degenerates you see who leave their kids in the car . . . or mug 'em off to spend time in some dingy amusements arcade or some shit like that. I gamble the same. I do it quite frequently, but it's not like I'm getting worse or doing it for some adrenaline rush or something. It's just something I do. I'm not spending huge wads of money. It's small amounts. £20 or £30 quid here and there.

In a defensive act of cognitive dissonance, both Dean and Tom invoke well-known traditional identifiers of the physical, land-based iteration of gambling addiction but, unlike the machine gambling addicts of Schüll's (2012) research, they were no longer compelled to organise their lives around gambling and had instead been able to flip that relationship, *organising gambling around their lives*, thereby disavowing the compulsive nature of the practice. In this post-disciplinary age, our participants were able to take on at least some of the monetary aspects of problem gambling without fully assuming many of its standout features to the extent that what we are perhaps looking at is a spectre of debtor-addiction absent many of its outward signs. Whilst still 'problem gambling', the special flexibilisation of the industry has allowed it to take on a more subtle form; our participants still had mounting debts, relationship troubles, and increased stress and anxiety but without many of the traditional breaks or markers like spending increased amounts of time secreted away in gambling venues or chasing the initial high by gambling ever-larger sums.

Unsurprisingly, perhaps, this has a number of policy implications attached to the changing nature of gambling, particularly as it applies to the design of games, the speed of play, and the necessity of re-evaluating the domain assumptions of problem gambling metrics in order to more closely align them with the new realities of a digital consumer culture. It is to these policy implications that we now turn our attention as we round off this chapter with a with a call for more research into theoretical accounts of contemporary subjectivity that can begin to provide more rigorous accounts of the neurological relationship between the individual, mobile gambling devices and the design of mobile games that are also carefully situated within the broader socioeconomic context of late capitalism. It is suggested that emerging work in the field of continental philosophy, specifically that of transcendental materialism (Johnston, 2008, 2014; Johnston and Malabou, 2013), offers promising opportunities for social scientists by adopting elements of neuroscience and combining them with psychoanalysis and critical analyses of consumer culture.

Policy implications and looking forward

In this concluding section we want to explore the policy implications of the gambling industry's shift into an explicitly digital, always accessible mode as it overwhelms and circumvents existing regulatory frameworks and market constraints in the UK and elsewhere. The rapid expansion of the online gambling market and the industry as a whole has resulted in a significant increase in public attention with contemporary policy debates fixing on the extent and growth of TV advertising, close partnerships with professional football and, perhaps most notably, the proliferation of B2 gambling machines commonly known as Fixed Odds Betting Terminals (FOBTs). This relatively new generation of electronic slot machines has been the subject of much debate over the last few years, most of it, until recently, centred on their relatively high stakes of up to £100 for a 20-second spin of a roulette wheel or hand of poker. Innumerable mainstream media articles assert (rather than explain) their addictive nature, offering lurid stories of derailed lives and gambling-related suicides whilst policy narratives have settled on a combination of maximum stakes, the concentration of betting shops, and their overwhelming placement in locales of acute socioeconomic marginalisation.

As a result, the gambling industry has entered into a meaningful dialogue with the UK government, signing up to a legally-mandated reduction of the maximum stakes on a single betting cycle, tying it down to a relatively limited £2 to reduce the scope for large-scale expenditure. It is our contention, however, that the nature of this debate, and its specific focus upon the FOBT machines found in high street betting shops, is deeply flawed in that it tends to obscure, downplay, and draw attention away from the harmful *design* of the games *within* these machines. At the level of design and the experience of play, many of these games are remarkably similar, if not identical, to the digital casino games that are played in the more profitable realm of remote gambling on laptops, mobile phones, and tablets. Both sets of games are geared toward high-speed, rhythmic play, both seek to funnel players into a trance-like affective state but with all the attention dedicated to FOBTs, the mobile version comes in for relatively little scrutiny, despite the fact that the latter produces substantially greater revenue. In the year to April 2018, UK gamblers lost more money on mobile casino slots *alone* (£2bn) than they did on FOBTs, while the total yield of the online casino sector exceeded the productivity of FOBTs by nearly £1bn (Gambling Commission, 2018c).

If we take the sector as a whole, we argue, it becomes clear that the true locus of harm and addiction is less a problem of specific hardware and more a common feature of distributed software. With such close attention to FOBTs, we are well on our way to implicitly suggesting and perhaps even tacitly accepting that the problem lies *within the physical object of the machine itself*, rather than the *design of the games* within the machine. The betting terminal, along with the bookmaker's shop, is falsely presented as containing something dark, mysterious, and addictive within its physical materiality that is alleged to be qualitatively distinct from the same games that are played on mobile, tablet, and laptop devices. This condemnation of the FOBT can be viewed in similar terms to the late-modern emergence of the term *problem gambler*, which Reith (2007) argues was actually beneficial to the gambling industry. While all forms of recreational gambling in western societies were traditionally seen as a moral vice, the liberalisation of the industry paradoxically coincided with the emergence of the problem gambler as a distinct type: an individually-flawed consumer that was different from and separate to the normal, safe, and morally acceptable gambling forms.

The idea of a problem gambler, in other words, has been broadly useful for the industry, reducing its problems down to individual pathologies rather than focusing attention upon the problems of embedded within the industry itself. With regards to FOBTs, we might even argue that as the bulk of gambling profits move away from spatially-fixed gambling venues and towards a post-disciplinary remote sector, the industry has all but submitted to the scapegoating the FOBTs in order to distinguish it from supposedly safe forms of remote gambling on devices that constitute a growing majority of the gambling industry's overall profit. In fact, the fixed odds betting terminal, despite its relative youth, is already a relic of a bygone age, soon to be rendered obsolete by digital capitalism's accelerated pace of change. The same games, producing the same affective states now exist without the geographical footprint of the traditional betting shop, cut loose from any kind of spatial mooring and free to work their way deeper into everyday life.

What's more, focusing on the maximum stake arguably skips over the problematic nature of the games themselves, steering critical discussion around their design in favour of another interminable debate about consumer choice. It's not the touchscreen or the ability to bet one amount of money or another that makes these forms of gambling so compelling that they are capable of producing an affective state of borderline catatonia; it's the software, the user interface, the tactility of the experience, the audio-visual payoff the win and the promise of the next spin. When Collins et al. (2016) set out to explore the promise of reduced betting limits on FOBTs, for example, they found that its only discernible effect was to reduce the speed at which gamblers ran out of money but it did nothing to alter gamblers' desire to continue playing, the enjoyment they received, or their level of absorption in the game. If this is the case, a policy debate that focuses on limited stakes might help mitigate financial harms, albeit at a relatively superficial level, but it's simply facing the wrong direction to fully address the interface between the player, the technology, and the game design.

It is almost as if the current policy disposition has tacitly assented to the proliferation of gambling-related harms, contenting itself with mitigating the worst excesses after-the-fact without really touching the true source of the problem. The changing face of gambling suggests that policy intervention should probably be trained upon the *design of games*, reducing the speed of play, making sure players are not borrowing money to gambling or ensuring appropriate safeguards on the deposit of funds into gambling accounts to structurally enforce 'breaks' in the rhythmic play cycle. Indeed, even the Gambling Commission's own report on the online portion of the sector, expresses much the same concern about game design:

> Our concern is that game characteristics can be used to encourage and incentivise consumers to play for longer and/or spend more. Whilst it has long been a practice to offer extra rewards for loyal consumers (such as bonus prize draws after a month of qualifying play, or tickets to sporting events for long term VIP players), *games can be designed to reward more intensive play within a gaming session.* That immediacy and incentive to increase the current gaming session spend might not allow the player to reflect on their activity as they might when playing over a longer period of time.
>
> (Gambling Commission, 2018b: 45)

This moves us onto our second point: the need to re-evaluate the ongoing legitimacy of risk assessment metrics as they apply to problem gambling such as the Problem Gambling Severity Index (PGSI). The assumptions about problem gambling underpinning the PGSI are largely at-odds with, and have pretty well failed to catch up to, the new post-disciplinary realities of the industry in its digital variant. Its most glaring shortcoming, perhaps, is the section that asks whether the individual needs to play with larger sums of money to generate the same level of excitement. This question alone is a hangover of increasingly aged studies that place gambling within a sphere of 'action', 'drama', and excitement, its problematic aspects the product of individual pathology and low-impulse control. As we have already suggested, the kind of immensely addictive gambling activity that takes place on FOBTs and mobile casino games does not appear to lead to a realm of excitement and monetary advantage but instead to kind of absorbed, time-skipping not-bored-ness.

While this is perhaps the most obvious shortcoming of the PGSI, many of its other questions also suggest a disconnect between the metric and the object of measurement, including one that asks whether others have criticised the individual's gambling behaviour, which clearly fails to acknowledge the isolated, sporadic, and easily hidden nature of gambling in the online realm. Many of our participants gambled on phones and tablets, literally and figuratively playing their cards very close to their chest, ensuring that their friends, families, and partners often had no idea that they gambled at all – let alone the capacity to drag them away from the roulette table or slot machine. In much the same vein, a question that asks gamblers how often they 'go back' another day to recover their losses singularly fails to capture the realities of post-disciplinary gambling to the extent that even the wording of the question is antiquated, suggesting a return to a specific venue. With the advent of high-speed, frictionless play, much less the capacity to add funds to an online casino at the touch of a thumbprint, many of our participants scarcely new how much they were winning or losing much less when and where. As Jordy explained:

> JORDY: I've got no idea over the course of a month how much I'm winning or losing. It's hard to keep track of really, 'cos you're not really thinking much about it. You notice you're out of money so you deposit another 20 or 30 quid. So bang that goes in. But it's amazing how quickly you forget when the last time you deposited or how much. I used to know because I would have like daily limits for myself. But now with the touch thumbprint thingy, it's just so easy to whack in another 10 or 15 quid.

Additionally, money deposited into mobile casino apps was rarely, if ever, withdrawn, further reinforcing Reith's (1999a; see also Raymen and Smith, 2017) observation that it is not the principal *object* of desire for the gamblers who contributed our research. It might be a necessary element, but it's just the price of zoning out, of not being bored for however long the individual remains within the app. Our participants were not depositing money to win more or even to recover losses, they were simply making an access payment to enjoy the experience of play and the affective states that went with it. If they accumulated enough, many suggested that they would consider 'cashing out' but acknowledged that it was unlikely they would ever extract such a sum from their app of choice because, at any given juncture, they were always coming back to play again. Repeated throughout our research, perhaps this clearest articulation of this came from Glenn:

> GLENN: I don't think of it in terms of putting 20 quid in and trying to double my money. When I deposit that money, in my head it's gone. I'm not getting it back. You're not even trying to really. You put it in so you can play the game. Obviously, if I win enough I'll think to myself 'yeah, nah I should probably take the money and run'. But then the game is over. I used to do that. I would win a bit of money and cash it out. I've done what I'm here for, I've made a bit of money. But then you want to keep playing. So you just end up putting it back in. Eventually you realise there's no point cashing it out. So I just treat that money as gone now. When I deposit it, I just accept that it's staying there.

When Glenn talks about the motivations behind re-staking his winnings or putting more money in when he has lost, he crucially does not talk of his desire to win or to 'get back to even'. Instead, he talks about the desire to *keep playing*. These are just a few examples of how the new realities of repeat-play gambling in a digital culture problematise what is now argued to be an out-of-date metric for assessing problematic gambling. Therefore, one key policy priority for the gambling industry should be the development of new problem gambling metrics that can better account for these changes in technology and their impact on the nature of gambling and problem gambling more specifically.

One final suggestion remains. If we are to grasp the true scope and impact of technology upon our subjectivities and consumer behaviours, it is imperative that the social sciences develop new and original accounts of subjectivity that can incorporate understandings of the neurological effects of technology upon our brains and adequately situate them within their wider political, economic, and social contexts. Only the most hardline social constructivists would deny that our unconscious or our material biological make-up has a significant role to play in our emotions, behaviours, and the formation of subjectivity. For any social scientist who claims to be seriously interested in the pursuit of more robust accounts of reality, turning a blind-eye to the life sciences is entirely unpardonable. Yet social scientists within the fields of criminology and beyond have either consistently scoffed at the notion of incorporating issues of biology into their study, or conveniently left this crucial and painstaking work to as-yet-unidentified others. To try and do so has been seen as committing social science's cardinal sin of 'biological reductionism', of pathologising individuals, and even risking implicit association with the dark and fascist politics of eugenics.

The life sciences have long been dismissed as too rigid and deterministic to have any explanatory power of the social world. However, developments within the life sciences – particularly neuroscience – mean that these dismissals have long been caricatures. Within the neurosciences, the notion of *neuroplasticity* has displaced the idea of the brain as a rigid, unchanging piece of physical apparatus, and has arrived at the understanding that all of our neural pathways and circuits – whether they're involved in feeling, seeing, hearing, thinking, remembering or emotions – are subject to constant change (Damasio, 2000). As the same experiences are repeated, certain synaptic links between neurons grow stronger as other synaptic links grow weaker. The most important issue is that our material-corporeal ground is subject to constant change and adjustment as it interacts with the social world. The constraints of space prevent us from going into much further detail. However, radical movements in the field of continental philosophy, such as transcendental materialism (Johnston, 2008, 2014; Johnston and Malabou, 2013), have firmly embraced such discoveries. Bringing these developments in neuroscience together with philosophy, psychoanalysis, critical understandings of political economy, and ideology, transcendental materialism theorises how 'more-than-material' subjects emerge immanently and ontogenetically out of an original material-corporeal ground (Johnston, 2008: xxiii).

Needless to say, such frameworks have substantial implications for future research in the field of gambling (not to mention a raft of other social fields transformed by the influence of technology), enabling social scientists to understand the scientific-neurological impact of electronic game design and their capacity for addiction, which can be adequately situated and critically theorised within the broader political-economic, social, and cultural context.

References

Albarran-Torres, C. (2018) *Digital Gambling: Theorising Gamble-Play-Media*, London: Routledge.

Apple Pay Casinos (2018) *The Complete Guide to ApplePay Casinos*. Available at: www.applepaycasinos.com/

Banks, J. (2013) Edging Your Bets. *Crime, Media, Culture*, 9, 2: 171–87.

Barthelme, F. and Barthelme, S. (1999) *Double Down*, New York: Harvest.

Boltanski, L. and Chiapello, E. (2007) *The New Spirit of Capitalism*, London: Verso.

Borrell, J. (2008) A Thematic Analysis Identifying Concepts of Problem Gambling Agency: With Preliminary Exploration of Discourses in Selected Industry and Research Documents. *Journal of Gambling Studies*, 22: 195–217.

Caillois, R. (1958) *Man, Play and Games*, Chicago, IL: University of Illinois Press.

Carr, N. (2010) *The Shallows: How the Internet Is Changing the Way We Think, Read and Remember*, London: Atlantic Books.

Cederström, C. and Fleming, P. (2012) *Dead Man Working*, London: Zero Books.

Collins, P., Barr, G. and Scott, L. (2016) *Report on Results of Research into the Likely Effects of Substantially Reducing the Maximum Permitted Stake of £100 per 20-Second Spin on Category B2 Electronic Gambling Machines in UK Betting Shops*. Available at: www.google.co.uk/webhp?sourceid=chrome-instant&ion=1&espv=2&ie=UTF-8#q=peter+collins+research+b2+bacta

Cosgrave, J. (2006) Adventure, Action, and Play. In J. Cosgrave (ed.) *The Sociology of Risk and Gambling Reader*, Abingdon: Routledge, 207–11.

Crary, J. (2013) *24/7: Late Capitalism and the Ends of Sleep*, London: Verso.

Cummings, L.E. (1997) A Typology of Technology Applications to Expedite Gaming Productivity. *Gaming Research and Review Journal*, 4, 1: 63–79.

Damasio, A. (2000) *The Feeling of What Happens: Body, Emotion and the Making of Consciousness*, London: Vintage Books.

Fisher, M. (2009) *Capitalist Realism*, London: Zero Books.

Foucault, M. (1995) *Discipline and Punish*, New York: Vintage Books.

Gambling Commission (2018a) *Industry Statistics: April 2015-March 2018*. Available at: www.gamblingcommission.gov.uk/PDF/survey-data/Gambling-industry-statistics.pdf

Gambling Commission (2018b) *Review of Online Gambling*. Available at: www.gamblingcommission.gov.uk/PDF/Online-review-March-2018.pdf

Gambling Commission (2018c) *Industry Statistics Machine Digest: March 2013-March 2018*. Available at: www.gamblingcommission.gov.uk/PDF/survey-data/Machines-statistics-digest.pdf

Geertz, C. (1973) *The Interpretation of Cultures*, New York: Basic Books.

Goffman, E. (1967) *Where the Action Is in Interaction Ritual*, New York: Anchor Books.

Horsley, M. (2015) *The Dark Side of Prosperity*, London: Ashgate.

Huizinga, J. (1949) *Homo Ludens*, London: Routledge and Kegan Paul.

Johnston, A. (2008) *Žižek's Ontology*, Evanston, IL. Northwestern University Press.

Johnston, A. (2014) *Adventures in Transcendental Materialism*, Edinburgh: Edinburgh University Press.

Johnston, A. and Malabou, C. (2013) *Self and Emotional Life*, New York: Columbia University Press.

Marx, K. (1993) *Grundrisse*, London: Penguin Books.

Raymen, T. (2019) Lifestyle Gambling in Accelerated Culture. In T. Raymen and O. Smith (eds.) *Deviant Leisure: Criminological Perspectives on Consumerism and Harm*. Basingstoke: Palgrave.

Raymen, T., and Smith, O. (2017) Lifestyle Gambling, Indebtedness and Anxiety. *Journal of Consumer Culture*. doi:10.1177/1469540517736559

Reith, G. (1999a) In Search of Lost Time. *Time and Society*, 8, 1: 99–117.

Reith, G. (1999b) *The Age of Chance*, Abingdon: Routledge.

Reith, G. (2007) Gambling and the Contradictions of Consumption. *Animal Behavioural Scientist*, 51, 1: 33–55.

Schüll, N. (2012) *Addiction by Design*, Princeton, NJ: Princeton University Press.

Svendson, L. (2005) *A Philosophy of Boredom*, London: Reaktion Books.

8 Toxic sovereignty

Understanding fraud as the expression of special liberty within late capitalism

Kate Tudor

Introduction

Depending on whether emphasis is placed on the social, cultural, economic, philosophical, or political features of late capitalism, our current epoch might be defined in myriad ways. While these ostensibly unrelated developments appear to have altered late-capitalist society in wide-ranging ways, both Badiou (2008) and Harvey (2007, 2008) demonstrate the way in which the various elements of the late-capitalist landscape are all underpinned by a shared vision of the 'restoration of class power' (Harvey, 2007: 31), each playing a role in its realisation. Thus, the wholesale transformation of the social, cultural, and economic landscape has served to remove barriers to accumulation existing both within the individual and society, allowing for the establishment of the 'Second Restoration' (Badiou, 2008: 26). Whilst the conditions present in late capitalism aim to facilitate the acceleration of elite acquisition, the requisite alterations to an individual's subjectivity and environment are not restricted to this group. Consequently, these changes have spilled out across the whole of late-capitalist society creating a vast array of harmful subjectivities and behaviours which are underpinned by the quest for acquisition. Numerous features of the late-capitalist landscape might be implicated in this process, but the current work remains focused on two in particular, namely the introduction of neoliberal economics and consumer capitalism and, more specifically, the importance accorded to the idea of sovereignty in these realms. The chapter will consider the harmful implications of contemporary capitalism's emphasis on individualised sovereignty and will suggest that, when combined with environments characterised by extreme economic and symbolic insecurity, barriers to harm within the individual can be eroded, paving the way for the proliferation of criminal and destructive behaviours. However, whilst these acts are sustained at the level of subjective experience by the fantasy of sovereignty, they are underpinned by its antithesis: the subject's fear of limitation. The avoidance of this reality forces the individual into the unrelenting pursuit of profit and distinction and thus, in reality, represents the severe curtailment of individual freedom by the psychic demands of the capitalist system. The article is based on a research project which sought to explore the motivations of those involved in acts of economic predation. The data was collected over a period of around eighteen months using in-depth qualitative interviews with fourteen men, all of whom had been convicted for their involvement in the perpetration of fraudulent high-yield investment (Ponzi) schemes.[1]

Neoliberalism and the revival of individual sovereignty

The introduction of neoliberal economics was the outcome of the work of a small group of historians, economists, and philosophers working in the Mont Pelerin Society who sought to revive doctrines of classical economics and philosophical liberalism as the basis for the transformation of the economic landscape of the west (Harvey, 2007). Within both of these early intellectual movements, the sovereign individual is placed at the heart of economic and philosophical considerations, with political change effected towards the promotion of their rights and responsibilities. From the perspective of classical liberal philosophers, the individual is considered to be a sovereign entity whose freedoms must be protected from excessive regulation or arbitrary interference, particularly those emanating from 'the king of the vultures' (Mill, 1964: 66), the state. The individual, therefore, must be granted maximum personal freedom and autonomy to determine his or her own fate, and the only possible basis for interference with this liberty is in the event that freedom might be used to harm the interests of another (Mill, 1964: 73–75). The definition of harm employed in this perspective, however, remains extremely narrow, with the responsibility for the avoidance of harm often falling to the individual who is expected to employ the maxim of *caveat emptor* in his or her conduct (Mill, 1964). This means that, in practice, the harmful outcomes of behaviour are often rendered secondary considerations to the primacy of ideals such as sovereignty and competition. Mill (1964) recognises, for example, the way in which the interests of the individual may be harmed in competitive struggles, but suggests that the 'general interest of mankind' (Mill, 1964: 150) is better served by the protection of competition than of individual well-being in these circumstances. So strong is the emphasis placed on the individual's right to self-determination that debates around self-governance appear to exceed notions of rights, crossing over instead into the realm of responsibility. Thus, Mill (2006: 59) questions the 'worth as a human being' (Mill, 2006: 59) of those who rely on the guidance of others. According to Mill:

> He who lets the world, or his portion of it, choose his plan of life for him, has no need of any other faculty than the ape-like one of imitation. He who chooses his plan for himself, employs all his faculties.
>
> (Mill, 2006: 59)

The work of de Sade (1990) reminds us that the exaltation of individual sovereignty and individual subjective judgement on the one hand, and rejection of external forms of control and collective notions of the good on the other, may just as easily lead humanity into the territory of evil and harm through the creation of solipsistic sybarites, as it might effect positive social change. Within philosophical liberalism the potentially harmful effects of individual autonomy are not without recognition. Mill (2006), for example, concedes that 'energy may be turned to bad uses', but suggests that 'more good may always be made of an energetic nature, than of an indolent and passive one' (Mill, 2006: 60). Consequently, he calls for the cultivation of character which provides the impetus for both good and evil and which represents the 'stuff of which heroes are made' (Mill, 2006: 60). Furthermore, Mill celebrates 'pronounced individuality', 'non-conformity', 'eccentricity' (Mill, 2006: 67) and 'intelligent deviation' (Mill, 2006: 60) on account of their ability to drive both individual and societal progress. That the assertion of sovereignty might lead to deviance, therefore, comes to be celebrated on account of its ability to drive development. Moreover, he accepts as collateral the ability of these same processes to produce harmful and criminal behaviours, suggesting that this represents a lesser evil than the curtailment of individual freedoms.

Indeed, this tendency to downplay the harmful effects of individual evils in comparison with those of the state continues to be a technique used repeatedly to champion the cause of individual sovereignty from the neoliberal perspective. 'Criminals' writes Rand (1964) 'are a minority in any age or country' but, she continues, '[p]otentially, a government is the most dangerous threat to man's rights' (Rand, 1964: 115). The minimisation of the eventuality of individual evil is also often achieved by stressing that humans naturally seek to please others. Rather than being underpinned by compassionate or altruistic motivations, Smith (1759) suggests that this desire to please is driven by self-love and self-interest (Eagleton, 2009). This conversion of self-interest into co-operation allows humanity to reduce the likelihood of harmful behaviours by restricting the range of actions available to the individual who seeks the approval of others. When operating in competitive capitalist markets, however, Smith (1759, Part 2, Section 3, Chapter 3) highlights the tension that exists between this impulse and the drive for economic success. Not only do the two often conflict, insofar as economic success might necessitate immoral behaviour, but Smith (1759) suggests that an individual may be precluded from receiving the approbation of others should he fail to achieve success, even when characterised by impeccable conduct. Consequently, he recognises the need for a degree of moral regulation in competitive economies in order to prevent the descent into unbridled competition and socially corrosive behaviours exacted within the pursuit of profit.

The atomised, sovereign individual is taken as the unit of productivity in classical economics and is given political rights and responsibilities which aim at the maximisation of his or her role in the production of wealth. Crucially, the negative liberty afforded to the sovereign individual in liberalism provides the space in which economic development can occur, but these conditions also serve to stimulate activity by withdrawing sources of support, giving responsibility to the individual for his or her performance within a wider competitive environment. By dismantling the forms of social and political regulation of the economic realm constructed during the social democratic era, neoliberals sought a return to this model of deregulated and individualised competition. Like their predecessors, neoliberals 'emphasised freedom as the ultimate goal and the individual as the ultimate entity in society' (Friedman, 2002: 5). Economic progress was to be driven by the efforts of individual 'wealth creators' (Rand, 2007) whose 'individual genius' (Friedman, 2002: 4) must be given space to develop through the implementation of deregulatory, negative liberty. The individuals operating in the space carved out by deregulation are imbued with sovereignty which allows them to determine their own conduct. Neoliberal sovereignty, however, represents a purer form of self-determination when compared with that of classical liberalism, primarily as a result of the extent to which individualism and economic logic has come to permeate all aspects of life (Davies, 2017).

Disregarding Smith's (1759) warnings about the potential dangers of excessive deregulation and individual empowerment in the context of competitive capitalism, many changes taking place across late capitalism have served to remove both direct and indirect forms of regulation which have traditionally influenced individualised conduct decisions. Exceeding formal processes of economic deregulation, wholesale social and cultural change has taken place in order to remove many of the barriers to accumulation existing within the individual and their social environment. As part of this process, informal sources of social control such as the family, the community, and the church have been systematically dismantled, discredited, and infiltrated by economic logic, undermining their ability to counter dominant competitive economic messages and to exert influence over an individual's behaviour (Currie, 1997; Messner and Rosenfeld, 2006). Consequently, contemporary capitalism has been able to 'redefin[e] social and ethical life in accordance with economic criteria and expectations' (Dean, 2009: 51). The result, Currie (1997) suggests is:

> the spread of a civilization in which the pursuit of personal economic gain becomes increasingly the dominant organizing principle of social life; a social formation in which market principles, instead of being confined to some parts of the *economy*, and appropriately buffered and restrained by other social institutions and norms, come to suffuse the whole social fabric and to undercut and overwhelm other principles that have historically sustained individuals, families and communities.
>
> (Currie, 1997: 151–152)

Alongside these changes to the nature of late-capitalist institutions, the development of post-modern thought has significantly contributed to the deregulation of the subject and the expansion of the notion of sovereignty. Through its attack on universal truth and collective identity and understandings, and its promotion of individual or minority identities and perspectives, postmodernism has dismantled the individual's relationship with the Symbolic Order. The result is that we are encouraged 'not only to accept, but even to revel in the fragmentation and the cacophony of voices through which the dilemmas of the modern world are understood' (Harvey, 2008: 116). With regard to the ethics of decision-making, late-capitalist subjects come to be characterised by an individualising logic that leads them towards solipsism. When combined with the extreme individualism of liberalism, Raymen (2019) suggests that late-capitalist subjects come to be characterised by 'ethical paralysis' whereby they are unable to engage with the conceptual apparatus required for making ethical decisions. Consequently, we have taken steps towards Kant's (1991), and by logical extension, de Sade's (1990), interpretation of self-determination whereby we are called upon 'to use one's own understanding without the guidance of another' (Kant, 1991: 54). Thus, we have come to reject the notion of any moral authority which is external to the self and whose judgement might be superior to our own individualised perspective. In determining what is right and desirable, we are left only with the subjective judgements of the sovereign individual of liberalism (Raymen, 2019). That hyper-individualist, ethical solipsism might lead us into undesirable, and potentially harmful territory is inevitable given the range of human proclivities, tastes, and interests. However, Eagleton (2010) suggests that those who exist in conditions which 'force their backs to the wall [and], confront them . . . in some room full of light with what terrifies them the most in the world' are 'generally incapable of being at their finest' (Eagleton, 2010: 153). Particular aspects of both the neoliberal economic model and consumer culture serve to replicate this function within everyday existence by subjecting individuals to extreme pressure in the material and symbolic realm.

Chronic insecurity: the forced choices of free individuals

From the neoliberal perspective, the highly competitive framework into which the atomised individual is embedded is understood to be 'a better way of guiding individual efforts than any other' (Hayek, 1976: 27) on account of its role in providing stimulus towards economic productivity. The competitive efforts of individual economic actors are seen, therefore, cumulatively to drive wider social and economic progress. Individuals are further 'incentivised' towards economic productivity by the grave consequences of failure following the state's retreat from its role in offering individuals protection against the excesses of market forces. The state's role, thus, moves from the provision of economic rights to that of political rights which facilitate economic engagement, but do not provide economic support for those in need:

> The right to life means that a man has the right to support his life by his own work (on any economic level, as high as his ability will carry him); it does *not* mean that others must provide him with the necessities of life.
>
> The right to property means that a man has the right to take the economic actions necessary to earn property, to use it and to dispose of it; it does *not* mean that others must provide him with property.
>
> (Rand, 1964: 114)

Increasingly, those who do not succeed on the unpredictable terrain of capitalism face the prospect of abject poverty. The economic logic of the neoliberal model thus draws heavily on the ideas of philosophical liberalism whereby the individual who has a responsibility to determine his or her own existence according to the implementation of personal judgement, becomes the economic actor who is responsible for their own economic survival. Within this context, the 'individual must become a self-entrepreneur, responsible for his or her own existence and integration into the market' (Amable, 2011: 15). Consequently, appraisal of one's economic position becomes deracinated from any wider socioeconomic context, with both success and failure coming to be interpreted as a reflection of an individual's characteristics, effort, and performance. In addition to the invigorating effects of individualised competition, its ability to construct a visible hierarchy of individuals according to their merits and efforts is espoused as one of the greatest achievements of the neo-liberal model. Consequently, both material *and* symbolic survival is at stake in the neoliberal struggle for enrichment, as economic position comes to operate as a signifier of an individual's value meaning that economic failure becomes a fate to be avoided at all costs. The outcome, Currie suggests, is the creation of 'sink or swim societies' (Currie, 1997: 152) centred on the principles of 'struggle and competition' of social Darwinism (Amable, 2011: 8). Moreover, Eagleton (2010) highlights that our existence in these 'desperately deformed conditions' (Eagleton, 2010: 153) stimulates our propensity to evil. As a result of the 'incessant struggle for resources' (Eagleton, 2010: 154), late-capitalist subjects become more willing to adopt ruthless measures aimed at their preservation in the vicissitudes of capitalist markets.

Competitive efforts aimed at sustaining symbolic survival within late capitalism are dependent not only on the pursuit of financial wealth but also on the conspicuous consumption (Veblen, 2005) of positional goods (Hirsch, 1978). Individual consumers are expected to symbolise their success, and by extension superiority, by visibly marking themselves off from those who have failed, through their consumption of exclusive goods and experiences. Rather than representing an opportunity for enjoyment, this process also comes to exert intense pressure on individual consumers, causing them to be characterised by extremely high levels of anxiety. That this anxiety is fuelled by the objectless desire which underpins the individual's relationship with consumption, and which precludes any form of lasting satisfaction, is well documented (Bocock, 1993; Hall et al., 2008; McGowan, 2016). The intense pressure to consume has also extended further into the lives of late-capitalist subjects through the cultural injunction to enjoy. Through the operation of this injunction, the responsibilised individual of liberalism is replicated in the cultural realm whereby they are called upon to maximise their own pursuit of pleasure and enjoyment (Žižek, 2008, 2009). Citizens of consumer capitalism are thus imbued with sovereignty which they are expected to implement in the identification and exploitation of chances for enjoyment and in the pursuit of their personalised imaginary ideals (Dean, 2009). Again, this process of liberation is underpinned by one of responsibilisation which exerts pressure on the individual as they come to experience feelings of guilt should they fail to exploit such opportunities (Hall et al., 2008: 189). As the engagement with pleasure in consumer capitalism comes to be characterised by compulsion, enjoyment can move beyond the pleasure principle, moving instead into the realm of anxiety and discomfort (Dean, 2009). Rather than triggering a withdrawal from the pursuit of pleasure, continued engagement is sustained by the role of fantasy which attributes the failure to enjoy to an external factor, rather than to an intrinsic and unavoidable feature of the process itself (Dean, 2009). Thus, the pursuit of the lost object which is inscribed at the heart of the capitalist system is perpetuated by capitalism's ability to alienate its subjects from the experience of satisfaction which ensures their eternal engagement with the 'illusory promise' of commodities (McGowan, 2016: 36).

However, whilst the anxiety that drives economic engagement may well be *stimulated* by contemporary capitalist markets, it is not *created* here. Becker (1975) draws attention to the way in which humans are characterised by deep-seated, innate anxieties around the fear of mortality and insignificance. These fears, Becker (1975) suggests, come to underpin the project of *causa sui*, whereby individuals participate in cultural projects which allow them to obtain lasting symbolic existence which extends beyond death. Hence, permanence obtained in the symbolic realm is used to assuage anxiety over the finitude of existence in the material realm, allowing individuals to achieve immortality through the play of symbols (Becker, 1975). Contemporary capitalism, however, has come to pervert the project of causa sui through its colonisation of immortality symbols, providing late-capitalist subjects with projects which *induce* rather than *console* anxiety (Tudor, 2019). The acquisition of capital offers an opportunity to engage with the infinite (Eagleton, 2010), while consumer symbolism is used to create symbolic meaning for the individual's life allowing him or her to escape the fate of insignificance (see Hall et al., 2008; Tudor, 2019). However, the zero-sum nature of economic competition and the 'in-built obsolescence' (Hallsworth, 2005) of consumer goods, mean that feelings of symbolic security and distinction can only be obtained fleetingly before necessitating ongoing engagement. The innate anxieties which underpin engagement with the causa sui project are, in the context of contemporary capitalism, intentionally stimulated and harnessed in order to drive economic dynamism (Hall et al., 2008). The system's potential to drive economic productivity is dependent, therefore, on the preclusion of the possibility of long-term satisfaction, serving instead to relentlessly stimulate anxiety whilst constantly referring individuals back to economic and consumer engagement in the pursuit of ontological security.

Owing to the dangerous fusion of the economic and cultural pressures outlined above, sovereign decision-making is compelled towards the prioritisation of the pursuit of profit, symbolic distinction, and pleasure. As the consequences of failure in these realms include guilt, anxiety, material deprivation, and symbolic annihilation, conditions in late capitalism combine to create dangerous subjectivities fixated on the achievement of material and symbolic survival within a brutally competitive landscape. Moreover, the range of possible behaviours open to the individual seeking to secure an escape from anxiety is greatly increased by the systematic processes of normative deregulation that have taken place under liberal capitalism. In his book, *On Evil*, Morton (2005) suggests that:

> *[a] person's act is evil when it results from a strategy or learned procedure which allows that person's deliberations over the choice of actions not to be inhibited by barriers against considering harming or humiliating others that ought to have been in place.*
>
> (Morton, 2005: 57; italics in original)

The conditions present in late capitalism, therefore, greatly increase our propensity to evil by imbuing us with feelings of individual sovereignty whilst simultaneously subjecting us to intolerable forms of pressure in the form of chronic material and symbolic insecurity. These pressures nurture our capacity for evil by eroding the barriers to harmful acts that ought to be in place within us. As a result, we are left with much less protection against the excesses of competitive capitalist engagement and personal enjoyment as individuals feel increasingly pressured to secure their own triumph at any cost. The participation in harmful behaviours is not however, dependent on a withdrawal of support for wider value systems which proscribe such acts, or indeed a restructuring of such value systems (Hall and Antonopoulos, 2017), but is instead based in a form of extreme exceptionalism whereby individuals view themselves as being above external forms of regulation. Consideration of the morality, propriety, or legality of their conduct comes to be subjugated to the primacy of their quest for profit and symbolic distinction allowing them to be characterised by what Hall (2012) terms 'special liberty'.

The harms of toxic sovereignty

Exercises in special liberty have thus come to visit a range of harms upon humanity including both those which have, and have not, been subject to legal prohibition. The current article seeks to contextualise the accounts of those involved in systematic economic predation in this wider theoretical framework. Interviews carried out with those who had been convicted for their involvement in investment fraud indicated that their ability to harm others was deeply related to their attempts to exercise special liberty in the quest for profit and distinction. Both business and consumption were central to the way in which the fraudsters defined themselves (Tudor, 2019), and both arenas represented areas of life in which they expected to be granted freedom to 'realise their potential'. As a result of the primacy accorded to their quest for profit, distinction, and pleasure in their narratives, the respondents found it inconceivable that their efforts might be tempered by any considerations which might limit their efficacy in allowing them to reach their goals. Consequently, they were unwilling to accept the limitations necessitated by compliance with legal and moral frameworks. The importance accorded to the consideration that their acts of economic predation might be both criminal and immoral, and might inflict palpable harms on others, was somewhat diminished by their fixation on attempting to secure significant personal enrichment, servicing their highly crafted identities based on the purchase and display of consumer goods and the pursuit of pleasure and, ultimately, establishing themselves within the role of successful entrepreneurs (Tudor, 2019).

Interviewees did not, therefore, claim ignorance regarding the legality or the consequences of their actions. Rather, they tended to discuss their crimes with a fairly resigned candour, regarding them as necessary in order to achieve success in the world of business. They also tended to depict their acts of criminality as being in keeping with wider economic practice and, rather than representing cynical attempts to neutralise their conduct, their observations were often incredibly sapient. They viewed the brutal nature of economic competition and the central role played by both criminal and unethical conduct in the mainstream economy and concluded that, to intentionally avoid such conduct, would be to put oneself at a 'disadvantage in business'. They routinely voiced the opinion that in order to make it, one must be willing to 'operate in murky waters', to 'push against the boundaries', or 'move into the corners of business which become grey and black'. Their decisions to take steps into these behaviours were always governed by considerations of the relative profitability of criminal enterprise when compared with legitimate business, and these considerations appeared always to eclipse others around the potential consequences of their actions.

Discussions of the harm caused by their crimes tended to be less candid than those relating to their legality. Some sought to significantly downplay the harm experienced by the victims of their crimes, whilst others sought to implicate the actions of the criminal justice system in the losses experienced by their investors on account of their intervention in, and subsequent unravelling of, their schemes. Some, such as Alan, admitted that it was 'unfortunate that people lost money' but sought to balance these losses against the consideration that the schemes 'made a lot of people very rich'. Others, including Mark, sought to construct their victims' willingness to invest in their schemes as being symptomatic of their greed or inherent dishonesty. During one interview, Mark went further suggesting that investors were too weak to break the law themselves and so they are forced into becoming 'prey' rather than having the strength to become involved in acts of criminality. He said:

MARK: It is also a truism that you cannot cheat an honest man, because they just don't fall for it. They just don't. They either have to be greedy, or in desperate need of something. Or, they'd know that out there there's lots of money, if they'd just come off the rules for a bit. But their view is that they're steaming angry that the people who are wealthy got there before them, because they broke the rules. So they've got to find their own way to break the rules without them having to worry. They know it isn't legitimate, but they don't care. They are too weak to go for it for themselves, so they have to come to an outfit like us.

The accounts of harm and criminality offered by the respondents were deeply entrenched in survivalist logic in which their actions were framed as a means of surviving or of remaining competitive. The respondents displayed a deep enchantment with neoliberal notions of sovereignty and self-sufficiency, and they sought to portray themselves as hard-working individuals who had struggled against adversity to achieve great things. They were self-made men whose achievements in enterprise were testament to their special talents and sagacious decision-making. Their accounts sought to construct themselves as heroes, whose significant business capabilities were employed in order to benefit and enrich both themselves and others, thereby portraying themselves as western incarnations of the anthropological 'Big Man' (Gilmore, 1990). Indeed, they regularly cited their ability to generate large sums of financial wealth as the basis for their belief that the world should turn a blind eye to their conduct. They suggested that, should they be afforded the freedom to conduct their business, then all would benefit even if this involved them 'coming off the rules for a bit'. The positions of freedom they carved out, therefore, were deeply excessive and were justified by the invocation of consequentialist logic relating to the production of profit. Ultimately, their criminality was explained by the levels of productivity it afforded. They regularly made assertions of sovereignty and appeared to view their ability to engage in business activity, and to produce profit, as an inalienable right. Whilst they disliked the idea and the experience of imprisonment, it was generally accepted as part of the risk associated with involvement in criminality. The subject of disqualification, and in some cases confiscation, provoked much stronger reactions among the men who viewed such practices as 'insufferable' and 'unjustifiable'. When discussing his disqualification from directorship, Richard found the idea of his compliance with these requirements 'inconceivable':

RICHARD: I've been inside. I served my time. I paid the money. Then the bastards try and stick a ten year ban on me . . . they can't do that. Who do they think they are? . . . There are ways round these things, obviously . . . and that's what I'll have to do. I mean, they can't expect you not to work. I'm in my prime. This is what I do. How can they legitimately interfere in your business once you have done your time? Of course they can't. It's ridiculous.

Similarly, as part of his sentence Monty had been banned from participation in business activities which involved taking deposits from individual investors. Over the course of our conversations it transpired that Monty was currently involved in money-renting schemes which involved individual investors. When the question of the legality of this enterprise arose, he replied:

MONTY: Who are they to tell me who I can and can't do business with? Who are they to determine the nature of *my* affairs? They have absolutely no right to speak on these matters.

Frank had been subject to a fifteen-year ban on company directorship and because he perceived this to infringe upon his right to make money, it was a source of extreme frustration to him. The revocation of his entrepreneurial freedoms was something which would impact negatively on the world as he would be prevented from employing his talents in the world of business:

FRANK: At my age . . . well, at my age it is essentially a life ban from directorship. A life ban from what I do, from what I'm good at. I mean, doesn't it seem ridiculous that they want £1m from me and yet they ban me from directorship? I could make the money in no time if it wasn't for that. It doesn't make sense. . . . All the time in prison, they talk about reform, giving back, changing and doing good. But with this, they are preventing me from doing all of that. . . . I'm a talented businessman and they try to stop me from doing good, from making money. It's absurd.

Thus, discussions around the legal and moral legitimacy of the respondents' conduct came to demonstrate the centrality of the notion of sovereignty to their understandings of their economic practice. Their vehement rejection of the restrictions imposed upon them by the criminal justice system demonstrated their unwillingness to allow external influences to detract from their economic goals. Instead, respondents sought to carve out individualised spaces of freedom in which they could exercise an excessive form of liberty which allowed them to act untrammelled by the restrictions of legal and ethical frameworks in order that they could compete effectively in the struggle for enrichment. However, whilst respondents sought to portray their unrestrained 'business practices' as an expression of their personal sovereignty, the reality of their situations suggested otherwise. Rather, their accounts indicated that their involvement in criminal economic practice continued even when it came to have significantly damaging consequences for them and their families including relationship breakdown, arrest, and victim reprisals. Pete, for example, continued to take deposits from members of his local community despite investors targeting him and his family when they became suspicious about the legitimacy of his investment scheme:

PETE: Well, I mean it wasn't like people round here didn't ask no questions [sic]. 'Course they did, man! It took time for those things to happen 'cause everyone was so excited about the money that was flying around at the time, but when people started to ask questions . . . that was when things got bad . . . I mean they torched my car; they torched my sister's car. That was their way of saying 'we're watching how this is going to pan out.' [Name of codefendant], well he got it bad. They actually kidnapped him and warned him that if things went bad, then, well, they wouldn't forget.

INTERVIEWER: Is that when you gave up on the scheme then?

PETE: No. No, that came much later. No, at that point . . . that was when things were really starting to take off for us.

During their careers, which spanned the boundary of legality, all but two of the respondents had attained fairly significant levels of personal wealth and economic security. However, none had chosen to cease their criminal enterprises at this point, reporting instead that they continued to be plagued by feelings of economic insecurity, desire, and dissatisfaction (Tudor, 2019). Instead, they all sought to continue their illicit acquisition towards the point of self-destruction, evidencing the way in which human subjectivity has become divorced and alienated from the experience of satisfaction (McGowan, 2016). The compulsive drive towards endless economic expansion thus not only imbued them with an ability to harm others, but also enabled them to pursue actions which significantly undermined their own interests. Therefore, whilst their accounts of their renunciation of external regulation evidenced the centrality of the notion of sovereignty to their *subjective* experience, their acts of criminality could be more accurately understood to be sustained by the *fantasy* of sovereignty which served to obfuscate the reality of their complete subjugation to the requirements of capital in their attempts to escape anxiety.

The terrifying spectre of insignificance

The renunciation of limitation was also a subject that respondents sought to repeatedly return to when discussing their engagement with consumption. The respondents' identities were deeply dependent on interaction with consumer goods and their attendant symbolism, and the pursuit, purchase, and display of these goods represented a central preoccupation of their existence (Tudor, 2019). Using key consumer goods and experiences, the respondents crafted narcissistic fantasy identities which were, they believed, reflective of their true selves and consequently, their pursuit of these items was characterised by an extreme intensity. During conversations, this intensity appeared in the form of a deep enchantment with consumer goods and experiences, expressions of entitlement in relation to these goods, and the descriptions of the way in which their consumption escalated significantly over time. Their ability to engage in the pursuit of pleasure was one of the key ways in which they attempted to symbolise their success and to demonstrate their ability to exercise sovereignty. During interviews, they constantly sought to impress upon me the ways in which they were able to pursue the indulgence of their interests.

All of the men were very open about the way in which their criminality served as a vehicle to access the things that they desired, both allowing them to obtain goods which would otherwise be out of reach, and as a means of expediting access. They also described how they sought out increasingly luxurious, exclusive, or rare artefacts and experiences over time as the revenues from their criminality increased (Tudor, 2019). However, this escalation in consumption did not only result from the pragmatic liberation afforded by the availability of greater resources, but also related to a form of symbolic liberation whereby they came to be driven by a deep sense of entitlement. They were not, therefore, consuming more because they could afford to do so; rather they actively sought to increase their criminal endeavours in order to facilitate increasing levels of consumption. The idea of sovereignty in the realm of consumption was deeply excessive in the sense that it surpassed the notion of the individual who is empowered to make choices which are informed by his or her personal tastes and interests, crossing over instead into the realm of the individual who is plagued by visions of excess and indulgence and who is willing to cause harm to others in order to achieve them. The way in which their identities had become fused with these goods and lifestyles meant that they considered engagement with consumption, as with business, as an inalienable right. The sense of entitlement that they felt was not simply a superficial, self-indulgent expectation of privilege, but was underpinned by a much deeper sense of anxiety owing to the fact that they felt their access to these goods was essential to their existence; their symbolic survival was dependent upon it (Becker, 1975; Hallsworth, 2005; Hall et al., 2008; see also Tudor, 2019). As a result, the prospect of being without these forms of symbolic adornment invoked a primal anxiety around the fear of insignificance, providing the impetus for the acts of criminality which ensured the continued presence of these goods in their lives (Becker, 1975). Rather than the assertion of sovereignty, therefore, the respondents' pursuit of pleasure and distinction was one that was based on compulsion, demonstrating the way in which 'imaginary identities' serve as 'key loci of operations of control' (Dean, 2009: 67) in contemporary capitalism. Crucially, this compulsion was underpinned by their failure to experience satisfaction in their consumption and display of commodities and was representative of the way in which 'the failure to accumulate enough is inscribed in the system' (McGowan, 2016: 21).

Conclusion

As a result of the recent revival of philosophical liberalism, the notion of sovereignty has played a central role in the transformation of the west under late capitalism. Both the establishment of neoliberal economics and consumer culture have been heavily underpinned by the notion of the self-determining, sovereign individual. Within this context, sovereignty has come to be elevated not just as a right, but also a responsibility, with self-governing individuals being called upon not only to determine their own life course, but also to be responsible for their own economic survival and for the maximisation of their own enjoyment in capitalist markets. Consequently, the notion of sovereignty has come to operate as a deeply seductive ideal which facilitates and mobilises participation in stark forms of extreme self sufficiency. As a result of their existence in cultures of extreme individualism which are characterised by the decline of Symbolic Efficiency, citizens of late capitalism are subject to processes of extreme deregulation, meaning that the type of sovereignty accorded to them comes to take on an excessive characteristic. The nature of this sovereignty ultimately leads towards ethical solipsism. From the liberal perspective, the individual operating in this deregulated space of negative liberty is free to choose his or her own actions, which ought only to be limited by consideration of the rights of others. However, the pressure exerted on the individual by late capitalism means that he or she is forced to operate under the constant threat of both material and symbolic annihilation. The intensity of the pursuit of profit and distinction which results from this pervasive culture of insecurity means that the individual strives for the assertion of a purer form of sovereignty which renounces the legitimacy of *any* form of external regulation whatsoever. In the declaration of 'special liberty' (Hall, 2012), the individual is therefore liberated from the requirements of ethical and legal frameworks meaning that the decisions they make in the pursuit of profit and distinction need no longer be constrained by barriers which prevent the slide into harmful behaviours. Thus, whilst the move into special liberty represents an assertion of pure sovereignty insofar as it signifies the extreme dislocation of the individual from regulatory frameworks, it cannot be considered a true expression of self-determination on account of the individual's complete surrender to the systemic demands limitless accumulation.

The notion of sovereignty was found to play a central role in the subjective experiences of fraudsters. The acts of economic predation for which they were responsible were an *expression* of this excessive form of sovereignty, symbolised by the renunciation of limitation of their business pursuits. Their criminality was also *motivated* by the ideal of sovereignty as they sought to attain positions in which they could consume without limitation, assuring their access to the goods needed to maintain the fantasy of their idealised identities. This preoccupation with sovereignty and self-determination, however, ultimately operated as fantasy, allowing them to escape from the reality of the anxieties which underpinned their quest for enrichment and distinction. The feelings of sovereignty attained through their complete immersion in the project of accumulation and display allowed them to transcend feelings of limitation and insecurity, albeit only temporarily. Even when participation in this perverted, late-capitalist incarnation of the casua sui project (Tudor, 2019) became disadvantageous, fraudsters remained committed to the struggle for enrichment. Thus, the sovereignty that was both expressed and obtained through their criminality was, in the end, an illusion which served to allay anxieties over the ultimate helplessness of mortal beings. Their drive to carve out spaces of extreme liberation within which they were willing to inflict harm upon others in their pursuit of profit was ultimately reflective of their complete enslavement to the requirements of capital, rather than of their freedom to self-govern.

Analysis of the conditions present within contemporary capitalism therefore, is crucial to understanding the way in which harmful subjectivities and behaviours are cultivated. The deeply individualising and deregulatory forces which stand at the heart of the project of liberalism open up the possibility of harm through the extirpation of universal and collectivist principles upon which politics and ethics are dependent. As a result, late-capitalist subjects come to be characterised by an 'incapacity . . . to name and strive for good' (Badiou, 2001: 30). The development of more positive environments which may reduce the incidence of harm and predation is dependent, therefore, on the move towards new modes of political thinking which 'reject finitude' (Badiou, 2006: 142) and which are 'engaged in rendering explicit the subjective infinity of situations' (Badiou, 2006: 143). Changes in this direction would enable us to abandon liberalism's minimalist framework of negative liberty, moving instead towards the construction of political projects which pursue notions of positive liberty and shared notions of the Good, which in turn might offer a platform from which to question the legitimacy of current economic arrangements and the harms that they generate.

Note

1 The term *Ponzi scheme* refers to a form of investment fraud whereby investors are offered high rates of return on financial deposits. Investors' money is then used to fund the interest payments to earlier investors. Such schemes are therefore dependent on attracting new investors in order to avoid collapse. The term *Ponzi* derives from the name of Charles Ponzi, who was arrested for his perpetration of this form of fraud in 1920 in the USA.

References

Amable, B. (2011) Morals and Politics in the Ideology of Neo-Liberalism. *Socio-Economic Review*, 9, 1: 3–30.

Badiou, A. (2001) *Ethics: An Essay on the Understanding of Evil*, London: Verso.

Badiou, A. (2006) *Metapolitics*, London: Verso.

Badiou, A. (2008) *The Century*, Cambridge: Polity Press.

Becker, E. (1975) *Escape from Evil*, London: Free Press.

Bocock, R. (1993) *Consumption*, London: Routledge.

Currie, E. (1997) Market, Crime and Community: Toward a Mid-Range Theory of Post-Industrial Violence. *Theoretical Criminology*, 1, 2: 147–72.

Davies, W. (2017) *The Limits of Neoliberalism: Authority, Sovereignty and the Logic of Competition*, London: Sage.

de Sade, D.A.F. (1990) *Justine, Philosophy in the Bedroom and Other Writings*, New York: Grove Press.

Dean, J. (2009) *Democracy and Other Neoliberal Fantasies: Communicative Capitalism and Left Politics*, London: Duke University Press.

Eagleton, T. (2009) *The Trouble with Strangers*, Sussex: Wiley.

Eagleton, T. (2010) *On Evil*, London: Yale University Press.

Friedman, M. (2002) *Capitalism and Freedom*, 40th Anniversary edn., London: University of Chicago Press.

Gilmore, D. (1990) *Manhood in the Making: Cultural Concepts of Masculinity*, Yale: Yale University Press.

Hall, S. (2012) *Theorizing Crime and Deviance: A New Perspective*, London: Sage.

Hall, S. and Antonopoulos, G. (2017) Troika, Austerity and the Reluctant Resort to Criminality in Greece. In D. Whyte and J. Wiegratz (eds.) *Neo-Liberalism and the Moral Economy of Fraud*, Oxon: Routledge, 113–29.

Hall, S., Winlow, S. and Ancrum, C. (2008) *Criminal Identities and Consumer Culture: Crime, Exclusion and the New Culture of Narcissism*, Devon: Willan.

Hallsworth, S. (2005) *Street Crime*, Devon: Willan.

Harvey, D. (2007) *A Brief History of Neo-Liberalism*, Oxford: Oxford University Press.

Harvey, D. (2008) *The Condition of Post-Modernity*, Oxford: Blackwell Publishing.

Hayek, F. (1976) *The Road to Serfdom*, London: Routledge Kegan and Paul.

Hirsch, F. (1978) *Social Limits to Growth*, London: Routledge.

Kant, I. (1991) *Political Writings*, Cambridge: Cambridge University Press.

McGowan, T. (2016) *Capitalism and Desire: The Psychic Cost of Free Markets*, Chichester: Columbia University Press.
Messner, S. and Rosenfeld, R. (2006) *Crime and the American Dream*, Belmont: Wadsworth.
Mill, J.S. (1964) *Utilitarianism, Liberty and Representative Government*, London: Everyman's Library.
Mill, J.S. (2006) *On Liberty and Other Writings*, Cambridge: Cambridge University Press.
Morton, A. (2005) *On Evil*, London: Routledge.
Rand, A. (1964) *The Virtue of Selfishness*, London: Signet.
Rand, A. (2007) *Atlas Shrugged*, London: Penguin.
Raymen, T. (2019) 'The Enigma of Social Harm and the Barrier of Liberalism: Why Zemiology needs a Theory of the Good'. In *Justice, Power and Resistance: The Journal of the European Group for the Study of Deviance and Social Control*, 3, 1: 133–161.
Smith, A. (1759) *The Theory of Moral Sentiments* [Online]. Available at: http://knarf.english.upenn.edu/Smith/tmstp.html
Tudor, K. (2019) Symbolic Survival and Harm: Serious Fraud and Consumer Capitalism's Perversion of the Causa Sui Project. *British Journal of Criminology*. doi:10.1093/bjc/azz009
Veblen, T. (2005) *Conspicuous Consumption*, London: Penguin.
Žižek, S. (2008) *For They Know Not What They Do: Enjoyment as a Political Factor*, London: Verso.
Žižek, S. (2009) *The Ticklish Subject: The Absent Centre of Political Ontology*, London: Verso.

9 Spy vs Spy

The surveillance state of social media

Leanne McRae

On 31 May 2019, a Belgian backpacker visiting Australia went missing at Byron Bay in New South Wales. At the time of writing, Theo Hayez has not been found (Australian Associated Press, 2019a). His family and police fear for his safety. On Monday 17 June, his father, Laurent Hayez, pleaded with messaging platform WhatsApp to give police access to his final communications (Australian Associated Press, 2019b). Hayez had used the application in the early hours of 1 June. It is his final digital communication before he disappeared. WhatsApp is not able to comply with this request. Due to the encrypted nature of the communications, WhatsApp is able to provide only metadata and not the content of the messages themselves. The platform utilises end-to-end encryption, which means only the sender and the receiver can read the content of the message sent. This is a promotional point for the app, as it protects the privacy of users from third parties. Importantly, WhatsApp had already provided the metadata to the police before Laurent Hayez made his public plea to reveal the content of the messages. Hayez was requesting that the company violate its own terms of service and hack its own platform to provide the actual content of the encrypted messages.

The pain and trauma a family experiences when a member goes missing in such a manner is palpable. The urgent desire to assist in locating a missing person stimulates public mourning and outrage, especially if a cold and distantly monolithic corporation who might help but does not is situated centrally in the conflicting and contested realms of public safety, terms of service, privacy, jurisprudence, policing, and harm. Company policy is denigrated and denied when a service to public safety can and must be performed. Yet this debate is taking place against a much larger privacy context of the routine violation of online users by corporations and governments, who obliquely yet overtly scrape, store, and supply reams of personal information gleaned from our digital media activity to third parties, both with and without our consent. The Cambridge Analytica scandal, which revealed a widespread and concerted program by the company to offer services that they claim can alter democratic elections, serves as a public punctuation point to the intersecting concerns of personal privacy, the power of social media, and online corporations to collect and cloud our online activities, as well as government spying on private citizens in order to protect and pre-empt harm. The use of Facebook profile data by Cambridge

Analytica to target 'persuadable' voters – without the consent of users – has become a catalyst in the current crisis facing social media and online environments more generally. In July 2019, Facebook was ordered by the U.S. Federal Trade Commission to pay a $US 5 billion fine (Shepardson, 2019) due to privacy violations that were revealed in the Cambridge Analytica probe. While this ruling was hailed as 'record-breaking', the fine itself was a pittance compared with Facebook's $US 15 billion first quarter earnings for 2019 (Lapowsky and Kelly, 2019).

Facebook's conduct is indicative of its continued trend of pushing the limits of social justice and jurisprudence. This behaviour is enabled by the contested reluctance of state authorities to hold it accountable. WhatsApp, having been acquired by Facebook as of 2014, faces questions about the status of its end-to-end encryption protocols in light of this acquisition and the revelation that data from the app will be shared with Facebook. In 2017, the European Commission found that Facebook had been misleading about the extent of information that would be shared between the apps post-takeover. Both founders, Jan Koum and Brian Acton, have indicated discomfort with Facebook's operational motivations. Acton has called upon users to #deletefacebook in a 20 March 2018 tweet after its alliance with Cambridge Analytica had been exposed. Koum left the company early in 2018 with a flurry of reports speculating that his exit was due to tensions resulting from Facebook pushing for WhatsApp to change its terms of service so that its data could be shared with Facebook (Statt, 2018). This has also led to speculation in the academic literature of the nature and intent of the codification of WhatsApp privacy and security protocols.

In the development of its end-to-end encryption, WhatsApp hired Open Whisper Systems, the same company that designed Signal's secure messaging system, which was recommended by Edward Snowden. Santos and Faure (2018: 6) muse that 'the current websites of both Signal and WhatsApp look surprisingly similar'. WhatsApp appears to be heavily leveraging Signal's reputation, indicating that messaging security is part of a carefully crafted façade to deliver marketable product to consumers concerned with their privacy. Santos and Faure also speculate about the roll out of the end-to-end encryption in 2016, which was announced via a system-wide message on the app.

> But one thing about this implementation seemed outstanding: WhatsApp sent a message to both users engaged in a conversation, warning them that the conversation was encrypted, though obviously the majority of the users do not understand well that meaning. So a few questions emerge: what exactly are the intentions behind such system message? Why make visible an invisible affordance such as encryption? Why should it matter to the mass of the App's users such information, besides the more tech-savvy users that are actually worried about the issue? Why focus so much on this decision when the defensive tactic of WhatsApp argued the nonexistence of stored data in the first place?
>
> (Santos and Faure, 2018: 1–2)

Such questions are pertinent to a pre-Cambridge Analytica context for social messaging, but they also raise concerns over the extent of WhatsApp's privacy, which has indeed been challenged heavily by some national authorities. A series of ongoing incidents in Brazil provide a spotlight on the emerging debates between social harm, criminality, privacy and the role of nation states in regulating these intersections. In 2015 the app was blocked for twelve hours in Brazil when it declared it was unable to hand over 'the content of conversations between suspects involved in some high-profile judicial case under investigation' (Santos and Faure, 2018: 1). This is not an insubstantial amount of time given that WhatsApp is the go-to messaging tool used by 120 million Brazilians due to the exorbitant costs of SMS (Nemer, 2018). Its popularity was used as a bargaining chip in the policing and judicial processes in Brazil. Law enforcement sought to recruit the company in criminal prosecution while the company sought to exempt itself from the debate and champion itself as a beacon of personal privacy.

Amid this tension, messaging apps are insulating themselves against perceptions of privacy failure by claiming the encryption does not permit the company's staff to view the content of messages, which releases the company from its responsibility to enter into debates about privacy versus prosecution. One key result from this twelve-hour ban was that Telegram, an alternative messaging service, received an increase of 1.5 million users from Brazil (Savov, 2015). Telegram occupies a controversial place in the messaging app stable due to its perceived utilisation by ISIS to commit and coordinate acts of terror. The app's enduring commitment to privacy and security – not only offering end-to-end encryption but also a self-destruction mechanism akin to Snapchat, where messages are deleted after they are read – has presented an attractive communication medium for those with nefarious intentions. These privacy affordances are causing nation states, policing, enforcement, and intelligence agencies concern. As a result, Telegram is banned in Russia and Iran – in Iran because of claims that it was being used to mobilise armed uprisings (*Radio Farda*, 2019), but in Russia because the company refused to hand over its encryption key (Akbari and Gabdulhakov, 2019). In both contexts, national security and policing are evoked as viable reasons to curtail, ban, or circumvent the security protocols of the app. The tensions between social media, private messaging, security, privacy, and policing offer up rich terrain for contemporary understandings of harm, the social good, and data rights.

This chapter investigates the relationships between harm, privacy, and jurisprudence, as they are managed via social media and messaging apps in a post-Cambridge Analytica environment. The argument asserts that the emergent focus on personal online privacy is a misdirection. By centring our attention on social media sites and their technological affordances we amplify atomistic customer consciousness. States use this focus, encased in public fear about harmful and criminal acts – and the needs of online transparency to curtail trafficking, terrorism, doxing, and digital deviance – to justify the legislation, management, regulation, and extension of a slew of neoliberal capitalist harms. Importantly, harm is not defined but rather evoked and imagined along the axes of the seen and unseen so that technological affordances and powerful interests remain obscured.

States enact their own 'special liberty' (Hall, 2012) in this space, where criminalised harms justify the collection, distribution, storage, and archiving of ever-expanding data points of non-criminals. The dragnetting of ordinary citizens is an integrated and fundamental part of not just policing and intelligence gathering, but also delivery of social services and public provisions. It is big business, global corporations, oil rights, and intellectual property agents that benefit from these activities. Extending these practices of fear mongering to encrypted social media and messaging permit cascading contexts of harm to intersect and provide the rationale for increasing and diversifying forms of surveillance.

In taking the messaging app Telegram as a case study, this chapter considers the role of terror in extending law and order, policing, and punishment into the digitised private sphere to correlate how 'big data' are being used to predict crime and manage harm. The effects of these practices are not confined to a *Minority Report*-like cautionary tale of the consequences of manipulating crime and pre-empting its enforcement. Crime, criminality, harm, and deviance begin to collapse into each other, providing a tangled trail of policy, practices, perceptions, and outcomes that exist in tension with resistances to the invasions of our personal privacy. The rhetoric of 'protecting' citizens is routinely deployed to affirm creeping violations of personal privacy as a small price to pay. Online messaging tools and their encryption provoke a point of tension between public safety, protection, and prosecution to scaffold harm into all digital interactions and interventions. Criminals can hide, states can surveil, and corporations can sell while citizenship is further eroded and consciousness is curtailed.

This chapter claims the computational prowess of big data is being hailed as a saviour for society-wide decision-making. Proponents aim to ensure that, when cross-referenced and computed, the data can act as a clear context for action, pre-emption, and protection. For states, prediction is seductive as expanding datasets offer the potential to commute risk and manage harm – an intent illustrated by the widespread surveillance programs revealed by Edward Snowden, which indicate a cohesive state and online media collaboration to scrape and monitor the personal information of millions of people. Terrorists' move into using encrypted social media messaging applications like Telegram and WhatsApp provides a fulcrum around which the anxieties of modern intelligence agencies and state actors dovetails with the outrage of social media users. The 'citizen' clashes with the 'consumer' while harm provides the deal-breaker. Data subjects emerge in a flexible and fluid space upon which 'harms' can be redefined, imposed, managed, and enforced. While the focus is on social media organisations offering robust and potent privacy protections for their consumers, the role of states in seeking to access, hack, and track their citizens' personal messages is encircled with protectionist paradigms about 'harm' and state responsibility – protecting us from the criminals and terrorists and also from ourselves as a service to public safety. At all levels the public discourse around crime and harm is enfolded within the potentials of big data and predictive technologies that work on the cusp of our personal privacy. It is the tensions between our fluctuating identities as citizen and consumer currently resisting and collapsing into the data-subject that peels open the space for a more proactive debate to occur. The intersections of big data, law, privacy, and social media are not easily reconciled.

The importance law enforcement attaches to its operations in the field of socially sanctioned expectations of justice has suffused its crime prevention and policing strategies with urgency and objectivity. A range of techniques, technologies, and devices are deployed to ensure fair and equitable distribution of the law enforcement milieu, not only for criminals but for their victims. This ensures the ongoing, just, and fair operation of a society framed by democracy, defined by freedom of choice, and underpinned by legislative rigor and appropriate punishment for transgressors. During the course of modernity, the development of various technologies has enabled a more weighted and reified mobilisation of justice to emerge. These technologies are attached to notions of objective fairness, rather than the emotional brutalities of medieval punitive performance, divine retribution, and caste consignment.

As early as the 1830s, for example, photography was harnessed for its perceived 'objective' rendering of the world in front of the lens. Alphonse Bertillon, chief of the Paris police, was the most famous advocate of photography in policing. Not only was he one of the first to begin photographing crime scenes, particularly those involving murder, but he pioneered a 'system of criminal classification and identification' (Gever, 2005: 451) involving 'mugshots' as well as 'anthropometric measurements of the bodies of criminal suspects' (Gever, 2005: 451), which could then be 'compared with a huge file comprising cards with the measurements and photos of previously detained suspects' (Gever, 2005: 451) that eventually included fingerprints. Bertillon constructed a database of information about people known to the police in an early form of precrime policing, where the potentialities for harm are imagined, and previous offenders or suspects who have not offended give up the right to privacy as they are subjected to random and state sanctioned surveillance. This early form of informatics fell under the eye of jurisprudence strategies and corporeal cache-ing that disciplines the subject and curtails consciousness. Such approaches to law and order, and now harm-prevention, deploy the rationalities of science, objectivity, data, and technology to anticipate, frame, and define how crime and harm are regulated, prevented, and punished. In the age of big data, the 'neutrality and comprehensibility' (Bridle, 2018: 32) of computation is now the frontier for policing. Bertillon's dataset is now global, accelerated, and encompassing.

This tethering of science, computation, and objectivity has moved us into an era where theory, contextualisation, and interpretation are suppressed. Data is presented as evidence and correlation trumps causality. These attitudes have been built through the coexistence and evolution of a variety of social and cultural tropes. It is significant that the development in the US of a national fingerprint database that could be searched and catalogued only came to fruition at the end of the twentieth century, just in time for the confrontation with the terror of 11 September 2001 and the perceived need for a widespread and cohesive intelligence and national security mobilisation as well as overhaul of the crime-fighting community, where there was 'an infusion of tax dollars for development of new surveillance sensors and data mining programs to produce strategic intelligence, and accelerated convergence of previously separate surveillance systems into a "surveillant assemblage"' (Brayne, 2017: 978). In popular culture there is an attendant explosion of police drama on television. *Law and Order* had been on the screen since 1990. *Law and Order: Special Victims Unit* began in 1999 while *Criminal Intent* was launched immediately after 9/11 in September 2001. This was followed by *Law and Order: Trial by Jury* in 2005. *Law and Order: LA* followed in 2010. Meanwhile, *CSI* had debuted in October 2000 with *CSI: Miami* following in 2003, *CSI: New York* in 2004, and *CSI: Cyber* in 2014. The popularity of these programs indicates an emerging desire for audiences to witness police fighting crime, pursuing justice, and catching criminals. These franchises were just a snapshot of the variety of police, intelligence, and crime TV dramas including *NCIS*, *Alias*, *The Closer*, *Castle*, *Bones*, *Cold Case*, *Criminal Minds*, *Crossing Jordan*, *The District*, *The Shield*, *Hack*, *Numbers*, and *The Wire*.

It is undoubtedly *CSI* that offers the greater insights into the shifting consciousness of viewers as it connects to the tensions and anxieties of the early twenty-first century. The program centres and celebrates the roles that technology, science, and machines play in not just capturing but convicting criminals. In the world of *CSI* 'the locus of truth . . . resides in expert applications of scientific technologies that organize and produce inscriptions, without troubling with problems of interpretation' (Gever, 2005: 456). There is a painstaking reification of the impartiality of the machines and technologies that scan for data, the minutiae of DNA evidence, and the empirical truth of the photograph that provides the unbiased 'evidence' unhampered by human interpretation or questioning. This security in the capacity of raw data to provide unshakable truths speaks to a time of increasing 'objectless anxiety' and insecurity (Hall, 2012), where criminals are invisible, unpredictable, and horrifying. The post 9/11 period spotlighted the nefarious insider, the home-grown criminal or outsider easily able to pass for 'one of us' embodied in the nineteen hijackers who trained on US soil for their attack. It was also hailed as an intelligence failure that not only sparked a reshaping of US police, surveillance, and crime prevention organisations, but also justified the massive surveillance programs that were green-lighted (Masco, 2017) as a result of the incident. This was a call to data, technology, and science to service a whole-hearted shift towards precrime interventions and a redefinition of harm motivated by a 'growing culture of fear and a rapidly increasing militarisation of public space and culture' (Giroux, 2004: 211) manifested in the securitisation of law and order.

The conscious move towards *harm* – to self, to society and to loved ones – was subsumed by the harm to the nation as the pictures of the collapsing Twin Towers were beamed around the globe. This made the attack not just about planes crashing and buildings burning, but a psychological trauma of witnessing murder, enlivened by images and spectacle – a 'visualization of social disorder' (Gever, 2005: 454) that burrows to the core of the psyche. It was a 'morbid symptom' of the manifestation of a 'changing real world and ossified ideologies' (Hall and Winlow, 2018: 107). In this moment, a concern with victimhood saturated the consciousness, mirrored in popular culture and *CSI* specifically where 'there is remarkably little concern with why people kill but a great deal with how people die' (Gever, 2005: 454). The emphasis is shifting onto systems and fractures of harm that are tethered to the seemingly random attacks of terrorists who create a cache of harmfulness, not just as a localised criminal event – a bombing or hijacking – but one that radiates outwards to impact upon multiple sites and people perpetuated by images and representations via multiple nodes of popular culture and everyday life. The fear of harm, rather than crime – for we know bad guys will be caught and punished in the increasingly militarised, reactionary, neoliberal society – gives the required ideological shape to neoliberalism's baseline objectless anxiety, driving ever more invasive surveillance cultures in order to prevent crime and minimise harm. Pre-crime and post-punishment become the widening focus of law enforcement.

Pre-crime focuses on the potential or possibility that a crime will occur. There are very real and rational reasons behind the emergence of some types of pre-crime modelling. For example, if a particular geographical area has reports of a series of burglaries, it is not unreasonable to predict that more burglaries may happen in the future and therefore an increased police presence in that geographical area may serve to prevent further burglaries (called 'prospective hot spotting') (Chan, 2016: 27). This type of anamnestic pre-crime activity gathers data about trends in geographical areas to facilitate decision-making about where and how to direct policing resources to ensure public safety. However, post-punishment falls outside the real and the rational. This is a punitive system designed to ensure that those who have already served time for their crimes continue to be punished and exiled. It is mostly framed as a public safety protocol in that past behaviour is mapped as a predictor of future behaviour, and as such it demonstrates a profound mistrust in the criminal justice system's ability to offer rehabilitation. The function of jail is punitive. Programs for rehabilitation or prisoner reform are defunded and diminished. The emphasis is on making criminals as physically, emotionally, and intellectually isolated as possible – to extirpate them from society at all levels as a form of punishment. Post-punishment also involves parole procedures and digital tracking, including, for example, circumstances where some sex offenders added to a public register and must also 'admit their crimes on social media such as Facebook' (Gurinskaya and Nall, 2018: 49) to ensure they continue to be socially punished long after they have served their time.

The increasing popularity of post-punishment practices' claim to ensure criminals do not reoffend dovetails with pre-crime initiatives designed to predict future crime. Both are motivated by fear, an amplification of harm and deviance, and are realised within a punitive criminal justice system. This symbolically shaped fear helps to shift the emphasis from crime – as anomalous human behaviour emergent out of specific trajectories of socioeconomic or interpersonal conditions – to harm as a foundational experience of modern anxiety and a failure of human resilience in light of the increasing complexity of perversions, injustices, and exploitations that pervade our daily lives. As those in affluent contexts are able to insulate themselves against harm, the shock of its presence is jarring when it comes cascading down on these individuals. The push to displace harm – onto the third world or the poor for example – serves to 'crime-proof' the middle class, sequestering them from the unpleasantness of neoliberal capitalism.

In the death-throes of capitalism, the maintenance of neoliberal continuity is fused into the emergent and cascading fear-of-harms that are perpetuated, all to assure us that the worst of all harms would await us 'should be instigate a process of transformation' (Hall and Winlow, 2018: 108) that might shift our priorities from growth and development to social care, stability, and equity. Ensuring the continuity of capitalist expansion and consumerism means constantly broadening the list of harms we risk should we opt for alternatives. As harm dovetails into a wider culture of fear, accompanied by rising militarisation of law enforcement in direct correlation, the desire to predict future crime becomes seductive. This desire is realised in big data – the ability to track, measure, and monitor people in unforeseen ways. The 'computational regime' (Bridle, 2018: 29) of number-crunching that by its sheer size and scale is conceived to reveal hidden 'truths' in its quantitative candour is codified as the key to predictive problem-solving. The extent to which big data can operate as a predictive system within law enforcement offers tantalising opportunities to manage, morph and monitor risk.

The origins of our contemporary understandings of big data are tenuous. There is tension over what types of data can be included. Most often, data types are categorised within the tropes of '*volume* (consisting of enormous quantities of data); *velocity* (created in real-time) and; *variety* (being structured, semi-structured and unstructured)' (Kitchin and McArdle, 2016: 1). Most importantly, they require large computational abilities to begin to analyse them, which therefore reshapes the relationship between data and their interpretation, placing computation over interpretation. This desire for more and more information is encapsulated in the Internet itself – a wide repository of almost all known knowledge that has produced 'simplistic narratives, conspiracy theories, and postfactual politics' (Bridle, 2018: 11) along with an increasing opacity of the nature and type of information architectures that filter through it. In this context, 'automated information is clear and direct, and confounds the grey areas that muddle cognition' (Bridle, 2018: 40). We celebrate data and the seemingly concise access to the truth it offers. As Chan suggests,

> [B]ecause of the availability of large volumes of data, (1) sampling is a thing of the past, Big Data is increasingly giving us access to all the data; (2) data accuracy is no longer a problem we need to be concerned about; and (3) there is no need to search for causality; correlation provides 'novel and invaluable insights'.
>
> (Chan, 2016: 22)

The increasing reliance on big data is changing how knowledge is being produced, and even what counts as knowledge. Information processed and packaged as big data yet uncritiqued or framed by interpretation is assigned as some sort of mythical 'pure' information category that allows entry into wholesome truth regimes. This increases the value of big data in the integration of 'algorithmic processing of datasets' (Ash et al., 2018: 10) that might offer a cleaner 'algorithmic governance' (Ash et al., 2018: 10). This means automation takes over thinking, polishes up policy decisions, removes insecurities about security, and generally 'ensures that we value automated information more highly than our own experiences' (Bridle, 2018: 40).

Underpinning this computational celebration is a core motivation – predictive ability. More data means greater and 'purer' datasets that enable algorithmic approaches to all life sectors. Yet, as more data is collected, greater concerns emerge over the role and place of social inequalities and critical thinking. Researchers and decision-makers obsess 'over the inherent limitations of a small class of mathematical and material conundrums rather than the broader questions of a truly democratic and egalitarian society' (Bridle, 2018: 34). These concerns filter and flow through debates about big data and privacy, and are integrated into the very systems at the centre of our everyday interactions that, when examined, reveal 'an ever-increasing opacity allied to a concentration of power' (Bridle, 2018: 34) such as that embodied by Google, which is undoubtedly the central player in our daily digitised interactions and has done much to lay foundations for the harvesting of big data and orientate its applications towards prediction.

Google began as a company offering users quick and effective ways to search the Internet to find information they need. This emphasis on user benefit changed with the dot.com bust in the early 2000s. The company had to radically reshape itself or risk collapse along with all the other start-ups of that era. They quickly realised they needed to monetise by offering advertising on their platform. Rather than clogging up their clean browser interface with ads, Google realised that they could leverage the technology they had developed to offer a better user experience. The technology that would complete search inquiries and correct spelling could be used to target advertising in very specific ways. Google emerged as a powerhouse at a crucial point in history when the Internet was like a digital Wild West – a frontier land where rules and norms were being contested. Google became 'the pioneer of surveillance capitalism' (Zuboff, 2019: 9) by deploying technologies aimed at users and activating them to sell products. The company harnessed the extraneous data produced when people search; 'in addition to keywords, each Google search query produces a wake of collateral data such as the number and pattern of search terms, how a query is phrased, spelling, punctuation, dwell times, click patterns, and location' (Zuboff, 2019: 67). This was the data that Google logged and stored without user consent and that could be collated to offer a specific and targeted advertising profile to organisations and corporations. Importantly, 'Google would no longer mine behavioural data strictly to improve service but rather to read users' minds for the purposes of matching ads to their interests' (Zuboff, 2019: 78).

These techniques were refined to create mobile and fluid datasets that could be adjusted according to the minutiae of behavioural nuances when users went online, creating 'user profile information' or UPI that 'would dramatically enhance the accuracy of these predictions' (Zuboff, 2019: 78). It is this predictive behaviour for which the data were being used that provides a fulcrum for a discussion around digitisation, privacy, social media, harm, and crime. Surveillance was dislodged from its criminal context and inserted into the consumer framework. This instrumental part of crime fighting involving 'close observation, especially of a suspected person', morphed into 'new surveillance [that] is more likely to be applied categorically, deductive, remote, low visibility or invisible, involuntary, automated, preemptive and embedded into routine activity' (Brayne, 2017: 979). In an era of 'coerced digital participation' where 'citizens are constantly forced to comply and provide personal data' (Barassi, 2019: 2) or miss out on essential social services and access to public goods because these are now all digitised, surveillance is an unexpected and implicit add-on. The data subject has overtaken the citizen or even the consumer as the dominant sovereign identity.

> In this framework, the 'data subject' is much more than an individual consumer or a user sorted by one's own choices; it is a citizen whose freedoms and rights are highly dependent on the ways in which he or she is being profiled.
>
> (Barassi, 2019: 5)

Citizen's rights are increasingly diminished in favour of not just consumer rights but a 'security state' where pre-emption and pre-crime tactics are routinely invoked to manipulate, mask, and manage law and order procedures so that the state may violate its own laws in the push to be perceived to protect its citizens from harm. It turns its own citizens into data subjects to validate the digital invasions it routinely deploys, simultaneously disempowering them in the opacity of these processes that make data subjects visible while making the datasets available to the institutions that develop them. The popular refrain that 'I have nothing to hide' reveals a 'resigned cynicism' (Zuboff, 2019: 11) that spotlights the perversions of contemporary law enforcement attitudes and state crime. These digital invasions operate in an increasingly fluid and unjust social context for law and order where the impositions foisted upon known criminals as part of racial profiling, post-punishment protocols, or pre-crime pre-emptions are now being widely employed against citizens of all types in an age of counter-terrorism where everyone is a potential suspect. Government institutions leverage the general condition of 'objectless anxiety' first forged in consumer culture but now intensified in the age of terror to violate rights on a routine basis. These violations are then protected under the guise of law and order, crime management, and harm prevention. For example:

> The NSA operated under an immediate new presidential mandate after the September 2001 attacks, one that overturned the long-standing legal requirement to restrict their intelligence-gathering to foreign sources. . . . The NSA operated for years in clear violation of federal law, leading to retroactive legislation by the U.S. Congress in 2007 to protect both the NSA and the telecommunication companies that gave NSA access to their networks.
>
> (Masco, 2017: 387)

The data-creep continued when the Obama Administration allowed 'the intelligence community to keep information on US citizens investigated in relation to terrorism for five years (previously, such information would have to be destroyed after 180 days unless a crime were discovered)' (Masco, 2017: 389). These perversions of the public interest were unmasked as part of the Snowden revelations and created a scramble to retroactively validate the privacy invasions on the basis of protecting the public, not from any actual crime, but from 'harm' embodied in the risk of random terrorist attacks.

Google's invasions and the illegal surveillance of citizens by government organisations like the NSA are part of a continuum of risk that assures us that we must tolerate 'some types of crime as the "price of freedom" whilst downplaying the harms they cause' (Hall and Winlow, 2018, p. 108). The invoice expands as the immersive, accelerated capitalist context of exchange and engagement that defines our everyday lives asserts that 'nothing is for free', and the large cache of freely available information, tools, and interfaces that we find on the Internet, must eventually be compensated:

> Eventually, companies began to explain these violations as the necessary quid pro quo for 'free' internet services. Privacy, they said, was the price one must pay for the abundant rewards of information, connection, and other digital goods, when, where and how you want them.
>
> (Zuboff, 2019: 52)

The attempt to normalise these privacy invasions intersects with the ongoing egregious violations of social media sites whose poor data management has seen numerous hacks and accidental releases of millions of individual's profile data and passwords. The Cambridge Analytica scandal was just one of the more visible incidents. In 2018, 29 million users were affected when a flaw in the 'view as' feature in Facebook enabled hackers to steal access tokens which let them take over individuals' accounts. Google+ had a breach that affected 52.5 million users when its personal information was exposed. Twitter discovered that passwords were stored in plaintext. This affected 330 million users. They were all asked to reset their passwords. This is attendant to the routine ways in which data is gathered, stored, and shared to third parties for revenue raising and other purposes. The extent of these violations (not just via social media, but the online environment in general) is such that the NSA advises its own employees to take great care when using a computer including 'recommending disabling Bluetooth and Wi-Fi and physically removing any camera of microphone capability from the computer' (Masco, 2017: 391) on which they are working.

The spill-over of personal and private information into the public realm via social media – not only by users gleefully offering this information in line with the sites' operational priorities but also the gross incompetence of social media platforms to offer the most basic protection of privacy as they data-scrape and glean as much information that they can, some of which is leaked through security missteps – is the product of a cavalier approach to security. It is this attitude that percolates through the social media landscape, accompanied by obscure notions about the role of corporations in this environment. The notion of 'responsibilisation' refers to the 'nonstate provision of security' (Gurinskaya and Nalla, 2018: 42). It describes the displaced faith we redirect into corporations and companies to protect us because the market dictates it, rather than demand that governments appropriately regulate and control these entities with rigorous legislation and enforcement. These attitudes allow the recurrence of the ongoing and egregious violations of our privacy in the digital environment. The neoliberal attempts to downsize government displaces responsibility onto third parties deploying a 'bait-and-switch' whereby regulatory capitalism asserts and inserts itself, 'coupled with the expansion of security concerns and preoccupations with risk minimization' (Gurinskaya and Nalla, 2018: 40) to 'lengthen the arm of the law'. Retroactively activated regulations function as a way to extend the state by situating prevention as its primary concern. It can then address a constantly and ever-expanding list of possible risks and make 'intervention possible at the earliest occurrence of the problem or even before the problem occurs' (Gurinskaya and Nalla, 2018: 41).

It is this obsession with appearing to diminish but simultaneously extending the role of the state that has led to tensions between regulation, criminality, and harm in digital environments. This discussion is not only motivated by the revelations of extensive data-mining of social media users, as well as breaches of their personal security and gross appropriation of their data without consent in ways that are counterproductive to basic democratic and sovereign principles. It is also being framed by a far wider concern with how states collaborate with corporations to exploit data-breaches and privacy loopholes to extend and command surveillance capitalism in an effort to brand, tag, track, regulate, sell, and police data-subjects. These issues can be starkly contrasted against the responsibilisation rhetoric that accuses social media of enabling bullying, trolling, deviance, and harm. These debates have cascaded into the mainstream deployment of encryption technology on messenger applications. This technology enables the restriction of access to our online conversations by both social media corporations and governments (protecting our privacy), but it also enables abusive and harmful content to circulate undetected and unregulated.

Until WhatsApp turned encryption into a marketing strategy, devices and platforms had largely been protected by unseen processes. Pretty Good Privacy (PGP) was invented in 1991 and remains a fairly standard encryption tool for most email software. When it was developed, it was considered a 'weaponised' technology. It evolved into an open source code, and it remains virtually uncrackable. Similarly, Apple's iPhone is regarded as a marvel of security. Although this has changed over time with the demands of greater interoperability and less sandboxing, efforts to ensure the iPhone remains secure from thieves has ensured that some impressive encryption protects it. Apple deploys full device encryption reinforced by full disk encryption:

> Not only is all of the data encrypted, it is done in a way that is combined or entangled with the hardware. Thus, the police cannot clone the encrypted

> data, then crack it offline using supercomputers to 'brute-force' guess all possible combinations of the passcode. Instead, they effectively have to ask the phone to decrypt itself, which it will do but slowly, defeating cracking.
>
> (Graham, 2016: 21)

Android phones also have similar efforts deployed to ensure a stolen phone cannot be cracked. Rumours abound about what types of activity intelligence agencies are funding to gain access to confiscated devices. Publicly, some intelligence agencies have taken Apple to court to force them to provide 'backdoor' access. Apple resisted the demand and, in one bold move, sought to become the champion of the people, setting the state against citizenry and the protection of rights. This was a shrewd move considering the FBI wanted access to the phone of Syed Rizwan Farook, one of the terrorist attackers responsible for a mass shooting in San Bernardino in 2015. The Snowden revelations in 2013 revealed that Apple, along with Google, Facebook, and Yahoo, had all acquiesced to NSA requests for the data stored on their servers. Apple was seeking to manage the public relations fall-out. However, many within the intelligence community have expressed doubts over the efficacy of backdoor access. Former CIA and NSA Director General Michael Hayden has famously disagreed with the imposition of backdoor access to devices, stating the importance of protecting citizen's rights and arguing that compromised phone security could also potentially create threats to national security (Lee, 2016). Nevertheless, an emerging narrative about the 'threat' of encryption in the hands of terrorists to plan and enact violence steadily gained ground.

Much has been made of the shrewd and clever machinations of ISIS in its deployment of traditional and digitised media. They have 'been repeatedly described as the most adept terrorist group at using the internet and social media to recruit new members' (Majid et al., 2018: 1). Until 2014, Twitter was their go-to platform for conducting these activities until public pressure serially shut down the ISIS accounts and the organisation withdrew (Weimann, 2016: 202). Since then, Telegram has been their medium of choice. Telegram was launched in 2013 by Nikolai and Pavel Durov, who designed VK (VKontakte) 'Russia's largest social network' (Bloom et al., 2017: 2). Its attraction was end-to-end encryption and other features, including a self-destruct mechanism where users could set a timer for messages to delete themselves. Due to these robust security protocols, Telegram has often been categorised as part of the 'dark web', 'a portion of the Deep Web that contains generally illegal and anti-social information and can only be accessed through specialized browsers' (Weimann, 2016: 196). The clandestine nature of the encryption of Telegram – as well as the role of ISIS in adopting the software – created the perception of its illicit nature. Software and hardware that make use of the Deep Web are constructed in contrast to the Surface Web – the one that we all use, transparently, and 'without deception'. This Deep Web is filled with criminals, abusers, paedophiles, arms dealers, terrorists, white supremacists, and drug dealers. Secrecy is therefore a staple of this environment. Privacy is paramount – serving to reinforce popular ideas about the Surface Web as open and honest, where people who 'have nothing to hide' exist, while the Deep Web is populated by criminals and deviants who must be policed. These are the people whose threat to us all means the gathering of our data and storing of our online identities is a necessity to protect against and pre-empt their harm.

Telegram was instrumental in a number of terrorist attacks in European cities since ISIL's declaration of the 'new Caliphate' in 2014. Telegram had been used by terrorists to plan attacks, maintain contact, and direct the violence as the attacks unfolded. ISIS uses Telegram as a broadcast media. It will use channels to broadcast audio and text files to an audience. It also deploys chat rooms where issues are discussed and planning can occur. Not only does ISIS use Telegram to broadcast propaganda about 'new the Caliphate' and the organisation, recruitment, and their invented 'proper conduct' of a Muslim, it also provides a space for chats to occur between recruiters and potential terrorists. While its success in recruitment is good, its operational success has not been so robust. Many operatives have been caught out by their own inexpert execution (reading a manual is no substitute for direct training in explosives or guerrilla tactics, for example). However, ISIS is rigorous in opsec (operational security) – their chat rooms and channels are rigorously monitored and regularly data-dumped while lurkers or potential infiltrators are systematically expelled. They have developed a smart approach to managing their digital presence on Telegram. While '99% of ISIS members do not use the Internet in sophisticated ways[,] [t]he 1% who might be more savvy are using Tor, PGP encrypted emails, encrypted sites and a variety of platforms' (Bloom et al., 2017: 4). They conduct counter-surveillance. They use anonymous browsers, VPNs, and self-destruct features that are 'probably one of the most frustrating features for intelligence services' (Graham, 2016: 25). While Telegram has consistently resisted calls to remove terrorist accounts, citing freedom of speech, it does have an 'ISIS Watch' channel where it lists the channels it deletes for violating the terms of service.

End-to-end encryption has been widely rolled out on other mainstream messaging applications such as Messenger and WhatsApp. While few users know of its presence on Messenger, it was rolled out on WhatsApp as a promotional feature. State actors have demanded that Facebook, which owns both Messenger and WhatsApp, release encrypted messages from the platform to assist in the prosecution of criminality or in the prevention of harm. As such, Telegram is not alone amongst messaging systems enabling terrorists or criminals to conduc clandestine operations. In fact, the encryption is commonly available and reg larly deployed:

> [T]he 'source code' itself behind end-to-end encryption is now widely av able online, which means that short of shutting down the internet, the nothing that can be done to stop individuals, including terrorists, from c ing and customizing their own encryption software.
>
> (Graham, 20

nuances of these debates are muted when agencies embrace clandestine activities that pervert the interests of national security and reify the exploitation of data subjects over citizens.

This changes fundamental rights and responsibilities in a democracy. When Snowden revealed the extent of the spying, he neutered many of these clandestine surveillance programs and as a result changed the shape of surveillance and intelligence gathering. The scandal of Cambridge Analytica was that all the speculations and outcomes of Snowden's revelations were suddenly revealed as an observable and comprehensible concrete framework – the data-scraping of our personal digital information could be used against us not just to get us to buy products but to change the very shape of society and its democratic processes. Selective fear-mongering based on the extension of spectacular types of harm normalises pre-crime strategies, situating big data processing as essential for crime prevention while it amplifies the harm of state surveillance yet distracts public attention from the everyday harms that befall citizens. Computation will reveal trends and truths that will mitigate risk. These risks are now in messenger services that can use end-to-end encryption to hide personal data and the content of messages. Access to these messages is becoming understood and accepted as essential not only to fighting terrorism, and Dark-Web deviance, but also for public safety. *Privacy versus prevention* is the defining debate of our times. This debate is being shaped by an evolving faith in computational systems that analyse data. In the warm embrace of the datasets that compute this truth, the privacy debates that exist in the tensions between harm and crime – the need to find a disappeared family member or to prevent terrorism – reveal the conflicting narratives about encryption, security, and surveillance that encircle online and offline realities.

References

Akbari, A. and Gabdulhakov, R. (2019) Platform Surveillance and Resistance in Iran and Russia: The Case of Telegram. *Surveillance and Society*, 17, 1–2: 223–31. Available at: https://ojs.library.queensu.ca/index.php/surveillance-and-society/index

Ash, J., Kitchin, R. and Leszczynski, A. (2018) Digital Turn, Digital Geographies? *Progress in Human Geography*, 42, 1: 25–43. doi:10.1177/0309132516664800

Australian Associated Press (2019a, July 3) Theo Hayez: Search for Belgian Backpacker Who Went Missing in Byron Bay Called Off. *The Guardian*. Available at: www.theguardian.com/australia-news/2019/jul/03/theo-hayez-search-for-belgian-backpacker-who-went-missing-in-byron-bay-called-off

Australian Associated Press (2019b, June 17) WhatsApp Joins Search for Belgian Backpacker Theo Hayez, Who Went Missing in Byron Bay. *The Guardian*. Available at: www.theguardian.com/australia-news/2019/jun/17/byron-bay-father-of-missing-belgian-backpacker-theo-hayez-pleads-for-whatsapp-access

Barassi, V. (2019) Datafied Citizens in the Age of Coerced Digital Participation. *Sociological Research Online*, 1–16. doi:10.1177/1360780419857734

Bloom, M., Tiflati, H. and Horgan, J. (2017) Navigating ISIS's Preferred Platform: Telegram. *Terrorism and Political Violence*. doi:10.1080/09546553.2017.1339695

Brayne, S. (2017) Big Data Surveillance: The Case of Policing. *American Sociological Review*, 82, 5: 977–1008. doi:10.1177/0003122417725865

Bridle, J. (2018) *New Dark Age: Technology and the End of the Future*, London: Verso.

Chan, J. (2016) Is Big Data Challenging Criminology? *Theoretical Criminology*, 20, 1: 21–39. doi:10.1177/1362480615586614

Gever, M. (2005) The Spectacle of Crime, Digitizes: CSI: Crime Scene Investigation and Social Anatomy. *Cultural Studies*, 8, 4: 445–63. doi:10.1177/1367549405051847

Giroux, H. (2004) War on Terror: The Militarisation of Public Space and Culture in the United States. *Third Text*, 18, 4: 211–21.

Graham, R. (2016) How Terrorists Use Encryption. *CT Sentinel*, 9, 6: 20–25. Available at: https://ctc.usma.edu/june-2016/

Gurinskaya, A. and Nalla, M.K. (2018) The Expanding Boundaries of Crime Control: Governing Security Through Regulation. *Annals, AAPSS*, 679: 36–54. doi:10.1177/0002716218778750

Hall, S. (2012) *Theorizing Crime and Deviance: A New Perspective*, London: Sage.

Hall, S. and Winlow, S. (2018) Big Trouble or Little Evils: The Ideological Struggle Over the Concept of Harm. In A. Boukli and J. Kotzé (eds.) *Zemiology: Reconnecting Crime and Social Harm*, Cham: Palgrave Macmillan, 107–26.

Kitchin, R. and McArdle, G. (2016, January–June) What Makes Big Data, Big Data? Exploring the Ontological Characteristics of 26 Datasets. *Big Data and Society*. doi:10.1177/2053951716631130

Lapowsky, I. and Kelly, C. (2019, July 12) FTC Reportedly Hits Facebook with Record $5 Billion Settlement. *Wired Business*. Available at: www.wired.com/story/facebook-ftc-fine-five-billion/

Lee, R. (2016, February 22) Michael Hayden: Making Moral Decisions on 'Gray Issues'. *CBS This Morning*. Available at: www.cbsnews.com/news/michael-hayden-former-director-fbi-nsa-fbi-apple-san-bernardino-2016-race-new-book/

Majid, A., Kaghazgaran, P., Caverlee, J. and Morstatter, F. (2018) *Measuring the Impact of ISIS Social Media Strategy*. doi:10.475/123_4. Available at: https://snap.stanford.edu/mis2/files/MIS2_paper_23.pdf

Masco, J. (2017) 'Boundless Informant': Insecurity in the Age of Ubiquitous Surveillance. *Anthropological Theory*, 17, 3: 382–403. doi:10.1177/1463499617731178

Nemer, D. (2018, October 25) The Three Types of WhatsApp Users Getting Brazil's Jair Bolsonaro Elected. *The Guardian*. Available at: www.theguardian.com/world/2018/oct/25/brazil-president-jair-bolsonaro-whatsapp-fake-news

Radio Farda (2019, April 11) Iranians Return to Banned Telegram as It Proves Effective in Flood Relief. Available at: https://en.radiofarda.com/a/iranians-return-to-banned-telegram-as-it-proves-effective-in-flood-relief/29874542.html

Santos, M. and Faure, A. (2018, July–September) Affordance Is Power: Contradiction Between Communicational and Technical Dimensions of WhatsApp's End-to-End Encryption. *Social Media and Society*, 1–16. doi:10.1177/2056305118795876

Savov, V. (2015, December 17) Brazil's WhatsApp Ban Is Driving Millions of Users to Telegram. *The Verge*. Available at: www.theverge.com/2015/12/17/10386776/brazil-whatsapp-ban-telegram-millions-users

Shepardson, D. (2019, June 24) Facebook to Pay Record $7.1b Fine Over Privacy Violations. *The Sydney Morning Herald*. Available at: www.smh.com.au/business/companies/facebook-to-pay-record-7-1b-fine-over-privacy-violations-20190724-p52ahu.html?fbclid=IwAR2s47xpaEBM7ZwGt2LR2z08nqxvZ4YtDI0uClG_TGr4ND6tONSV5SdwG28

Statt, N. (2018, April 30) WhatsApp Co-Founder Jan Koum Is Leaving Facebook After Clashing Over Data Privacy. *The Verge*. Available at: www.theverge.com/2018/4/30/17304792/whatsapp-jan-koum-facebook-data-privacy-encryption

Weimann, G. (2016) Going Dark: Terrorism on the Dark Web. *Studies in Conflict and Terrorism*, 39, 3: 195–206. doi:10.1080/1057610X.2015.1119546

Zuboff, S. (2019) *The Age of Surveillance Capitalism: The Fight for a Human Future at the New Frontier of Power*, London: Profile Books.

Index

www.ingramcontent.com/pod-product-compliance
Ingram Content Group UK Ltd.
Pitfield, Milton Keynes, MK11 3LW, UK
UKHW011014180926
475701UK00004B/745
* 9 7 8 1 0 3 2 0 8 1 7 5 5 *